To Jan
Best
J Mandel

SPEED
WITH STYLE

SPEED WITH STYLE
The Autobiography of Peter Revson

by Peter Revson and Leon Mandel

DOUBLEDAY & COMPANY, INC.
GARDEN CITY, NEW YORK 1974

Parts of this book have appeared previously
in *Sports Illustrated* and *Car and Driver*

PHOTO CREDITS

Betty Collins - 1
Bernard Cahier - 2, 7
Bahamas Ministry of Tourism, photo by Roland Rose - 3
Ashland Oil & Refining Company, Ashland, Kentucky - 5
Jeanne Beeching - 6, 16, and 25
Edsel B. Ford III - 8
Leon Mandel - 9-11, 14, 21, 23, and 27
Edwin Ingalls - 12, 18-20, 22, 24, and 26
Dutch Mandel - 13 and 28
Bill Fant - 17
James D. MacQueen - 30-31
Caroline Hadley - 34
Mike Hart - 32-33
No credit - 4, 15 and 29

Library of Congress Cataloging in Publication Data

Revson, Peter.
  Speed with style.

  1. Revson, Peter. 2. Automobile racing.
I. Mandel, Leon. II. Title.
GV1032.R47A37   796.7′2′0924 [B]
ISBN 0-385-06166-8
Library of Congress Catalog Card Number: 74-9201

Copyright © 1974 by A. Harry Kupersmith, Executor of the Estate of Peter J. R. Revson, Deceased, and Leon Mandel
ALL RIGHTS RESERVED
PRINTED IN THE UNITED STATES OF AMERICA

To *Olivia Lee*
and to *Peter*

Publisher's Note

Peter Revson and Leon Mandel delivered the manuscript for *Speed with Style* to Doubleday & Company on March 15, 1974, after fifteen months of work. On March 22, the day on which this book went into production, Peter Revson was killed in a testing accident at the Kyalami circuit in South Africa.

Because it is our feeling that this book offers immediate and vivid insights into the world of a grand prix driver, it appears as originally written.

Contents

Foreword ix
Introduction xiii

PART ONE

Revson · One 3
You can be friendly, but it's hard to be friends. Racing is just a job.

Mandel · One 18
If everyone around thought the profits from 100 million tubes of Orange Flip lipstick were buying your car, you'd be testy too.

PART TWO

Revson · Two 45
If I don't do it in the next two or three years, I won't do it at all.

Mandel · Two 62
The driver is lying in some enormous bed that is swarming with naked women who are feeding him sugared grapes and cognac.

PART THREE

Mandel · Three 83
Indianapolis is a ceremonial gathering, a terrible kind of tithing, the biggest shuck in the hucksters' carnival.

Revson · Three 88
In this business, a mistake can ramify itself into something terminal.

Mandel · Three Continued 110
As Revson walks by, he whispers, "A hawk has very stiff lips." Revson's lips are pretty stiff, too.

PART FOUR

Revson · Four 141
I had won my first grand prix. I was earning better than $300,000 a year, and there I was looking at the unemployment line.

Mandel · Four 170
Sentiment greases the economic wheels of racing. Sentiment and large inheritances.

PART FIVE

Revson · Five 187
I was no longer a part of the family. It had been a long relationship and a good one. But I asked for my release and I got it.

Mandel · Five 207
One of these days the racing people are going to drive out a race track access road to the main highway to find nothing but wisps of smoke, some blackened fields, and a twisted tree.

Footnote 220

Foreword

Even at night, in the still of its abandoned garage and swathed in its dust cover, a grand prix car is an awesome presence.

There are no people around it, none of the swirl of the crowd nor even the intimate and familiar shadows of its crew, but still the car seems to breathe and tremble.

A race car is a lean and terrible thing. Delicate, highly bred, it is like a fine horse but with an immense strength no living creature can have. In the sunlight you are blinded by the splendid, bright colors of its paint. Not a rough weld, not an obtrusive seam jars the conviction that what you are looking at is an enormously accomplished product of the craftsman's bench.

But at night, in repose, the car is at its most impressive. All that strength, all that power is quiet and isolated. Even then, however, it is not alone.

For all its ability to shake the trees with the shriek of its engine, to destroy the thought of time and distance by flashing incredibly from end to end of the viewer's horizon, for all that, the car is only paraphernalia.

It is nothing more than a fiberglass pole in a vault. A number-nine iron. A Head competition racket.

It is the driver who counts.

I have been frightened simply standing next to an Indianapolis car, knowing how the ground feels when it screams by at 220 mph. And I have been much subdued in the presence of a CanAm sports car, $175,000 and 1200 horsepower worth of turbocharged wedge which can outaccelerate even the hopes of its owners.

I'm unashamed to feel that way about their cars, but it's embarrassing to stand in awe of the drivers. I need no one to demonstrate to me that race car drivers are often unexceptional human beings. Drivers, like anyone else, can be rude (A. J. Foyt), obsequious (Wally Dallenbach), one-dimensional (Mark Donohue), or egomaniacal (Jackie Stewart). These human failings are common to stock car drivers and championship car drivers and sports car drivers. To grand prix drivers as well.

They are failings particularly visible during moments of stress, and it can be said that almost *all* a grand prix driver's working hours are filled with stress. For most of the year 1973, life on the circuit was difficult. It was one of those years when the landscape seems to fall away, to seethe and finally to rearrange itself. Jackie Stewart, one of the legends of the sport, retired. François Cevert, a certain future champion, was killed. Jody Scheckter, conceded by almost everyone to be the towering driver of the next generation, arrived. If there was a year in which the awful weight of reality forced the drivers to look inward, it was 1973.

That was the year during which Peter Revson and I chose to do this book. And if there was a time when Revson's failings might have shown themselves for anyone to see, it should have been that one. If the cars cloaked in the garages or standing bright in the paddock sunlight still put me in awe, surely the drivers in this difficult year—and Revson in particular—should not have.

That was not the case.

In a way, it's a pity, so far as I'm concerned, that Revson is a race driver, because if his job and my job didn't get in the way, I have the feeling he'd be a fine friend. As it is, during the course of this book, he's become someone I've enjoyed and someone who has taught me a good deal about manners and decency and dedication.

Unlike many professional athletes, Revson is a man of education and vision. When his ever-present self-approval doesn't get in the way, he is surprisingly realistic about the lasting worth of his contribution as a race driver (not much) and about his own shortcomings (many).

One of the pleasant things I discovered about Revson is his nice way with words. This is not an "as told to" book at all. It is, of course, Revson's story, but his was an equal voice not only in the accounts of the events but in the ways they should be talked about.

Finally, although Revson was properly allowed to express anger, annoyance, or displeasure over the words that are entirely mine in this joint effort, when he did so it was with characteristic humor and patience.

I thank Russ Goebel, who turned a blind eye to my absence from his company for months at a time in order that I might travel with Revson and write my chapters—instead of complaining, he offered encouragement; Caroline J. Hadley, a managing editor, tape transcriber, goad, and amanuensis; her designated hitter, Margaret Stallings. Peyton Cramer, Peter Revson's business partner and friend; almost all of Team McLaren, but mostly Teddy Mayer and Tyler Alexander; Danny Folsom; D. O. Cozzi; two staffs of *Autoweek*, who went serenely on doing a superb job in the happy knowledge I wasn't there, first David Abrahamson and Claudia Hosepian, after them Dave Clark, Jim MacQueen, Steve Thompson, and Mike Faulknor; Vicki DeVines; a variety of press officers at a variety of tracks; Pete Lyons, to whom both Peter and I hope proper credit is given as the finest motor sports writer ever to carry a typewriter; Charles Fox, Bob Brown, and William Jeanes of *Car and Driver* magazine, neither of whom did very much but both of whom were fine company at some pretty depressing races; Edwin Ingalls, who remained more or less cheerful for thirty days at The Speedway, thus setting an all-time record; Jeanne Beeching, who had a fine file on McLaren and who gave permission to use some photos, including several she might have used for her own book *The Last Season;* Bud Stanner, a co-operative source of information; Jacques de Spoelberch, Dr. Georges Seligmann, a man of wisdom and patience; Avie Mandel, who was willing to read parts of the manuscript that could only have bored her to tears; Dutch

Mandel, who spent much of the 1973 season with a tape recorder on his back, a spare note pad and spare pens in one hand, and fourteen cups of coffee for the McLaren mechanics in the other; and finally Olivia Mandel, who was almost as critical as she could have been, which was a great help. More important, she endured the sounds of a typewriter firing up at 4 A.M. for months at a time, met a lot of airplanes, and did a lot of dirty laundry. The point is, she was there.

L MANDEL

Reno, Nevada
March 11, 1974

Introduction

After eight months of following Peter Revson around the world, I finally discovered his real name.

For eight months I stared at him over his platter of sea bass (Weight Watchers style) in New York restaurants, hung around the pits at Watkins Glen and Indianapolis wondering whether his driving suit was tailored by the same London people who cut his slightly flared flannels, and watched him ease his executive chair back to full rake in his office in Harbor City, California . . . all this thinking his name was merely Peter Revson. It isn't. It's Peter Jeffrey Revlon Revson.

In all his fourteen years as a race driver, he had reacted in the same, predictable, outraged way whenever he read newspaper stories referring to him as "Peter Revson, the Revlon heir." It was as though they were calling him some kind of faggot. Now, I discovered, "Revlon" was his middle name.

Even two years ago, the words above would have pissed off P. J. Revlon Revson almost beyond calculation. But something's happened to him since he won the Canadian-American championship, won his grands prix, almost tied ex-heavyweight champion Joe Frazier in a coast-to-coast-TV weight-lifting contest, and became recognized in Brazil, South Africa, Sweden, and England (if not quite yet in the United States) as one of the three absolutely top drivers in the world— not to say one of the great international sports presences at 21 or on the beach at Juan-les-Pins. He laughs a great deal more, and now that he's rich by his own hand he's openly boastful about being careful with money, even as the Kennedys and the Rockefellers.

As for the lipstick connection, well, if it's there it's there. Is it *his* fault that his father Martin and his uncles Charles and Joseph were compulsive empire builders? Besides, more people in supermarkets in Belgium recognize the name Peter Revson than the names of either his father or his surviving uncle. In France and Germany and Italy too. Perspective has come to Peter Jeffrey R. Revson. Moreover, he's pretty busy these days, not really enough time left for petulance. For example:

Saturday morning, November 17: the Revson apartment in Redondo Beach, California, 9 A.M. It's the off season, time to relax, do all the work necessary during the three-month grand prix break, sign the contracts, negotiate the deals, film the TV special, rejoin the real world, and, not incidentally, complete taping for this book, which is three months behind. P.J.R.R. has sworn he will get down to it at last. Of course, yesterday was more or less filled with priority problems. There were some trade books and training films to review, bills to pay, letters from fans to answer, autographs to put on two hundred or more photos (a name stamp won't do, that's cheating—if someone has taken the time and trouble to write and ask for a photo, he gets the real thing in reply), and a decision to make about whether the new parts-and-accessories company will carry a decal saying "Peter Revson Turbocharger" on its new Capri turbo or "Revson Turbocharger" or "Revson-Charge" or "TurboPeter." Seventeen minutes of contemplation and it comes out "RevsonTurbo."

By 8 P.M. the effects of the steamed clams at luncheon have worn off and it's dine or die. We dine. Finally, at 9:30 P.M., we get down to work in the Revson apartment. At 9:33 the doorbell rings. Revson sighs, goes to the door, looks through the spyhole, and opens up to reveal an attractive lady in jeans, a double-layered shirt, a tall scotch and soda, and a 30-degree list to port. "I don't believe I know you," she says.

The opening so intrigues Revson that he invites her in. She is indeed drunk, she is surly, she is hostile, and she has a friend, who, seeing the moat crossed, has wandered in behind her and is worse. The famous chill is turned on.

Revson can manage to be a puritan, and drunken women

exacerbate that prudish inclination no end. So the frost is on the host, and drunk as she is, the lady begins to notice her fingers and toes are freezing and leaves, taking her friend with her. Back to work. Five minutes later the doorbell rings and it's the drunken lady again, back for some more scotch and ice. I go out for a long walk.

But now it's the following morning and there are jeans, half-stockings, and some oddments I have never seen before scattered around the Revson living room. Shortly, the lady, still a little cross-eyed and wearing only an abbreviated tee shirt, comes down, parks herself across from me, borrows a cigarette, and, exposing only the most demure vista of pubic hair, begins to discuss the failure of her previous marriage. She has, it turns out, been married to a former major-league baseball player. Later on, P.J.R.R. will tell me she complained all night that her ex-husband could go neither to his right nor to his left in bed, that he was a disappointing husband as well as lover, and that the ex-wife was well rid of him. As for the ex-wife, whatever the reason, her enthusiasm exceeded her capacity, and her own performance was reportedly not historic. At any rate, the lady seemed clearly to like professional athletes and to go after them with some vigor no matter what her degree of sobriety. Revson referred to her thereafter as "The Collector."

We taped all day Saturday.

On Saturday night, Claudia from my office in Reno and two of her friends called. Would we come to Balboa Island for dinner if they bought? Thank you, Claudia, but no two-hour round trip tonight; we're too tired. An hour later they are in Redondo Beach, three Armenian girls from Fresno, just out of college, very young, still with that awkwardness that can occasionally be most appealing but is usually nothing but humiliating to its possessor and embarrassing to her dinner companions. Zits and laryngitis and compulsive talking about Norman Rockwell being an idol: dreadful stuff. Revson is charm itself. Leaning back, puffing on a Monte Cristo, he listens attentively to every word, makes the right inquiries at the right times, beguiles, flatters, mystifies: in general, acts as though he were with the three most fascinating women in the universe. At dinner's end, they walk out of the restaurant about an inch beneath the ceiling. Revson pays the check with pleasure. He has not been acting.

On Sunday, I have a business/social dinner in Huntington Beach. After a day of taping and an evening of renewing old friendships and trying to be subtle about selling something, I return exhausted to the Revson apartment. Into the bathroom assigned to me; in the dark I reach for my Dopp kit and discover a Gucci bag in my hand instead. Jesus, not another one.

On Monday morning, with some work left to do and a 10:35 plane to catch, I go out, buy a couple of sausage-and-cheese omelets from the Saroyanesque restaurant next door, and yell upstairs to the sleeping loft that it's time to get the hell up. In about five minutes, down floats an absolute vision. Small, long clean blond hair, exquisitely groomed, dressed so that it's hard to tell if she's Italian or French or Finnish, the lady comes into the living room and makes it her job to put me at ease. I am a welcome guest in her Alpine chalet. She is delectable in every way, witty, feminine, educated, a deferential hostess. . . . I begin to understand how the Fresno girls felt last night. Maybe I can delay my flight a month. The lady is a Harvard graduate, a publishing brat, and a citizen of Milan, where she is doing research for her doctoral thesis.

O.K. A refugee from baseball land, three sorority girls from a Central Valley, California, town, and a gentlelady from Verona.

Says Revson: "Goddamn it, it only happens when you come down. You seem to cause these things. My life is dull the rest of the time."

Bullshit, Revson. I've been standing around for eight months now, remember?

* * *

If a grand prix driver is worth anything at all, other than as an extremely quick entertainer, it is as a man who is living out our dreams.

His life is a magic round of first-class flights, commuter hops in chartered jets, dazzling women, legendary hotels with magnificent kitchens, and people crowding in from all sides pressing money into his hands.

It's true. That's the way a grand prix driver lives. He also lives with boredom, terror, dirt, danger, and fatigue.

The young understand grand prix drivers. They take them for life models, to the distress of many of us, who would rather they looked to NFL quarterbacks or establishment lawyers. Perhaps the young are telling us their understanding of American life goes deeper than ours.

The young know that race cars and racers—and particularly grand prix cars and grand prix drivers—are the visible edges of a totally pervasive theme in American life. Consider:

. . . Of every six people employed in this country, one is involved in some way with the automobile.

. . . Racing is the second-largest spectator sport in the nation.

. . . General Motors' annual sales are about equal to the gross national product of Belgium.

The young sense something even beyond that: They seem to recognize the symbolic importance of the grand prix driver; he is engaged, they are aware, in a quixotic pursuit.

The rest of us are resigned to being dominated by machines; the young are not. They want to feel a sense of control of their lives.

That is why they see a motor race as a contest not only between drivers, but between drivers and machines. They understand that the driver is taking a complicated and unpredictable device to the limits of its performance . . . and his own.

This is the story of a year in the life of a man who spends almost every weekend testing his own limits. In the end of the story, his life turns sharply, not because he failed to meet the challenge of his machinery, but for the same reasons yours or mine might: his own or someone else's pride, stubbornness, impatience, and greed.

The annual grand prix play has three acts. The curtain opens in South America, in January. In Brazil and Argentina, it is the time for experimentation. The first faint outlines of the year begin to appear.

In South Africa, the second act is played. Now the adventure becomes serious. Here the last modifications are made, the final adjustments to strategy are arrived at. Here, too, the relationships between driver and manager, driver and driver, driver and crew chief crystallize. From now on, if envy or trust, hatred or admiration it is to be, that's what it will remain.

The real year begins in Europe, in the spring. From now on there will be no time for testing, no time for change. From Spain in April until Watkins Glen in October, there will be time only for practicing, qualifying, racing, loading up for the next race, and doing it all again. It is during the summer in Europe that the Ken Tyrrells and the Colin Chapmans turn serious, lose the pleasant patience of the Southern Hemisphere, and speak in the harsh imperatives of professional racing men.

This is the life that Peter Revson lives, and the young understand it. The young know too that the establishment lawyer and the NFL quarterback are prehistoric lizards. Adapt or die.

The young are at the race track because the racers have outsleeked the stick-and-ball dinosaurs at Candlestick and Shea, who were fine for a slower, smaller, more rudimentary age. But now (they know) it's style. Speed and style.

There's this about the young: They may be brash and they may be impatient, but perhaps that's because they know a great deal about the tempo of their times.

PART ONE

Revson · One

You can be friendly, but it's hard to be friends. Racing is just a job.

Sometimes racing becomes so much of a job, sometimes I become so preoccupied with what I've set as my goals in racing, that I don't spend any time enjoying it any more. Sometimes I don't take time (especially when I'm in a race car) to sense the exhilaration that racing can bring.

For example, the noises become something you want to drown out; you even use earplugs. For another example, you're annoyed by the people who pass you in the pits: the photographers and the journalists who want to see you. You just wish to hell they'd get out of your way. And the other drivers: you know they're being sociable, but you know that they're only being superficially pleasant in order to find out what you're doing with your car so they can glean some information that will help them.

When you're absolutely single-minded about the job at hand, totally preoccupied with it, these things become an annoyance and you want to shut them out.

But when a new season starts and you've been away from the journalists and the race car noises and the other drivers for three months, you realize that they are things you relish. You've missed them.

PART ONE

The noise of the cars sounds good. It gets the adrenalin going. I'm happy to see the familiar faces. They belong to people who are interested in doing what I'm doing. The journalists' questions may get a little repetitious—after all, most racing journalists are ignorant, their questions plain stupid more often than not—but at least the people who ask them want to talk your language. That is gratifying.

As for the other drivers, what the hell, there's nobody else you can talk to about what you're doing.

This year, 1974, Jackie Stewart, one of my closest friends among the drivers, has retired. Although he will be around as a representative of Goodyear and Ford, he won't be driving and so that will automatically eliminate one person I have been able to communicate with over the years.

Jean-Pierre Jarier is my new teammate at Shadow. He is an experienced driver but he has spent most of his time in Formula 2 and I don't know him that well.

As for the others . . . I know them, but at least so far as Ronnie Peterson, Emerson Fittipaldi, Jacky Ickx, and perhaps Carlos Reutemann are concerned, I view them as my principal competition for the world championship this year, and so there is a certain restraint.

It is not as though I don't find them good company. But I have my own professional appraisal of each and I must keep that foremost in my mind.

I know that Emerson has as much natural talent as anyone in the grand prix circus. He was not as confident of the Lotus 72 as the other top drivers were of their cars and so he would not throw the car around like Ronnie Peterson. But this year he has switched to my old team, McLaren, where he could be more comfortable. Emerson is a very polished driver.

Jody Scheckter, who is in his first year with Tyrrell, is naturally somewhat quiet. He is all raw ability. But he hasn't shepherded it yet, he hasn't nurtured his ability or refined it, and he is someone who is going to be quiet off the race track until he does.

Clay Regazzoni is a pretty decent guy. He's a very aggressive driver, but despite our little run-in in the first race this year, I don't think he would take advantage of you on the track.

Peterson too is very aggressive. But I've never had any trouble with Ronnie and I've always found him a gentleman.

Chris Amon (who will be with us when his car is finished) and Denny Hulme, my roommate and my teammate respectively in past years, are both gentlemen. I've known those guys a long time and they drive with a great deal of manners and sportsmanship. Denny doesn't give ground easily but that doesn't mean a lack of manners on the track. Off the track Denny is a very pleasant and simple man with the other drivers, although he has a deserved reputation as being extremely difficult in his public personality.

Reutemann's tough, but so are most of the guys in Formula 1. Most of them have great regard for what they're doing. Almost all of them understand the implications of what they're doing in a car. All of them, at least all those who are really good, understand the potential hazards.

So this is to say that while I know these guys and I respect them, they are my competitors in a sport that is an individual effort. You can be friendly, but it is difficult to be friends. And while I am pleased to see them again, I know how formidable they can be, and therefore the kind of closeness you have in other sports, perhaps, does not exist here.

At the first race of the year, too, you look around and see some new faces. Sometimes you see faces not exactly new, but faces that represent new presences. It has not been long since three or four highly regarded young drivers in competitive cars have joined us.

They must have had a race or two before they made themselves known, and in those races they did surprisingly well. They have made some of the so-called established veterans think a little bit.

Perhaps it's not so curious, now that Stewart has retired, that the drivers who seemed to appear suddenly last year at the British Grand Prix appear to be larger in stature this year.

For instance, there's Jochen Maas, who is with Surtees. At Silverstone last year he was the fastest of the Surtees', and this year he's a regular. James Hunt was the fastest of the Marches at the British Grand Prix last year as well, and of course he's now known as one of the brightest of the newcomers. Jody Scheckter almost tied my time at Silverstone. It's interesting to see all these new faces but it's also somewhat disquieting.

Every three or four years the turnover begins, as several new people appear. Suddenly the whole circus seems to change, then stabilize, and then, in a couple of years, you'll have a turnover again.

I think the turnover now is due to the younger and better talent coming along to push some of the older guys out. I don't want to be one of the older guys who has been pushed out.

George Follmer is one who has been. I've been racing against George for a long time. George and I raced together in 1968 on the American Motors TransAm team, and if I was not aware of it before, it was at that time that I saw clearly George's very determined driving style . . . he was very aggressive and not altogether, well, accurate. I like to give George the benefit of the doubt, and very likely I will be driving on the same track with him again. But as his teammate there were times when it seemed as though I was being forced off the road and I have to think he was merely being imprecise.

Thereafter, when we were no longer teammates, I had to conclude that it was his aggressive style that did not allow him to give another driver the benefit of a doubt in a wheel-to-wheel situation. George doesn't have the classic techniques of a boxer. Rather, he is a street fighter. But there are two George Follmers. He is a different man off the track, very pleasant and very nice.

This year, George is not with us. George is gone and so is Jackie Stewart. But there are still the others, and some of them I genuinely like. To be back with them and among all this for the first race of the season is encouraging. It adds to my conviction that this is what I want to do. I'm happy to notice that it remains enjoyable.

And yet, even as I am taking pleasure in what I see and hear around me, I know that as the season wears on some of these things I now view sentimentally will become annoyances again, because they will be interfering with my job. I won't have time to be romantic. Instead of rejoicing, come midseason, racing will be just a big job. Because that's what we make it. That's what *I* make it.

It was a particularly hard job in 1973. When I look upon last year, I can't say it was a good one. Sure, I won two grands prix and it's good for an American to win two GPs in a year; but it isn't enough. Even though I won those races I finished fifth in the world championship. I had done as well the year before. So although I had at least two really good races in '73, I also had more poor races than the year before. Also I have to admit that there were more grands prix, so there were more chances to do well.

I didn't win any races in 1972, but each race I ran had a tone of quality about it. Of the fourteen races in 1973 there were quite a few totally without that tone of quality. And it was frustrating, because I had a good car, particularly after the Spanish Grand Prix, when I had the McLaren M23. But for one reason or another I didn't get to test the car. Teddy Mayer, the McLaren managing director, and I differed on how the car should be set up, and we had some bugs in the car (for example some small handling problems) that were never revealed.*

In racing with the United States Auto Club, Indianapolis was one of the worst races of my career. In the Gulf McLaren M16C, I was dealing with and battling a very balky car. It

---

* Revson says, "For one reason or another . . ." he didn't get to test. McLaren's Teddy Mayer feels, as most team people do in Formula 1, that the ability to test is almost as important in a race driver as the ability to win. According to Mayer, Revson's teammate at McLaren, Denny Hulme, is an extraordinary car tester, as good, or better, for example, than Jackie Stewart. But Revson's no slouch. When he switched to the Shadow team there was general rejoicing by the mechanics and the designer that finally they had someone who could take a new car out and not only find out what was wrong but tell them some directions to search to correct it. Testing is a pain in the ass for most drivers; it's dangerous and it's dull. But it's a plum as well, because apart from the necessary early car tests, the sponsoring tire companies do their tests with their contract drivers. And those tests are conducted only by the favored, who are handsomely paid. More about testing farther on. L.M.

was a car that didn't feel right from the beginning. No amount of changing and chassis tuning and dismantling and inspecting could resolve the problem. Maybe there was some compensating for it, but the car was never truly competitive. I started tenth in the race, ran a few uncomfortable laps, and finally lost it in the fourth turn and hit the wall. That was the end of my 1973 Indianapolis.

Despite putting the car on the pole at both of the remaining 500s, Pocono and Ontario, things got no better. I failed to finish both races due to engine failures.

Sports car racing was, if anything, worse. Even though I was signed to drive Alfa Romeo prototypes in seven races, I drove in none. In every case but one the cars weren't ready, and in the exception I had a race conflict. So *that* season was non-existent.

It does not require close scrutiny on my part to conclude that the 1973 season revealed failure. The two grand prix wins saved me from a very bad year. As it was, my racing in '73 ended in disruption, since for the first time in four years I wasn't going to continue with Team McLaren.

These reflections occupied my mind during the off season, as such things always do, but the atmosphere of the first race, the noise and the other drivers, and being back at work again somewhat dispelled them. Although the first race of 1974 with my new employers, Don Nichols and the Shadow team, ended badly when I was run into on the first lap by Clay Regazzoni, the start of the season gets the blood flowing again.

We stayed in the same Sheraton hotel in Buenos Aires as last year, and as usual, considering that Americans have a habit of disappearing suddenly in Argentina, people were extremely solicitous of our welfare—which was appreciated. It went through my mind, remembering the number of kidnapings of American businessmen lately, that I could be considered a target. Looking at it from the layman's point of view, I might well be thought of as being in danger. But I did not feel that way at all. So far as I'm concerned, I'm not worth the trouble and expense of a balls-to-the-wall kidnaping. With my name and my connections, it could, I suppose, be thought that I am a direct pipeline to a lot of Revlon Company money. In fact, of course, I'm no such thing. Perhaps those kidnapers did their homework. Hopefully so.

At any rate, the hotel had all the amenities: swimming pool (which I didn't get to use), two tennis courts, several restaurants with fine service, and security people on every floor and in the elevator as well. As I said, they took good care of their guests.

One of the most spectacular things about racing in Argentina is the drive to the track and back and to the airport. The automobile club supplies the driver. This year mine was named Joseph, and he did a spirited job of getting us to and from the circuit. Even my teammate, Jean-Pierre Jarier, who is used to energetic traffic in France, was prompted to say "*¡Por favor!*" to Joseph when he started to get too enthusiastic weaving in and out of traffic.

Last year, we went out to the track for the race en masse with a motorcycle escort. I have never seen such brave riding as those motorcycle cops displayed. If the leader thought the oncoming traffic was veering too close to our cavalcade, he would swerve his bike into the oncoming lane and stand up on the pegs and wave the cars away . . . all this while going sixty or seventy mph! Denny Hulme, who has been World Champion and is as brave as they come, got down on the floor of the car he was riding in.

When we got to the circuit, I got out and shook my driver's hand and then went up to the leader of the motorcycle escort and congratulated him. I hope he was not then (and still isn't) aware of my reputation for a somewhat dry sense of humor.

By the way, the vaunted efficiency of the Argentinian police did not stop at getting us to the track in the shortest possible time. At one point, just before the race started, a dog ran out onto the track. One of the cops assigned to control the crowd dispatched it with his machine gun. Evidently nothing is spared in making the track safe for the visiting GP drivers in Buenos Aires.

At any rate, although Joseph had Jean-Pierre thoroughly uncomfortable, I watched his driving and I knew he was very alert. I was convinced he was not driving to impress us, but to get where we were going quickly. He had a feel for traffic, even though some of his driving was inefficient. He would use the access sidings to the expressway to pass two or three cars on the inside—swerving, braking heavily, and generally conducting himself in a herky-jerky style that involved some discomfort, I'm afraid, for his passengers.

But he did it with 100 per cent concentration. He had owned his car, a Peugeot, for a year, and he loved it. He had put 19,000 kilometers on it, and when I checked it out surreptitiously, after the first ride, for dents and found no trace of bodywork or scratches, I concluded he knew what he was doing.

Later, Joseph really felt for my unsuccessful weekend. It was almost as if it had been a blow to *him*. He, among all the others, was probably the most sympathetic. Even though my Spanish is halting, Joseph and I exchanged some views while weaving through the Sunday night traffic of Buenos Aires after the race, on the way to the airport. I commented on the craziest driving I'd seen during my whole stay. It was even worse than usual, I said, and attributed it to heavy Sunday consumption of wine. Joseph thought for a moment seriously, then said straight, *"Vino no es un problema, es mujer!"* Siestas can have a bad effect. When we said good-by at the airport, and he asked if he might be my driver again next year, I was considerably moved.

A bad race and a late plane are not a good combination, especially when there is an eighteen-hour trip ahead. At the airport I discovered Rikky von Opel, whose plane to New York was also delayed, and we sat down for a couple of beers and a wait.

I'd never talked to Rikky much. I knew, as did everyone else, that he was independently wealthy. His family name, after all, was attached to the German car that is now manufactured by General Motors.

But Rikky pays the bills on his car for grand prix racing. He's the living definition of an amateur. He says he doesn't have any consuming desire to win the world championship, all he wants to do is go out there and give a good account of himself. He told me that in Formula 3 racing, where he had some success, he never thought about winning, only about going faster and improving.

Maybe, I said to him, when he had been in racing for several years, as I had been, winning would become everything. I told him that when that happens, when you get some years under you, that you begin to think very objectively and analytically about yourself and your car, all to the end of winning. That's why I'm still at it, I told him.

He answered that after three or four months away from racing and after another disappointment this year in the first race (his car didn't start—some sort of malady—and he qualified last) it seemed to him things weren't going to be any different from the way they had been.

Last year he didn't get to do any testing, because the car was always prepared late and they just barely had time to make each race, much less test in between. He'd like to get someone else to sort out his car, he said. He'd just like to step in the car and drive.

All the while we were talking and he was saying those things, I was thinking, "Well, that's expecting a lot. But, on the other hand, he's willing to pay for it."

Rikky was telling me how many other things there were in life besides racing. I didn't know how long he'd been at it (he is twenty-six now). He was talking like a guy who'd raced enough and had decided perhaps that the rewards weren't worth the risk and sacrifice any more. It seemed to me that he was thinking (although I wasn't going to come out and say it) that it was time to give it up and go on to some of the less risky pleasures of the world—which, God knows, he could certainly well afford.

But perhaps Rikky was resigned because he couldn't hack it and his car couldn't hack it either. I told him he wasn't going to get anywhere in racing unless he stayed at it, perhaps became a little more dedicated.

"There's so much more to life than racing," he said again. And I was thinking to myself, "Yeah, you're right. With an attitude like that, you don't get anywhere."

My flight was called prematurely and the additional delay gave me a chance to remember that it hadn't been very long since things had gone badly for me. I had poor cars. I would jump from one car to another. I was telling myself that there was a lot more to do in life than to jump from one bad car to another without making much money.

Someone once said it's an artist's prerogative to have momentary lapses: to fall down, to rise again to new heights. It could be that this is true of other things as well, but I don't think it applies in racing. In this sport you have to dedicate 100 per cent of your faculties all the time. If you have spells when you are not doing well or spells when you are not successful, it may *seem* like a lapse, but because the sport is so mechanical and so complex, it's very likely due to accountable reasons rather than some mysterious and so-called artistic lapse.

I used to think (a long time ago, when I was racing without much success and without recognition and without encouragement from anyone) that if I persisted long enough, I'd be sure to make it. I don't know how much persistence had to do with it, but the philosophy served me well. I'm making it now, but this is my fourteenth year of competition.

Fourteen years ago, even ten, my thoughts, while much the same as now about sticking to things, were also less tolerant. I thought that a racing driver's career was fairly short. I was very young and I figured that by the time I reached my so-called peak driving years, most of the guys at the level I was trying to attain would be retired.

And of course, I was very cold about it too. I knew some of those guys would have been killed. But I also knew there were enough smart drivers around who would have retired from the sport so that not only would there be room, but there would be proof for me that when I did reach a certain level of success the road wouldn't literally turn into a cul-de-sac.

I still feel that way. I'm almost where I want to be. This year, which has started with bad luck, can end with the world championship, given good luck.

Mentioning luck isn't to imply any lack of confidence or lack in conviction about my own ability. In racing you need luck, since you're working with a very complex mechanical device. You can have all the best people in the world and you still need luck.

I have often heard it said about some driver or another that he would have made it big if . . . and that "if" usually means if someone had come along and given him a good ride. Probably the most frequent question I am asked is how does somebody make it into grand prix racing.

There, I was thinking on the plane, was Rikky von Opel, and he made it with money and didn't know what to do with it and only part of it had to do with talent or lack of it.

If I had had the talent Jody Scheckter has, maybe I would have done it a lot sooner. Who's to say?

Everyone says, "Well, I didn't get this break, I didn't get that break," and some of the guys I grew up with still probably aren't going to get that break.

But if you look at the record, they always got that one racing-career opportunity. It always came, perhaps not once but twice. They never took advantage of it. And that's something they won't admit. In racing, if you persist long enough, if you persevere, you are going to get the opportunity. And you'd better be ready for it.

My opportunity came in 1970, when Chris Amon couldn't get the McLaren Indy car up to speed and went home to England. I had ten laps to prove myself. Ten laps. If I had screwed up, if I hadn't been able to do any better than Chris, the opportunity would have been gone. They were probably the most important ten laps of my life.

But people say they never have the chance to get even that far. My answer is that if they want to get out of their Camaros or their sprint cars or their sportsmen, they can. It isn't easy, but if racing were easy everyone would be doing it. It takes persistence and it takes enterprise.

PART ONE

I am also asked what it takes to be a successful racing driver, and what that is leading up to is the most frequent question of all: "How do I get started?"

The answer to that question is: Go to school and then buy a Formula Ford.

The cars are readily available, more so than anything else. They're the cheapest cars you can buy and the easiest to maintain. A lot of people are in the class, so if you're any good at all you'll have a chance to show it. So far as I can see, it's not true that you have to go to England to learn to race. Sure, the racing there is more frequent and more localized. But there's plenty of racing in the United States if you're up to it, and the competition is very good.

Now, as to how to learn what to do when you get in your Formula Ford, go to drivers' school. Jim Russell is one that I would recommend. Then start your round of weekend racing.

There is such a thing, by the way, as proper stature for racing. It's hard to say exactly what's too big for a racing driver. Dan Gurney was 6'3" and he was about the biggest Formula 1 driver on record, sort of a Kareem Abdul-Jabbar. If you're going to grow to be 6'5" I'd say you're going to have a problem.

So far as attributes, the ability to concentrate is the most important thing you can have. You really can't go fast until you learn to concentrate 102 per cent. And this is something it takes a while to learn; it took a while for me to learn it. You have to anticipate, you have to be ahead, you just have to concentrate every step of the way. It's this simple: If you don't learn to concentrate, you're just not going to be able to go quickly safely.

It's hard to relate size to racing. Today, for example, the wider tires take considerable effort to steer. For the two hundred miles of a grand prix race it requires a great deal of physical effort to do well. You have to be in good shape. You need stamina. You *don't* need power, because racing is not a power sport in the sense that golf and tennis are power sports.

So, in that regard, racing is an equalizer. Some of the very greatest of drivers have been little men. But you do need to be athletic. You need hand/eye co-ordination. You need good reflexes and you need stamina.

And you need purpose and you need attitude.

From turn to turn around a race course, you are dealing with perfection. There are ways of bringing yourself to a state of preparation to accomplish that. I know I have to be perfect in order to win and so I get very edgy. Before a race I am not communicative, perhaps even a little sullen. And on the grid, no matter what anyone thinks or supposes, there are butterflies. But what we are dealing with here is attitude. It is the pressure I put on myself to win. It is self-imposed before a race. You must know what you have to accomplish and be prepared mentally and physically to accomplish it. I know I have to maintain the highest degree of excellence from beginning to end in the race. I know how good I have to be. If I am not good, it is very hard to take. There is a lot at stake and you must realize it. There's reputation, there is pride, there is money. If you are not prepared to understand that, to sacrifice for it, you are not prepared to be a winner. If I just went out there to run a race there wouldn't be that kind of pressure, and I don't think I'd feel the butterflies.

You must be prepared to be apprehensive about being hurt or killed. That feeling exists. This is a difficult thing to explain. The way to understand it, if you are going to be a racing driver of any consequence, is to see it in terms of the edge of the road being a buffer. I know if I make any mistakes, go off the road at all, it's going to penalize me in the race. I'm going to lose time. I'm going to lose. And that's as bad as anything I can visualize. It's the thing I relate to most: the only thing I see as relevant.

Understand this: Losing really hurts. To fail in the race is the most painful thing imaginable. The physical fear is another matter. You get shaken when certain things happen on the race course, but during a race you are protected by a certain resilience. Perhaps if you gave much thought to some things that happened during a race you might faint—once the race is over. But those things don't register emotionally during the race itself. What does register is that something almost happened to you and perhaps you should concentrate harder to prevent any similar thing from happening.

The thought of being killed does occur to you if you're a racing driver. But if it occurred a lot, you couldn't drive. Although it's ever present it can be made to serve a purpose. What we do is fairly dangerous, and that's why I feel we should make as much money as we can.

And I would be lying if I said accidents don't worry me. They mean I won't finish a race. I don't like pain, but I have a high threshold for it. If I were to be in a serious accident, I've decided I could live with the consequences, and some are very unpleasant. I have heard people say they'd rather be dead than disfigured. I don't agree. If I were in a really bad wreck, I'd spend some of the money I've saved on a plastic surgeon. I've seen racing drivers who have had very bad accidents and who are back driving race cars. They don't look like Valentinos, but people don't turn away from them in horror either. I'd be thankful my faculties were still intact.

These are all thoughts I had on the plane after I talked to Rikky von Opel. Maybe these black thoughts were caused by my bad mood, because, even though I was in first class, we weren't fed anything for hours and that didn't help my attitude much. I kept thinking, if I had had Rikky von Opel's money when I was going from bad car to bad car I could have accelerated my racing career. Maybe then, three or four years ago, I would have done enough so that I might have been saying with conviction then what he said to me at the airport: "There are other things to do."

But I didn't, and I told Rikky just before my plane left, "You know, you're twenty-six. I'm going to be thirty-five next month and I'm still looking for the big prize." He didn't say a thing to that.

Perhaps he understood that it's not going to happen overnight even if you buy your way. It takes time. It takes experience. I don't know if Rikky is going to be able to use his money to help himself achieve something in racing. Even that requires a certain amount of diligence, intelligence, and dedication.

I wonder, too, if Rikky's money doesn't insulate him from the sounds of racing I find so stimulating early in the season and so hard to take as the year goes on. Certainly it must make it difficult for him to know the people as I know them or to see some of the special and basically private things I see. It might make a year like the one I had in 1973 a lot easier to take, to be sheltered by Rikky's money and his uncommitted attitude. But even that kind of year, which all of us sooner or later have, was filled with some moments that you can find probably only in a job like mine.

Mandel · One

If everyone around thought the profits from 100 million tubes of Orange Flip lipstick were buying your car, you'd be testy too.

If 1973 came as a nasty surprise to Peter Revson, 1967 had come as an even nastier one to his brother Douglas, although perhaps he never knew it. It killed him.

Doug Revson died in a small single-seater race car in the rain in Denmark. The news of his death saddened the racing community for the obligatory moment, but it didn't distract them much from whatever they were doing at the time. After all, Douglas Revson was another rich kid playing at racing, and that kind of thing can be expected to happen. Too bad, of course, but Denmark is far away and the race wasn't an important one. Not much of an opportunity for dipping into a little self-importance by letting people know what a good guy Douglas had been. Few people outside sports-car racing on the East Coast knew Douglas. When someone is killed, the least he can have done is to have provided the survivors with something to say to their friends in the bar at the Holiday Inn in Speedway, Indiana, or at the monthly meeting of the San Francisco Region of the Sports Car Club of America at the boathouse in Oakland. Doug Revson hadn't had the consideration to do even that.

Now *Peter* could have killed himself in 1967 and that would have been worthwhile. People knew Peter. He had already made his mark. Peter was a rich kid in the minds of the racing people too, and if by the year of his younger brother's death he hadn't exactly become a superstar, there was still something about him and something about his driving that demanded he be taken seriously. Well, at least not completely written off as just another preppie making noises about being a race driver instead of going into his father's business. "Yes," those people tend to say at Southampton and Pebble Beach somewhere between races no one has ever heard of, "actually, I'm a racing driver. A professional." By their languid manner and the cut of their J. Press madras, they're denying it at the same time.

Douglas Revson never quite escaped that. He was an intense, moderately good-looking young man. His rides were at least acceptable but the problem was they were *his* rides, which is to say he owned the cars he drove. If you're any good at all, if you even promise to be any good, you don't have to buy a car to go racing. Did Johnny Longden or Willie Shoemaker ever have to own their own horses? In '68, when his legs and his eyes and his reputation were still intact, did Willie Mays have to have a piece of the Giants franchise to play ball?

It's damn near as cut and dried in racing. But of course a race car is a lot cheaper than a National League ball club or even a small piece of one. So to get a leg up the ladder, sometimes you buy your ride. But Doug Revson owned everything he drove, even the red, white, and blue Porsche 906 that he surprised everyone with at Laguna Seca.

By then, though, his elder brother was being paid to race somebody else's cars and was very much a man of his own.

That surprised a lot of people. At least the ones who were willing to look and see a real race driver beneath the tailored jackets and the transatlantic accent. CIA directors may come from the Ivy League, even the occasional New York Knickerbocker or Minnesota Viking, but race drivers don't. Ask A. J.

Foyt about the Ivy Leagues and he'll probably think you're getting around to calling him a flaming faggot and punch you in the mouth just in case.

So Cornell would have been explanation enough for Peter Revson's truculence from time to time among his fellow racers. It could also be that if everybody in the pits thought that the profits from 100 million tubes of Orange Flip lipstick were buying your car, you'd tend to be a little testy too.

Whether they thought that or not didn't matter. Because, at the time, Revson was convinced they did, that everyone figured he was floating to his successes on a sea of Intimate.

For example, it is true that Martin Revson, Peter's father, is one of the three Revson brothers who founded Revlon. And surely Revlon is one of the extraordinary postwar business phenomena and made an astonishing amount of money for its major stockholders.

But after these two facts, matters begin to get a little confusing: The people involved start to have a curious way of appearing in one context and reappearing in another; the paths of truth and the zigzags of legend begin overlapping until tracing the course of Revson history is as difficult as mapping the Bridger Range.

Take something as innocent as the appearance of RevUp (The Vitamin for Men), "something they've asked me to endorse," according to Peter, who spent four days before the Indianapolis 500 wandering from shopping-center drug store to shopping-center drug store smiling and autographing 8x10 glossies. The deal was put together by the number-two man in the office of Revson's business manager, Mark McCormack. It looked like any other deal that any other of McCormack's athlete-clients (who include Jackie Stewart, Rod Laver, Evonne Goolagong, Arnold Palmer, Larry Csonka) might have had. Give a slightly commercial nod in favor of Wilkinson Sword Blades or Oleg Cassini sunglasses. What it is supposed to do is double your sports earnings in any given year. Mark McCormack's organization is very, very good at that sort of thing.

Except . . . the number two man in Motormarketing International, which is the automobile racing division of

McCormack's International Management, is Peter Revson's longtime friend George Lysle. Nothing very strange about that, of course. It's reasonable that McCormack might hire a qualified friend of one of his big earners. We make some money, you make some money, right?

On the other hand, RevUp (The Vitamin for Men) is marketed by Commerce Drug, makers of Detain (numby dummy as Revson calls it—"First a RevUp, then a little Detain"). And Detain is marketed by Commerce, and Commerce is a subsidiary of Del Laboratories, a toiletry and chemicals company. And Del Laboratories' major stockholder is . . . Martin Revson.

Now there's nothing here to conclude about scandalous conduct or a fraud upon the public. But there *are* three recurring patterns that make life extremely interesting for Revson-watchers: The Revsons operate like the Rothschilds or Exxon or Great Britain—they are very fond of interlocking directorates and vertical integration although, socially, they are detached from one another. Second: if you take notice, as you cannot help but do, of Peter's fierce need to acquire independent wealth, you also can't help but remark that he's willing to pursue that goal even to the point of accepting an alliance with his family. And, finally, the same people keep popping into the Revson warp and woof no matter where you look, no matter about what you inquire.

It could be that all this is to the account of the incestuous world of rich New York. Peter and Peter's family became a part of that as Revlon's worth soared. They lived in White Plains, New York, in Westchester County. Nelson Rockefeller lives in Westchester. A notoriously bad state school for retarded children is there too. The Martin Revson family could see neither from their large house in White Plains. Peter, Douglas, and sisters Julie Ann and Jennifer could see billows of comfort around them and an unlimited future. They could see their mother, Julie, a lot, because Julie was around wherever they went . . . although she spent considerable time doing good works as the children got older.

They didn't see much of Martin though. Revlon was growing enormously, and the three Revson brothers lived and breathed the business. (When brother Charles began, with fingernail polish, his significant contribution was to popularize colored as distinguished from colorless lacquer. "It made women aware of their hands," said one of his suppliers later. Charles was so taken with his heavy responsibilities that he would paint his own nails in the variegated colors he was contemplating putting into Revlon bottles and go home on the subway gazing at the effect.) "Charles was the hardest-driving man I ever met," said a man who sold him raw materials early in his career. "A genuine bastard, as a matter of fact." Like a child's wrinkled brow, Charles Revson's early business attitudes left an impression. "How do I assess Charlie Revson?" muses a New York social arbiter. "Simple. He's the biggest son of a bitch in town."

The Revson kids knew that their father wasn't around much. (Although Martin protests, "I played with the boys, I used to go out in the backyard and play ball with them," Peter says, "Sure he remembers that. He even did it seven times." But he laughs with affection at the thought, because nowadays he understands the worth of his father's days in the city and admires him for it.)

Probably it didn't make much difference. The kids were too busy fighting with each other. Peter and Doug were intensely competitive. Their fights were awesome. Martin remembers several of classic magnitude. George Lysle does too. "Christ, I thought they were actually going to kill each other a couple of times."

When you're poor and miserable you fight a lot; it's the only way you can object without getting stomped on by the establishment. When you're rich and bored you fight a lot too. Peter Revson fought some in Country Day School, but by the time he got to Hotchkiss he wasn't fighting so much any more.

At Hotchkiss, an elegant preparatory school in the fine eastern tradition, in Lakeville, Connecticut, Revson discovered he wasn't going to be able to get into Yale. When you're ninety-sixth in a class of 101, nobody wants you, much less Yale. But the Yale imperative, or something like it, was still there. "Revlon was in cosmetics and cosmetics had gotten very hot. Peter's father and his uncle were really starting to make a buck. The company had gone public and there was just a shitload of money being made," explains George Lysle. Revson disagrees. It was not the company success, not the money, not his father's longing to have a qualified son follow him in the cosmetics business that propelled Peter into yet another prep school to lift his grades; it was his mother. His mother was a stubborn woman, and she insisted that so far as the vision of success of her children was concerned, they were to be stubborn too. "It was bred into me," says Revson, "that what you started, you had to finish. I don't know whose idea it was that I was to be an engineer, but once the idea was there, it stayed there. My mother didn't like quitters."

Lysle ended up at Williston Academy, "kind of a step down when you're making the tour [of prep schools]." So did Revson.

Lysle is not at all embarrassed about his tour of the eastern educational establishment; his friend Revson views his own travels more modestly. At Williston, Revson was a jock. "He was a chubby guy and he was a fullback" is the way Lysle puts it, as though somehow the two go together. Lysle was the captain of the hockey team, Revson remembers, and until the ice formed he would lead a long line of apprentice skaters off into the countryside until they were out of sight of the schoolmasters and then call a cigarette break.

But Revson was more serious. Williston's was a "pretty rummy football team," in middle-'50s argot, which meant reasonably good, probably more the effect of some of the children of the Massachusetts Polish/American population than any inherent athletic prowess of the paying aristocracy.

Anyway, Revson played a lot although he continued to be overweight. "Not a superstar, but a pretty competitive guy, not fantastic at anything but a good football player. He tried."*

Revson's prep-school days then set a pattern: trying and traveling. He was in and out of, not Yale, but Cornell. And

---

* Lysle was jealous. He was so small he had to play on the Canary football team, where he was the oldest guy by three years. P.R.

the University of Hawaii. And Columbia. Wherever he went, he tried. But what he tried was someone else's concept of what he should do and what he should be. It was not the road to success.

In his social life, his direction was equally aimless. Revson may not have followed Lysle over hill and dale to a shaded spot for a cigarette, but he followed him into the parlors and swimming pools of the East.

George Lysle might well have posed for the picture of Dorian Gray. At least he could now. And surely the man who invented the ascot and the man who invented the blazer both used Lysle as a mental tailors' dummy. George Hamilton is a pale Lysle; George Montgomery is the prototype. But Lysle is real. He speaks out of the corner of his mouth in a triple-fast, machine-gun monologue spiced with whatever the current idiom of the sports world combined with the favorite adjectives of this week in the international set and . . . delightful to hear; vivid inventions of his own. George Lysle's speech, like his thoughts and in fact his presence, are out of context.

George Lysle has an endless capacity to amuse. He is always correct and proper among people of substance. He has been a tow-truck driver and a stockbroker, so he knows protocol. Charles Revson's wife, Lynn, is delighted to see George at the race track, and Martin Revson's new wife, Eleanor, is even more pleased. George will offer his arm, provide a hamper filled with chicken, deviled eggs, and champagne, shield them from the dust, the noise, and all those terrible people, while whispering the most delectably awful rumors about their private lives, hum some Beethoven, get a suite in the best hotel in town even when everything is booked solid, lay on a helicopter to the track, and play backgammon with their kids all at the same time.

Well, little wonder that this social scourge was irresistible to Peter Revson.† Lysle was in the middle of a kind of Waspy

---

† As a joke, Lysle would go through Connecticut reception lines with his P.F. high-top keds, an Eddie's Greenwich Esso T shirt beneath the jacket of his dinner suit. P.R.

country-club crowd.‡ No sooner would Lysle's parents be off to Florida than Revson would kind of come over and kind of move in. It all sounds very protective and very altruistic and maybe even a little condescending. But the trouble is that Lysle is an appealing if morally whimsical man. And honest enough to admit it wasn't one way. "Of course, his family have always taken care of me. They have flown me places, taken me places. When I've been hung over or fucked up they've had a place for me, or a bowl of soup for me when I'm broke."

It makes a fascinating picture.

A slightly overweight Revson arriving bag and baggage at Lysle's house the moment Lysle père and mère are chauffeured to the airport for Palm Beach.* A gay round of house parties with Revson standing slightly off in the corner. And in the middle of it all, George Lysle in blazer and ascot, champagne glass in hand, twirling one exquisite creature after another in the Scarsdale waltz.

That is the way *Lysle* would have you picture the Revson early social years. These days, a socially secure Peter Revson, thumbing through February *Town & Country* to the photo spread of the legs of the beautiful people (among which he easily identified his own), smiles tolerantly and says little to contradict his friend. Pressed, he admits it was something like that, but does a lateral arabesque and laughs at the memory of Lysle stopping his parties in mid-course to look at his watch and announce to everyone that he had to leave in order to take his mother to the roller derby.

The Westchester young have their legends, and as social legends go, Lysle is fairly strong stuff. But, to a substantial degree, it was just legend. Sure, Lysle got through to the Kremlin on a long-distance call once, and probably a couple of unattended cars did roll down the Lysle driveway to crash into someone else's backyard and the following morning's newspapers. But, in fact, George Lysle's father is a much respected

‡ Well, sort of; they really didn't want him in the middle.   P.R.
* George would raise a flag and there was a convergence of people from many counties.   P.R.

New York banker and it is hard to imagine Lysle broke and seeking soup from anyone's family but his own.

While all this intoxicating whirl was going on, Julie Revson was contemplating the alienation of her husband. Martin was busy too. Martin, the executive VP of Revlon, had said he would leave the company if Charles, the president, would not make substantial operating changes, the principal bone of contention apparently being a review of officer bonuses.

Whatever happened, and neither surviving brother will speak of the matter, Martin took his stock and left the company. "Martin was deemed the culprit," claims a *post hoc* George Lysle. "Martin left with his stock, millions of dollars' worth. Remember that Martin is a very shrewd businessman, an enormously sophisticated investor. If he got several million in settlement when he left, he's got many more millions now."

The brothers did not speak for thirteen years. Not until 1971, when Peter won the pole at Indianapolis, when as a result of two phone calls Peter's father and his uncle met at the track and reconciled to make it a clean sweep of astonishing accomplishments by Revson family members in central Indiana.

Says George Lysle now, "Why they showed up I couldn't tell you, but when somebody pointed to an older man with gray hair and said it was Charles Revson, I thought he was pulling my porkchop."

In the interim, Peter's father was not speaking to his brother; worse still, he was not speaking to his wife. Lysle thinks Peter began his long-standing role as a mediator early. "It was a very sticky, messy, sad, drag-it-through-the-mud affair. Peter showed great fortitude, a very big set of balls, because he has remained the arbitrator and mediator in the whole situation."

"What d'you mean, Peter says his mother took them camping?" demands Martin about his eldest son's memory of these unpleasant years. "Why, his mother was a Christian Scientist!"

Revson's response to the *non sequitur* is amusement. By now, he has had a long time to practice.

Revson's patience, his role as mediator, is due as much to his regard for his mother as to forbearance. Revson's father had said to his wife that she must raise the children until they reached the age of reason, at which point he would take over. As a result, it was Julie Phelps Hall Revson who bought Peter his first rifle and his first motor scooter. And if Revson learned discipline and determination from his father, it was his mother who provided lessons in culture and manners.

Julie Revson had adequate credentials to be a model of social rectitude to her eldest son. She traced her ancestry from William Phelps, who arrived in America in 1630 and founded the Congregational Church in Windsor, Connecticut. She was confirmed as an Episcopalian but converted to Christian Science before her marriage. Thus, although Martin Revson is a Jew, Peter was raised as a Christian Scientist.

For health reasons, Julie Revson moved to Hawaii. Peter, having left Cornell, went along, and it was in Hawaii that he began his racing.

He started in a Morgan, before he was twenty-one, with the Associated Sports Car Club of Hawaii, but the relationship didn't last long. From the first, Revson was a vigorous driver. He finished second in his first novice race, and won his second. But the Associated Sports Car Club of Hawaii sent him packing after his third because he was "too aggressive." When the Old School Tie steward set him down, Revson remembers being told he was talking like a "loose lunchbag." That was not calculated to leave fond memories of Hawaii for Peter Revson. But it's amusing to speculate what the Old School steward says now about having been there when Peter Revson ran his first races.

Revson came back to the mainland wanting to enter the Vanderbilt Cup in 1960, and bought a Taraschi Formula Junior from a Pontiac dealer on Long Island. The Taraschi, an early single-seater in a class meant for learning drivers, was a beautiful car: chrome wire wheels, chrome megaphone exhaust pipe, handsome black and white paint, wood-rimmed Nardi steering wheel, turned-steel dashboard. But it had a stock 1100cc Fiat engine and it was a pig.

Rodger Ward, Carroll Shelby, and the Rodriguez brothers

were entered in the Vanderbilt Cup; even Lorenzo Bandini came over from Italy to run it. Revson was lying fifth until he had fuel-feed problems; he finished seventh.

He was able to parlay his good finish and his Hawaiian license into a permit to run with the Sports Car Club of America, which was the sanctioning body for all major road racing in the United States at the time.

The Morgan had been on consignment in Hawaii but nobody was interested, so Revson brought it back to the United States and decided to run it in production-car races on the East Coast. Classes for production cars were determined by engine size, and the Morgan put Revson in with some people he would keep seeing for the balance of his career. John Cannon and Jay Signore had Elva Couriers in the same class, and Bob Tullius had a Triumph. But the king of the class was a newcomer named Mark Donohue.

"Mark was winning a lot of races. His car was particularly fast and well driven, although we questioned its legality. In those days in SCCA racing there were a lot of ways to beat the rules and Mark was clever enough to do it."

They raced at Thompson and Lime Rock, Connecticut; Vineland, New Jersey; Watkins Glen, New York—all over the East. Revson and Donohue ran in race after race, and Revson would invariably finish second. Donohue went on to win the 1961 class championship; Revson was fourth.

That year, Revson made two mistakes for which he is remembered.

On the grid at Watkins Glen he put his Morgan in reverse instead of first and started the race backwards.

Then, at Thompson, he flipped his car spectacularly and barely managed to find another one to buy for the next weekend's national race at Bridgehampton, on Long Island. "Now my old man was coming to the race that weekend," Revson remembers. "He knew my car was black with gray fenders. This other car was red. So he comes to the race track and he's standing by the fence on one of the downhill turns with some guy as I'm running around with Mark having a hell of a tooth-and-nail battle, passing and repassing, until I finally get a stone in my radiator. After the race, the old man comes into the pits and he says, 'I thought your car was gray with black fenders,' and I say, 'I painted it.' So it turns out the guy he was standing next to is the guy who sold me his car and I have to tell my old man about my horrible wreck."

Martin Revson was not pleased anyway about Peter's racing career. After that weekend at Bridgehampton, any thoughts Peter might have had about parental subsidy must have vanished forever.

By the end of the following year, Revson had used up all the money he could earn or coax from a sympathetic banker, but he had barely begun to use up his ambition to become a racing driver. With a fine disregard for the consequences, he emptied his small bank account, cashed in an accumulation of twenty-first-birthday presents, and sold the little amount of stock meant to pay for his college. The result was a twelve thousand dollar fund he intended to use to go racing in Europe for 1963.

Revson ordered a Cooper Formula Junior with a Holbay Ford engine, hired on Walter Boyd from Southern California for fifty dollars a week and keep, and set off.

Boyd and Revson arrived at the grandly named Cooper factory in Surbiton, England, to find it was nothing but an oversized garage and that their car had not even been started. "We were told, in the classic tradition of Coopers, that there was no reason why we couldn't help pitch in and build the car. The result, of course, is that we built the whole thing."

Nevertheless, John Cooper did at least one favor for Revson. He told him that a well-known car owner and team manager named Reg Parnell had lost his previous year's sponsorship and was looking for some way to help meet expenses. Parnell might be willing to rent some garage space, Cooper suggested.

Revson and Boyd were given space, and Jack Brabham sold them an old Thames bread van with a diesel engine and a governor that limited its speed to 48 mph. The van had been a race car transporter before Revson got it, and it had two frame racks inside. Revson put his Cooper on the top rack so that spares could be put on the bottom, along with a cot. Revson and Boyd slept as much in the van as anywhere else that year, partly because of necessity, partly because of the downward drift of their treasury.

The van, which Revson named Gilbert, was reliable, but that didn't mean it was without eccentricities. For example, Walter Boyd couldn't keep its head gasket sealed. The gasket would blow, invariably, as far away as possible from places that sold sealants. So the engine would begin to stream out water, which would come pissing out the back of the block, through the firewall, and all over the occupants of the driver's compartment.

In 1963, international racing was not so complicated as it is now. There were two formulas: Formula 1, the major leagues, and Formula Junior, the minors. There was room for only a few top drivers in Formula 1, and so the Junior circus was large and populated by very fine young drivers. During all that season Revson raced against the likes of Peter Arundell, Denny Hulme, Frank Gardner, Mike Spence, Jo Schlesser, Gerhard Mitter, David Hobbs, and Jochen Rindt. It was a fine, carefree life. On one trip to the Continent, Revson and Boyd went to Monte Carlo, where there were almost seventy entries for the preliminary race to the Grand Prix. With the other Junior drivers, they camped on the beach in front of some high-rise buildings, a band of gypsies living hand to mouth. Revson remembers looking up at one of the buildings, which he identified as the Hôtel de Paris, and realizing that it was where the grand prix drivers stayed. He remembers almost not daring to hope that he might be staying there himself one day. It was too much of a contrast to the life he was leading at the time; dungarees for eight months, sleeping in the back of the bread van. Besides which, he was terribly busy.

After Monte Carlo, Revson bought a Cosworth engine for eighteen hundred dollars of his diminishing funds, went to Zolder, in Belgium, and led the race until he spun. He and Walter Boyd packed up immediately and went on the long and beautiful drive down the west coast of Italy, heading for the race at Enna. Revson remembers waking up sometime during the night to great scraping and sliding. They were

1. The four Revson children with mother, Julie Phelps Revson, in 1953. From the left: Peter, Julie Ann, Jennifer, and Douglas.

2. In 1965, Revson drove for Ron Harris' works Lotus team in Formula 2 behind Jim Clark and Mike Spence. He also drove several Formula 3 events, including the classic preliminary to the Grand Prix of Monaco, which he is shown here winning.

3. Start of the Nassau trophy race in the Bahamas in 1966, with Revson already on his way in one of George Drummond's McLarens. Revson allows as how it was one of his better starts.

4. The superdrivers on the factory Cougar team in 1967, Dan Gurney and Parnelli Jones, combined to just equal the number of wins of their substitute, Peter Revson. Here he leads the first race of the season at Lime Rock, Connecticut, a race he won.

5. In 1967 Revson drove for the Ford Motor Company, whose cars were entered b Carroll Shelby (right) and Holman and Moody. Shelby's Ford career was cut shor when he flew a Mk IIB prototype at twenty-five feet over the Daytona race track

Revson drove in the United States Road Racing Championship for Peyton Cramer's Goodyear team. Another USRRC driver was Masten Gregory, who was just coming to the end of his career. Revson's intense stare is an almost exact imitation of his father's everyday expression.

Revson teamed with Steve McQueen to take a second at Sebring in 1968 in an outclassed Porsche. As good as Revson is, he by no means placed the car that high himself; McQueen is a fine race driver.

With friend, co-boat owner, competitor, and sometime employer Roger Penske during the Javelin TransAm days.

9. Teddy Mayer, boss of McLaren Racing.

10. "George Lysle might well have posed for the picture of Dorian Gray."

11. Tyler Alexander (right) is a perfectionist. Not only must his race cars go fast, they must be shiny and clean. This is the moment before the first of three Indianapolis starts in 1973. Tyler has on his flameproof jacket and his CB radio set, with which he keeps in touch with the drivers when they are on the track. At the left is Edgar The Incredible.

12. Danny Folsom, an Indiana businessman, is a superfan who has adopted Pet Revson. At Indianapolis he is Revson's governess, companion, bodyguard, and cheering section. Folsom opens his house to the McLaren team during the month of Ma and keeps the team's garage refrigerator stocked. In recognition, he was awarded team jacket.

going down a mountain and Walter Boyd was sliding the truck in great sweeps and slides to scrub off speed, because he had run out of brakes. Revson recalls thinking he'd better not watch much more of Boyd's midget techniques in an English bread van on an Italian mountainside than he'd already seen, and going back to sleep.

At Enna, Revson gained his first real recognition by setting the lap record and dueling with the French Champion, Jo Schlesser. After Enna, with no preparation other than loading the car into the van, they drove north to Copenhagen to run an eight-tenths-mile circuit in a quarry. They stayed in a motel in Denmark, one of the first in Europe, but they had no place to work on the car. So they used the shower in the motel room as a work stall. Revson qualified on the pole and won the race and five hundred dollars.

From Denmark, they went to France for a full international, where Revson was second, behind Hulme, in his heat and fifth in the final.

Back in England, Reg Parnell, who had been following Revson's progress on the Continent, offered him a place for the following year on his Formula 1 team. Parnell was going to run a pair of ex-works Lotus 25s for Chris Amon and Mike Hailwood in order to develop his own car. He would use Revson as a test driver.

Before he left, Revson had one drive in Formula 1, his first. It came at Oulton Park in the Gold Cup, and, despite bad brakes, he finished seventh.

Revson went home at the end of the season much satisfied. He had gained experience, he still had six thousand dollars left, and it looked as though in 1964 he would actually be making money and be on his way into the big leagues.

Reg Parnell died during the winter.

Parnell's son Tim took over the team, but it wasn't the same; Tim was not experienced and he was not paternal. Revson and Tim Parnell made a deal for Revson to drive a Lotus-BRM in Formula 1, but it would have to be under the name Revson Racing, because that way it would sound as though it were a different team altogether and that would mean additional starting money.

Revson paid the mechanic and his own expenses, but got 25 per cent of all starting money, which varied from four hundred to six hundred pounds a race, and a quarter of all prize money as well.

The prize-money share was academic. It was not a successful year. In practice for one of the early non-championship races, Revson vaulted some hay bales in the rain. Since starting money was only paid if the car actually started, Revson's hay-bale adventure put Tim Parnell into an anxiety fit, and from then on Parnell restricted Revson's practice severely. No sooner would Revson begin to get familiar with a circuit than a sign with a big arrow saying "IN" would be put out and the Patented Tim Parnell Practice Drill would begin. Revson would bring the car in, Tim Parnell would tell him to go off and take a rest, the mechanics would take off one wheel and remove the spark plugs, and then they'd disappear too. About ten minutes before the end of practice everyone would come back and the car would do one more lap before the session ended.

To be accurate it wasn't only Revson's exuberance that worried Parnell. They had absolutely no spare parts for the car, so if anything broke before the race, they were through.

But sometimes even starting the race was no guarantee of anything else. At Syracuse, in Italy, Revson didn't manage to complete even the first lap before he spun the car.

Tim was furious despite Revson's apologies and ranted and raved, all the while dragging Revson to the prize-giving and swearing he would have his head. Despite his bluster, Parnell was a worried man. The organizers could have balked at paying any money at all to someone who may have started, but whose retirement on the first lap made it look suspiciously as if the only reason he started at all was to collect the appearance money.

At the party Parnell was all charm toward the promoter, a very swarthy man with an enormous swarthy daughter. He brought the daughter over to Revson, the young American, and it was very clear that Parnell expected Revson to save the day even if it meant eloping with the daughter. "We started dancing and she was a big, big girl. A *huge* girl. I could just about see around her and every time I'd swing in a certain direction I'd see Tim glowering at me. Every time I'd grab her hand to walk her away from the dance floor, Tim would come over and glower some more, so I'd ask her to dance again. All night long I was under the gun. I was dancing with that broad until I was ready to drop."

But it worked. The next day, Tim Parnell walked into the promoter's office and collected his money.

The Parnell school may have been fine training for the foreign service, but Revson wanted to be a racing driver. So, for '64, Revson signed on with Ron Harris, who was a film distributor and also found time to run the Lotus in the new Formula 2. Harris would use Revson in Formula 2 when Jim Clark and Mike Spence, his two top drivers, were running Formula 1 events. As it turned out, Harris occasionally ran a third car even when Clark and Spence were driving, so Revson got in quite a few races. Although there wasn't an official Lotus Formula 3 team (another new formula for even less powerful cars) Harris entered a couple of the big races including Monte Carlo, the most important Formula 3 race in Europe. Revson was entered for it and won.

By this time, if Revson wasn't making a fortune, he was at least a full-blown professional. Harris paid him seventy-five pounds a race for the Formula 2 races in England and within short traveling distance, and one hundred pounds for races farther away. He also got 40 per cent of the purse.

Despite the status and the pleasure of driving for a works team, Revson felt the future in Europe was becoming less and less promising. Bill Kay, a friend of the promoter at the track in Lime Rock, Connecticut, had just bought a Formula Junior and asked Revson to drive for him in the United States. When Revson agreed, Kay went to Europe and bought the fastest small-engined sports car available, a Brabham BT8, for the new fall sports-car series in the United States.

The fall series was the forerunner of the Canadian American Challenge Cup, which Revson was to win with McLaren in 1971. Although Revson was the top money winner in the small-car category, he was out of a ride at the end of 1965.

That was the year Skip Scott came along. Scott was an eccentric figure in American racing. He was a driver of considerable talent himself, but he was a much better promoter. Scott had put together a sponsorship deal with Essex Wire, which made wiring harnesses and whose best customer was the Ford Motor Company. Ford was involved in racing in an increasingly extravagant fashion. Nineteen sixty-five was the heyday of the muscle car and the youth cult, and Ford marketing people were convinced there was a strong positive correlation between racing successes and the car-buying habits of the young.

Scott told Essex Wire it would be a fine public-relations gesture to sponsor a team of cars and that Ford had developed a race car called the GT40. He signed Revson to a contract to become his driving partner in Europe in the Manufacturers' Championship for sports and prototype cars at five hundred dollars a race plus expenses. And although Revson didn't think he was being overpaid, he does admit now that they lived well. In Paris they stayed at the Crillon. "I lived well because I was with Skip and Skip liked to live well." Scott had a very high opinion of himself, he was ambitious, he thought on a grand scale, but, withal, he was poor on detail. One of the details he was forever overlooking was paying Revson. So one night at the Crillon, in the room they shared, Revson waited until Scott was fast asleep, then suddenly began to yell at him at the top of his voice about what Scott owed him. Scott was so startled he agreed. Revson had no money troubles with Scott thereafter.

That season, Revson qualified first in the GT (Grand Touring) class five times and the Revson/Scott Ford won at Spa, in Belgium; and at Sebring, Florida. Because of a transmission weakness, the Ford failed to finish several times, but the Essex Wire car led Daytona; Monza, Italy; and Le Mans before it broke.

Ford had three teams entered, and their placings all counted together toward the championship. Ford of France had a team with Schlesser, and the Belgian Fillipinetti team was entered as well, but the Skip Scott Essex Wire car contributed more than any other to winning the championship for Ford in '66.

Revson was very fond of the GT40. "It was a very well balanced car. Very easy to drive. It responded beautifully. Until then, I had never driven a sports car that handled quite as well, as forgivingly or as controllably as that one. It stopped well, and for a car of its size and weight, it was very comfortable to drive." The GT40 continued to win races for three more years, an absolutely incredible accomplishment, almost as if a distance man were still winning Olympic gold medals at age sixty. Revson is not alone among the people who drove the car in thinking that the GT40 will go down as one of the great sports cars in history.

If the big factories were in racing, it was indispensable for any ambitious driver to get to know the people who were running the factory racing programs, and the man who ran Ford's was a grim dandy, with the smile of a barracuda, named Jacque Passino.

In addition to the independents, the factory also ran its own teams, although they were frequently disguised under someone else's name. Ford had been successful with the modest GT40 and now was going after the title with the biggest, hairiest sports cars it could build. Carroll Shelby was to enter three cars, and the North Carolina firm of Holman and Moody was to prepare three others.

Shelby and Holman and Moody were bitter rivals. Shelby had become virtually a part of Ford Motor Company as a result of his converting the Mustang into the Shelby GT350; Holman and Moody was as close to being the racing subsidiary of Ford as it could come.

Passino sat in Dearborn egging them both on, hoping for some kind of racing civil war, on the theory that mortal conflict off the race track meant winning on it.

Ford signed Revson to a Ford Mk IIB ride for three thousand dollars a race for 1967. At the same time the International Championship for sports cars was being held all over the world, the TransAmerican Sedan Championship for so-called "pony cars" had begun on American circuits, sanctioned by the Sports Car Club of America. The series was designed to take advantage of the Detroit factories' insatiable hunger after a "performance image," and provided for a cross-country series for cars that fit the specifications of Mustang, Javelin, Camaro, Cougar, and Barracuda.

Although Lincoln-Mercury Division's Cougar was essentially the same car as its sister the Mustang, put out by Ford Division, and both divisions were integral parts of the same company, it is important to understand that the rivalry between the two was—and is—intense. They are treated almost as separate companies, and it is not Chevrolet that the Ford people hate . . . it is Mercury.

So when Revson signed on the Cougar team for the TransAm as the third driver behind Parnelli Jones and Dan Gurney, it was made very clear to him that his rivals were the people across the hall at Ford.

The TransAm Cougar team contract provided for five hundred dollars a race and all the prize money, and it turned out that, far from being the third man on the team, Revson drove most of the races and won two of them, twice as many as either Jones or Gurney.

The Cougars were prepared by a shrewd veteran of southern stock-car racing named Bud Moore—slow speaking, sleepy-eyed, and about as mild as a raging wolverine.

The TransAm was a bitterly fought series filled with courage, tenacity, and inventiveness. For example, TransAm cars had to conform to a weight minimum, and they were put on the scales before a race to make sure they complied. A driver with one TransAm team had a special, lead-filled helmet he'd toss casually in his car when it was being pushed to the scales. Another team had weighted Gatorade bottles ready just in case. And a third used weighted wheels and tires.

The TransAm championship came down to the last race of the season in 1967 with Cougar and Mustang both in a position to win. Revson doesn't know what went on behind the scenes at Ford before the last race. He does know there was a lot of politicking, and he knows the people in charge of the Cougar team, who worked directly for the factory, were prepared to defy any instructions and go all out to win. It was academic; Mustang won the last race fair and square.

Meanwhile, in international racing, things had not gone well for Ford. Revson and Mark Donohue co-drove a Holman and Moody car at Daytona in the twenty-four-hour race, but it was another case of bad transmissions, only ten times worse than before. Ford knew about the problem and had brought truckloads of spare gearboxes with them for the race, and they went through almost all of them.

Two cars were sent to the next race at Sebring, and Ford won it with Mario Andretti and Bruce McLaren co-driving, but neither Revson nor Donohue was entered.

And then, in preparation for the twenty-four-hour at Le Mans, a race Henry Ford always considered the most important international event of them all, Revson was bounced off the first-string Ford team in the most dramatic way possible.

"We were having a private Ford test at Daytona for the Mk IIB and the Mk IV and I was coming off the banked fourth turn when the car started to get a little wormy. It was losing a little of its stability coming over the turn where there is a hump in the road. A tire was going soft and the car slid a little further than it should have. The tires started to lose adhesion when the whole car just sort of swept toward the wall. It scraped the wall very lightly, it didn't even hit the tail end, it was almost as though the whole car brushed the wall at once. What that did was to grind off the right rear tire. I was going maybe 185, and the whole car dipped down. The air got under the front and it took off like an airplane. I just put my head down and waited for the banging to stop. I thought I was up in the grandstands. As it turned out, I took out a light pole 25 feet in the air, but I didn't get in the grandstands and I didn't jump the fence. The car went bicycling down the track and it landed, according to the odometer on Lloyd Ruby's bicycle, a third of a mile from the point where it first made contact with the wall.

"Just previous to my accident Ford had put rollbars in the car. They hadn't been in when Ken Miles was killed in a Ford testing accident and they hadn't been in when Walt Hansgen was killed in his Ford practicing for Le Mans.

"I remember getting out of that thing, popping open the door and pulling myself up out of the car, and I've never seen so many shocked people in my life. They were all standing in a semicircle about 50 feet away from the car, kind of poised, waiting for something to happen and never in their lives expecting anyone to get out . . . much less uninjured."

Insisting it was a precaution, the Ford people put Revson in a hospital. But it is Revson's conviction that it was a matter of keeping word of the accident from leaking out. To Revson's surprise, since he had always considered the elegant life-style of Henry Ford to pervade his corporation, Ford did not arrange for a private room in the hospital. That was particularly disturbing when Mario Andretti came to visit and gave Revson, an avid cherootist, a cigar. Revson's roommate was dying of emphysema.

When the team got to Le Mans, Revson was demoted to backup. About noon, with a good part of the race still to run and a very clear obligation to stick around in case he was needed, Revson got bored and, figuring he had done his duty, asked Skip Scott to give him a lift to Paris. Scott had borrowed an Eldorado to drive down to the race, one of perhaps two Eldorados in all of France and no more visible than the Goodyear Blimp. It's hard to sneak out of a French race track in an Eldorado, but Scott and Revson were managing it when Scott spied Henry Ford on his way in.

"Of course, Skip wanted to say hello mainly in order that Mr. Ford could acknowledge Skip's presence. But I said, 'For Christ's sake, Skip, if he sees us leaving now he's going to tell Passino and we won't get the 3Gs.' I needed the 3Gs but Skip wanted to say hello to Mr. Ford. So he deliberately rerouted himself to drive in the same path in the heavily crowded pits as Henry Ford, who was coming in the other direction.

"I took one look and saw that Skip was serious about saying hello to Mr. Ford and got down on the floor of the back seat.

'What's the matter with you?' Skip asked me and I told him, 'just forget I'm here.'

"'How do you do, Mr. Ford,' says Skip. And Ford answers, 'Hi, Skip, how're we doing?' Skip tells him, 'we're doing great, Mr. Ford, we're leading.'

"I don't think it ever entered Ford's mind what Skip was doing and I told Skip, 'O.K. you asshole, you've said hello to Mr. Ford, now let's get the hell out of here.'"

Revson and Scott were just checking into their suite at the Crillon when they heard that Ford had won Le Mans.

Revson had a Mk III McLaren entered by Drummond Racing for the last three races of the 1966 CanAm, but it wasn't the racing that made the fall season important in his life, it was his meeting with Larry Truesdale. Truesdale was the racing chief for Goodyear. Like Ford, Goodyear was performance minded, which meant involvement in racing, and the head of its program was by definition an important man. But the fact that the job belonged to Truesdale made it even more important.

Truesdale is a tallish, reddish man whose warmth and good manners are fine complements to his tough, quick mind. When a company as large as Goodyear decides it's important to win a race, it does not take chances. Although no one has ever been able to document it, it is common knowledge that for several years at least half of the cars entered at Indianapolis were owned by Goodyear, which is the world's largest tire company. The other half were owned by the world's *second* largest tire company, Firestone.

Every Goodyear driver of any consequence was signed to an exclusive contract, which meant he could use no other tires. Control of the top drivers in the world through contracts meant a heavy edge when it came to winning races. Since Goodyear had only recently begun to challenge Firestone for dominance on the race track and it was doing so by offering up-and-coming drivers large contracts, so far as drivers were concerned Larry Truesdale was the most important man in racing.

Truesdale's influence, as enormous as it was with drivers,

did not stop there. Since it was winning his company was after, and since Goodyear intended to corner the market on drivers, that meant the company was in the marriage-broker business when it came to getting car owners and drivers together. A driver whom Larry Truesdale wished to sign was assured not only of a fat contract but of a first-class ride.

Truesdale had been well aware of Revson's career; he met him during the fall races in the CanAm in 1966 and offered him fifteen thousand dollars to sign a Goodyear contract.

"I was very cool," says Revson. But it was a great break and Revson knew it. Truesdale told him he'd be at Nassau for Speed Weeks and he'd bring the contract with him.

When Revson saw the contract, he discovered that it called for him to drive the following year in the United States Road Racing Championship for a man named Peyton Cramer, who had been the General Manager of Carroll Shelby's company and was going out on his own. Cramer's program was a wholly subsidized Goodyear team.

In 1966 Cramer was a partner in a Chevrolet dealership in Southern California. Today he owns part of a Lincoln-Mercury dealership in Harbor City, California, and part of a sports-car store in San Pedro. His partner in both is Peter Revson.

The team was only moderately successful, and the contract was cancelled after the '67 season. In the ensuing seasons Revson drove for Shelby, Boyd Jefferies, Carl Haas, and others . . . all on Goodyear tires.

But the Truesdale connection was more happily fateful than that. Revson says now that his big opportunity came at Indianapolis, when he was offered the factory McLaren that Chris Amon couldn't get up to speed. Revson may have known McLaren director Teddy Mayer as well as any other man in racing, but the odds are that the ride could never have come unless Truesdale was somehow involved.

From that moment on, Revson was in the big time.

Nowadays, Revson remembers 1963, his first year in Europe, as the time that racing was sweetest. He spoke no foreign language, he lived like a gypsy. Everything was an adventure: traveling, ordering in restaurants, going through customs in the Thames bread van with Walter Boyd. The results of 1963 were mixed, but at least by the end of the season people knew who Peter Revson was.

These days when he goes to a race at Monte Carlo he doesn't camp on the beach; he stands on a balcony in the Hôtel de Paris, a place he very much doubted he'd be.

Those are clear memories to Revson. The difference between 1963 and 1973, the balcony and the beach, mark a clear path of accomplishment to him now.

He also remembers, but does not talk about, a moment in 1967. That was the year, as mentioned, that his brother Douglas was killed, and he and his friend George Lysle changed from their dinner suits to go to the funeral. Afterward, Lysle drove him to Bryar Motorsports Park, in New Hampshire, where, expressionless, he won the second race in a row for the Cougar racing team.

PART TWO

Revson · Two

If I don't do it in the next two or three years, I won't do it at all.

It's a fourteen-plus-hour flight from London to Johannesburg and it's not one of your great trips. We had surprised everyone in South America and not in the way we had intended. We started slowly in Argentina with the McLarens. I was eleventh on the grid, and Denny, who didn't seem to be having the problems I was, started eighth. The fact is, we were a little worried. But, after that, we realized we could have been better. We would certainly have to be, since the Lotuses and the Tyrrells dominated the race and put on a hell of a show besides. Emerson Fittipaldi followed Jackie Stewart for many laps and didn't get around him until there were only eight laps to go. But he promptly caught François Cevert, who was leading him, and went on to victory. I passed Denny pretty early in the race and started battling Jacky Ickx first for sixth place, then for fifth, and finally for fourth. We went hammer-and-tongs for a number of laps and either the power in my engine was falling or Ickx was improving markedly. At any rate, I was fifth all along behind Jacky and about thirty seconds ahead of Denny when the ignition started failing, with six laps to go.

And so it goes. I made an unproductive pit stop and was hardly running at the end, winding up eighth.

Compared to Brazil, though, Argentina was terrific.

I'd gone home after Argentina to shoot an Aurora Toy Company commercial at Riverside and then immediately boarded a plane for Sao Paulo. I hadn't been in my hotel more than four or five hours when I woke up from a nap feeling really shitty. Stomach cramps, dysentery, and dizziness. I managed to make it out to the circuit on Thursday, put in a few laps, and promptly stopped, deciding I'd feel better the next day.

On Friday I felt worse and decided to pass up practice altogether. To help matters, Teddy Mayer, who runs the McLaren show, was a little abusive, saying I should take better care of myself and stop burning the candle at both ends. This kind of talk is typical of Teddy. He tends to be sarcastic and not altogether accurate about some things, particularly when he's frustrated. I was feeling a little frustrated myself, particularly since I had absolutely no idea of what brought my sickness on. Not only hadn't I had a chance to misbehave in Brazil, but since I'd only been there a few hours and spent that time napping, I hadn't even eaten anything.

On Saturday it was boiling hot. It must have been 95 with very high humidity, and two or three laps around that busy circuit quite exhausted me. Still, I managed to get up to twelfth on the grid on a day when the track was slightly slower than on the day previous.

On the other hand, Teddy had arranged for an interested spectator. The day before, not being sure about my ability to drive, he had contacted an English driver who was in Brazil on a holiday. Teddy's prospective new employee had never driven much of anything but Formula 5000—still, Teddy was ready to put him in the car in order to get two McLarens in the race. That's Teddy. He plans for all eventualities, and he wasn't going to be caught short.

This poor kid actually looked disappointed that I showed up feeling reasonably well. For my part, I knew that, one way or another, I was going to drive that car even if it meant I was going to vomit over the side of it every other lap.

Sunday morning was even hotter than Saturday. Although I was feeling better, I was dehydrated and a little weak and very much worried about the heat. I went to one of the seventy military doctors they had posted around the race track in eight different infirmary units. The doctor told me that not only were they (military police) expecting a lot of heat exhaustion with the spectators, but they were also very much prepared for riots.

This doctor was very agreeable, saw that I was dehydrated, and gave me a shot of glucose, water, and salt. That made me feel a hell of a lot better almost immediately, and I was feeling pretty chipper for the race.

On the second lap a crown wheel and pinion failed, and that was my race. Denny continued after having started fifth and came on to finish third. So goes Brazil.

During the long plane trip from London to Johannesburg for the South African Grand Prix, I was giving the first two races a lot of thought, and that thought was not cheerful. There were two interruptions in my black speculations.

I noticed some guy hanging over the seat behind me. After a little while, he interrupted my talking into the tape recorder wanting to know what I was doing, who I was, and made it clear that he thought I was acting suspiciously. He seemed to be satisfied with my explanation and walked away. But I can't imagine what he thought I was reporting on, particularly if it had anything to do with the plane and its passengers. There just wasn't anything worth talking about there. When we flew over Angola, according to the pilot, I saw that they're right about the vast dark continent. When you look out the window it's both barren and dark.

Ken Tyrrell was on the plane too. He's the man who is behind Jackie Stewart and François Cevert, as he has been behind a number of other fine drivers in the past. Some years ago he had a car designed and built for Stewart and managed to keep the whole thing a secret until they rolled the car out for practice. That, what with the fact that everybody knows everything that goes on within two seconds of its happening in the world of racing, was a considerable accomplishment.

Anyway, Ken came over, sat down, and wanted to know about our new McLaren M23. He was very casual about it, and I told him I hadn't driven it, but, from all reports, from the first test it was a better car than the M19. Slightly faster down the straightaway. Ken asked me who was going to be driving it in South Africa, as there's only one. I answered that since Denny has done most of the testing, as much because of his availability as anything else, it's likely he would. Besides, Denny's probably still considered the senior man on the team.

Maybe from the tone of my voice, Ken thought there was some resentment on my part that Denny was getting the car. So he picked up on that and said he thought this might be Denny's last year, particularly in the light of his disappointment in his performance in South America. Besides, said Ken, Denny just about wilted in the hot weather in Brazil and, although he hung on to third place, his lap-time curve went off drastically at the end of the race.

Denny retiring didn't seem to me to be likely, and I told Ken so. Denny probably doesn't have any plans for the future at all. If he didn't race he probably wouldn't do much of anything, one of the reasons being he doesn't have to. He lives frugally and he's got ample money for whatever he might need. For want of anything else, Denny probably will continue to race until either he isn't wanted any more or until he can't command the amount of money he thinks he's worth. He's got enough talent to carry on for several more years.

Ken thought about what I was saying, and the conversation got around to Jackie Stewart. Jackie has said that if he has a particularly good year he might retire. But nobody knows for sure. Ken thinks if Jackie retired, he'd miss the life, miss being the center of attention. It would likely take him several years to find something else that would give him what he gets from racing: money, a lot of money, and attention.

I probably know Jackie about as well as any other driver on the circuit, and my feeling is he'd give it up if he could find something to take its place. But whatever he finds will have to be the same thing to him that racing is. It would have to be challenging and it would have to allow him to express himself as completely as he does with motor racing. But that is a pretty tough problem, a big order. It won't happen immediately. He'll have to explore a few situations, and there'll be a period of transition for him. When I think about it, I realize the same period of transition would exist for me.

My own plans at this point are to continue for a couple of years and try to win the Indianapolis 500 and the world championship. But if I don't do it in the next two or three years, I won't do it at all, and therefore it would be time to give it up.

I'm getting to be like Jody Scheckter. Every place I go I get a different sickness. In Brazil it was flu, here in South Africa it's a reasonably good head cold.

There doesn't seem to be anything worse in a hot climate than having a head cold. The weather has been warm, the sun's shining, and there are only slight hints of clouds.

The track at Kyalami is just outside Johannesburg, which is inland and at an altitude of about two thousand feet. It's a sort of new city and it's very bland and not at all colorful. The architecture is strongly European, but you can see that when people build they're very cost conscious. The streets are very broad and they are the only common ground for the blacks, the colored, and the whites. The whites, who control the government, refuse to liberalize the *apartheid* policy, although there are liberal factions in the government that want to make strides toward integration. But the Afrikaners, who control the government, are very hard in their stand.

They feel *apartheid* is necessary because if you even start to liberalize, if you introduce any civil rights at all, you are going to create a monster that will mean the end of their way of life.

The blacks have their own lives. They live in their own quarters, they have their own villages. Actually, they seem to have their own little government within a government. But they're not allowed to own property, they're not allowed to keep a job any more than six months. They have to keep moving. The government won't let them settle in for fear that once they do they will unite. They would organize and become too powerful.

When I'm in South Africa, I don't see their poverty and actually the black people seem to be happy. But it is probably happiness that comes from ignorance. They're free to emigrate by the way, but once they leave they can never come back. If I were a black in South Africa, I'd leave. I'd go to some black or co-operative country: Kenya or Mozambique.

The Afrikaners are like their city, very drab. There's nothing stylish about their stores or what they sell inside. They are very Germanic-looking people—blond and stout—and their language has got to be the worst-sounding language I've ever heard.

The English in South Africa are opportunists. They live very well. They have servants and very nice living quarters. The most expensive thing in their budget is rent. But food's cheap and servants are very cheap. There are apartment houses in Johannesburg with servants' quarters in the basement. I know a gal down there who is divorced, has a child, and is living in very moderate circumstances when it comes to money. Yet she has a full-time servant.

The currency unit is called a Rand and, as I figured it, a dollar only bought about .65 Rand. The mechanics on the team, by the way, called Rands and all foreign currencies "funnies." So when they're calculating something they'll say, "Let's see, that'll be ten funnies."

We went to the Mala Mala game preserve, about 250 miles northeast of Johannesburg. You get there in a light plane; ours was an Aero Commander. They have a dirt strip and next to it a very nice lodge. The food at the Mala Mala and the accommodations were certainly as luxurious as any we had in Johannesburg. They had a swimming pool, and each living unit was sort of a separate little thatched house with air conditioning. Breakfast was buffet style. Dinner was in an outdoor compound with a big fire built at the center.

All the guests would sit at little individual tray tables in a circle surrounded by trees overhanging the compound. They served impala meat, which is much like venison, perhaps even better. For those who wouldn't venture into impala meat, there was lamb roast.

We got up very early, 5 A.M., before it was hot, and the day was for swimming, playing cards, and, after lunch, taking a nap. Then, about 4 P.M., we got up to go out in the Land-Rovers again and look at the animals. We could get within twenty feet of lions dozing in the grass and sunning themselves. Surprisingly, the animals weren't spooked at all. The guides had given all the lions names and recognized each. I gave some thought to whether or not the animals had been drugged. There was a wildebeest named Fred who was always around. A very spoiled wildebeest, who was always gnawing on something. He was an old fellow who used to get up only when the Land-Rover came around and then lie right back down.

The rhinoceros were fantastic, although they spooked quite easily. We didn't have to worry about one charging the Land-Rover, because they wanted very much to run away from us and not toward us at all. The impressive thing about rhinoceros is how thick their skin is. It looks like chain mail. They seem to be completely armored, and they move with such stiff movements that their skin has to hurt. Their joints don't even seem to flex. They're badly engineered, but they really get a hustle on them.

The highlight of the evening was being driven to the blind, where a couple of servants in white jackets were serving drinks. We sat behind an opening in the blind eating hors d'oeuvres, being served drinks on a silver tray, and watching the lions gorge themselves on impala carcasses. I had a drink and a cigar and leaned back in the chair just digging the little cubs, and it didn't bother me at all that the animals were so close or that I might be thought of as doing something decadent.

We were quite safe, and particularly from snakes. I made

sure of that. If there had been any question I'd have been sleeping in a hammock, because if there's one thing I'm afraid of it's snakes. I am absolutely fucking terrified of them; I'd just as soon meet Joe Frazier in a dark alley as a snake.

We were at Mala Mala two days, but that was enough. I was nodding off the last ride in the Land-Rover, thinking of dinner. When you've seen one lion you've seen them all.

We began unofficial testing of the new car at Kyalami, and the M23 seemed to be doing very well. As a matter of fact, it seemed to be making a sensation with everyone else, but we preferred to be reserved about it until it raced. Denny claimed the car was good immediately. That's the sign of a successful race car. If you roll it out and it's good right away, it's going to be a good car. If it's not good then, it's never going to get good.

As the week progressed, Denny continued to be better and by the middle of the week, which was the first official practice, the McLaren team was one, two, three on the grid. Denny was first in the new car, I was sitting number two, and the new sensation, Jody Scheckter, was third.

Jody is a local boy whom everyone considers world-championship material.* Even the drivers admit that, at

---

* Peter considered him championship material too. Especially after he spent almost the whole race in South Africa practically on Revson's lap. It came as something of a surprise, despite Scheckter's early reputation, to find he was so fast. Early in the year, when Scheckter was the new boy with McLaren, Revson was highly complimentary. But as the season wore on and Scheckter began to make an enormous name for himself in the United States, winning the L&M championship here, Revson mentioned his name less and less. The reason was obvious. Team McLaren could afford to carry only two drivers. Denny Hulme was set; that left a choice between Revson and Scheckter. In an interview in midsummer, I asked Scheckter if he knew what he'd be doing the year following. He replied that he did, but since it involved many decisions and many other people, he absolutely would say nothing about it. But his grand prix races with McLaren were disastrous. He had an accident in France that took out World Champion Emerson Fittipaldi, an accident in England that involved nine cars and destroyed the whole Surtees team, and an accident in Canada with François Cevert. Still, he was a good bet to be brought up from the minors for the following year simply because of the abundance of his talent. As it turned out, the year was even worse for Scheckter than it was for Revson. Both drivers ended with teams other

twenty-three, he's probably the brightest thing to come into racing in many years . . . probably the brightest since Emerson Fittipaldi.

The one-two-three positions made that practice day the best single day McLaren had ever had, although on days following, Jody dropped to fifth and I dropped to fourth as a result of the improvement in the Lotus times.

Noticing their improvement, I thought back to some of the things Ken Tyrrell had said on the airplane about Lotus.

To explain requires a little background. Argentina is a particularly tight course. It's only two miles around, and it's characterized by a lot of tight turns. Brazil, on the other hand, is a longer course. It's almost twice as long, with longer straights, but it's bumpy and has a lot of challenging turns. On a bumpy circuit, where handling and braking are at a premium, the Lotuses excel.

The Lotus, with Emerson driving, just walked in Brazil. Having dropped out myself with a broken crown wheel and pinion, I had a good chance to observe what was going on. I'd walked the circuit as well. Emerson just seemed to have time in hand, while Jackie Stewart in the Tyrrell, who drove a hell of a race, still had to extend himself to keep up. I think he did a fine job in just staying sixteen seconds behind Emerson.

With this in mind, Ken was saying that the Lotus was a highly developed car and carried more wing and had more downforce but at the same time a reasonable straightaway speed. With our car, for example, if we put too much wing on it we do so at the sacrifice of straightaway speed and the lap times drop.

But the Lotus seems to get away with carrying a lot of wing. In fact, Ken thought they were perhaps carrying an illegal amount of wing, and as soon as the race was over it took them only a minute to drop it.

That seemed interesting. It was interesting, first of all, to

---

than McLaren in Formula 1, indicative of the shuddering change in the international racing scene that made it one of the most unsettling years in recent memory. L.M.

cheat in that particular way. If you're going to cheat, you've got to cheat and have it work for you. If we did that, we'd probably slow ourselves down, because the drag would be too much.

But here, in South Africa, the straightaway is much longer, and since the McLarens did their testing here we were able to adjust before anyone else. In practice, Lotus obviously realized it would have to do something about its straightaway speeds and they flattened their wings off. In consequence, they started to improve their lap times.

The last day of practice I had more mechanical problems and dropped to sixth on the grid behind Denny, who kept the pole position. Emerson was second, Jody third, Peterson fourth, and Regazzoni fifth.

Starting sixth wasn't disturbing. It's a long race and I've started first and I've started twelfth, and particularly here it wouldn't make much of a difference.

Jody and I were driving the M19. Denny, as I've said, had the new M23, which is faster down the straightaway without sacrificing any of the handling qualities our cars have. The M19 used to be truly competitive only on circuits with relatively little straightaway, but the new car is going to be very good everywhere.

Here, my car is right on the pace, unlike my experiences in South America, and I look forward to this afternoon. I have a chance to win this one. Hopefully, from here on I have a chance to win them all. I've worked a long time to get to this point and I want to be a contender; I don't want to be an also-ran.

But I *am* worried about a three-car team. I don't know about the contract that Jody Scheckter signed with McLaren's last year, although I am aware it was for three years. I think there are certain performance clauses in there to be met by Team McLaren. I suspect they have to provide him with a certain amount of racing. For sure, they want to keep him, and that's why they're making every effort to get him into a few races this year. Besides, the organizer here is enthusiastic about having a home-grown product in this race and is probably willing to pay for a third car to accomplish it. But when we get to Europe, Jody won't be driving any of the grands prix except the one I have to miss in France in July because of the date conflict with the Pocono 500.†

While I don't think running three cars is really responsible for any lack of attention to my car (I have the same people working on it), to someone looking on it would seem we're spreading our resources thinner and thinner.‡ Maybe, though, the engine shop has had to build the engines more quickly because there are more of them to build and maybe that's the reason my engine has been getting problems it normally doesn't get.

Of course, according to Teddy my problems have absolutely nothing to do with running three cars. Still it seems to me that trying to do too much manifests itself in things that don't become evident until after the race, because everyone is so hopped up, so intense and preoccupied beforehand. Maybe, after this race, Teddy will look back on it and say we tried to do too much . . . maybe not.

In addition to the problem of a third car, there is the fundamental problem that led McLaren to hire Scheckter in the first place. I wish I could be certain I knew what it was. Simply because Denny is going on thirty-seven and might retire is certainly no reason. I plan to continue, if everything goes well, with Team McLaren. I don't like to think that Jody Scheckter's been added to the team to act as a needle. Or to make Denny and me more competitive. Or to make me feel I have to put out a little bit more to keep my job. I don't really think he's here for this reason.

I think the press has written a lot about Jody as a newcomer with a lot of ability. McLaren's aware of this, and the South African tide for him seems to have swept McLaren along. I think Teddy has been caught up in it somewhat.

† Revson was soon enough to find out that he was wrong on this one. Scheckter also drove in England . . . to Surtees' everlasting regret. L.M.
‡ No small irony here. In the convulsive negotiations at the end of the year with Team McLaren, it was over exactly this point, the amount of attention needed to run a third car, that Revson, sponsor Yardley, and Team McLaren split. L.M.

I'm still at the pool at the hotel near the track, which is a lovely garden setting. A footnote on Brazil emerges from some information I've been given.* Teddy didn't say much more to me about being sick down there and I wondered why until I found out that he had the same thing that attacked me, the day he got home to London. Alestair, the crew chief, got it too and so did Denny. I guess to turn off Teddy's sarcasm what you need is a good plague.

Of course, by the time the race was ready to start, the sun was gone and the good weather with it. Since the weather changed abruptly every afternoon at three, you would think the organizers would be wary of scheduling the race to start at that time. But they weren't, and, sure enough, at three the clouds were swirling around the track and the rain started, stopped, intermittently sprinkling on different parts of the circuit.

But we started on dry tires and luckily the rain held off the rest of the day. I got off to a good start and was fourth after a couple of laps with Denny leading from the pole. It was particularly nice to see Denny moving the way he was; it gave me a thrill to see the potential of the new car. Scheckter got a good start from the front row and moved into second, followed by Emerson.

Ronnie Peterson was behind me in the other Lotus and we got into a dice, passing and repassing each other, only to have Stewart come from rather a poor start position to join us.

If Stewart was a bit frustrated at the start I can understand it. He had crashed on Friday and had to start in François's car,

---

* That's not the only footnote that emerges out of the jacaranda in that lovely garden setting. Revson fails to mention that it was the scene of his near-rape the year before by a particularly determined female journalist. Her cover was an interview. But a McLaren mechanic who saw the whole thing, or almost the whole thing, seems to remember that the lady kept creeping closer and closer and suddenly began to shed her clothes. When Revson realized what was happening he took one horrified look, and fled behind the hotel, with the lady, notebook still in hand, in pursuit. The McLaren man is unsure what happened out of his sight, but he has his suspicions. Revson has reason to be retiring about this incident since the lady is notorious on the grand prix circuit for her democratic tastes and her voracious appetite. L.M.

in which he had had limited practice. As a result he was gridded fourteenth, but here he was right behind Ronnie and me. That set the stage for the famous Stewart yellow-flag incident.

At the beginning of the sixth lap, the yellow flag was out and waving for a third-lap accident involving Clay Regazzoni, Mike Hailwood, and Jacky Ickx. We'd seen the flag on the fourth and fifth laps and now on the sixth as well. I couldn't pass Ronnie on the straightaway, and as I was about to pass him in the braking area, I saw the yellow flag still waving. I pulled back behind him and, much to my surprise, Jackie came down and passed both of us in the braking area even though the yellow flag was waving.†

Jackie proceeded to gain positions right up to the front of the pack behind Denny . . . and just then Denny got his first puncture, very likely because of the debris on the track from the accident.

Denny pulled out of contention and Jackie assumed the lead. As for me, I got by Ronnie, I got by Emerson, and eventually I gunned down Jody, who was driving very well. But, in the process, Emerson went by as well, only to chase me for the rest of the race.

When Denny came back on the circuit with fresh tires, he came up behind me and I let him by thinking I could manage to stay in his slipstream on the straightaway, where he was quicker than I was. That way I hoped to gain some time on Emerson, who was hounding me.

Then Denny's engine started going a little better and he pulled away slightly. I had been able to get about seven seconds on Emerson, but with Denny gone, Emerson came back to within about three.

Finally, at the end, I was balked by Denny, who was bogged by slow traffic. That let Emerson get within a second and a half and that's the way we crossed the finish line. Jackie, I twenty-four seconds back, then Emerson.

† Revson's shock at Stewart's breach was justified. A waving yellow flag indicates an extremely dangerous situation ahead and carries with it an absolute prohibition on passing. L.M.

It was a satisfying race. I had to drive hard throughout because of Emerson, and one of the reasons I'm happy about it is that I know the new car will go even better. I feel as good as I felt two years ago, when I had the McLaren CanAm car and knew that, one way or another, I was going to win a whole lot of races.

The third-lap accident involving Hailwood, Regazzoni, and Ickx was quite serious and could have been more than that for Clay, who wound up being trapped in his car.

Although I heard about four versions, the way I reconstruct it is that a local driver went wide with Hailwood right behind him. Mike stayed in his groove, but the local man got crossed up, causing Hailwood to spin with Regazzoni coming around the turn. At the last moment, Regazzoni got sideways and went broadside into the front end of Hailwood's car.

Being T-boned in that fashion caused Regazzoni's cockpit to simply close around him after the impact. That, in turn, resulted in rupturing of the fuel tanks and some flash fire.

While all this was happening, Ickx came on the scene and didn't quite make it either. Although he didn't get involved with the other two, he did get out of control and wound up some yards away off the race track.

Hailwood managed to get out of his car immediately and went to Regazzoni to try and get him out. He found himself on fire as a result and quickly moved away and rolled around on the grass and then went *back* to Regazzoni and helped pull him out of the car. A very courageous act.

What Mike did doesn't surprise me, because ever since I've known him, which goes back to about ten years ago, when he and Chris Amon and I lived together, I've always thought him a very honest, straightforward, and good character. I've always appreciated him and I'm proud he acted as he did.

After the race, I got out of my car giving some thought to what Jackie had done under the yellow flag. I had noticed also that there was a second time he had taken quick advantage and that involved the appearance of an ambulance on the track. Denny and Jody were the two leaders at the time, and Denny was slowing up with his puncture. Both he and Jody hesitated at the appearance of the ambulance, there was a shuffling of cars behind them as everyone sort of bunched up, and Jackie took the opportunity to pass Jody, which seemed to me to be a questionable interpretation of the flag rules by Jackie.

Anyway, at the end of the race my first thought was to remind Jackie quietly that he'd passed under the yellow, and I didn't think it was fair for him to take advantage of the flag. He was lucky to get away with it, because evidently the observers were otherwise occupied, with the accident itself, and the man who was charged with waving the flag didn't have the authority to make a report.

On the other hand, I was incensed that Jackie, of all people, would take advantage of what was a fairly dangerous situation. The cars in the wreck occupied half of the road on the exit of a turn, and if anyone should have been aware of the potential danger it should have been Jackie, who is a veteran and the foremost proponent and spokesman for safety among the drivers.

It seemed to me that if I had refrained from passing, he should have as well. Unless, of course, he had a different interpretation of the flag rules. Now, inasmuch as I've been caught out on this several times when I felt I wasn't under the control of the yellow flag only to find myself overruled by the interpretation of the steward, I was interested to know what Jackie knew that I didn't know. So I got Teddy Mayer and told him about it. Teddy decided to make a formal protest.‡

The stewards heard both sides, with Jackie saying he didn't see the flag and that it was an honest mistake. Of course there

---

‡ Teddy Mayer making a formal protest is one of racing's truly imposing sights. Teddy is a lawyer, and litigious by nature anyway. I have seen him spend an hour drafting a protest just in case he might have reason to file one. He uses long yellow legal pads, isolates himself somewhere, twists his face into awe-inspiring grimaces, and laboriously writes his briefs. Once, in a genuinely historic moment, I watched Roger Penske and Parnelli Jones join Teddy at the pit wall in Ontario, California—all three threatening protest. Although this must have been as close as we can come in modern times to a joining of the Visigoths, the Mongol hordes, and the 101st Airborne at the gates of some frail country village, the three were summarily dismissed and they slunk away. L.M.

was the fact that the yellow flag had been flying for two laps prior to his pass. The flag marshal came in and testified that Jackie did in fact pass at the point at which the flag was being waved.

Jackie was quite open, claiming he wouldn't do anything that seemed dangerous to him. Evidently the stewards accepted his point of view in making their decision, because the extent of his punishment was a reprimand.

But obviously the reprimand only served to remind Jackie of his infallibility in such situations. So he and Ken Tyrrell decided that even the reprimand would sully Jackie's reputation. They decided to appeal.

That came as a surprise. On Sunday morning we were all convened again in front of the stewards, and Jackie's appeal was based on his contention that it didn't make any difference whether he saw the flag or not, because his pass took place before he got into the flag control zone.

The stewards took a long time deliberating and finally decided to uphold the appeal on the theory that under the international rules a car does not come under the control of the yellow flag until it reaches its braking point. So if I was surprised before, I was even more so then, at what I considered a very loose interpretation of the rules.

Now, Stewart must have braked a lot later than he said he braked, when he was first in front of the stewards. (It's curious that, with a full fuel load, we all brake in pretty much the same place . . . about 240 yards before the apex of the turn.) Because, as sure as I was standing there, Jackie didn't complete his pass until we got down to about the 100-yard mark, well inside the braking area, the area that was established as the yellow-flag control zone.

In making his appeal, Jackie kept reassuring the stewards that, after all, with his reputation in matters of safety, he certainly would not do anything that was dangerous and that he was the one who could best interpret the rule.

It was a clever appeal. Jackie has been the most outspoken voice in crusading for safer racing. Without him, the Grand Prix Drivers' Association wouldn't be nearly so effective as it is now in having changes made to improve the standards under which we race. Jackie has been much maligned for his crusading by track owners, who have had to spend a lot to make improvements he has suggested. I stand behind him 100 per cent and I think the criticism of him has been unjust. But in this circumstance, I'm disappointed that he took advantage of his reputation to help himself win a motor race.

In Jackie's book *Faster!* he comes across as infallible. The book is filled with moments and circumstances over which Jackie had no control and which resulted in his being uncompetitive. As a driver, though, according to the book, he never made any mistakes.

Perhaps he believes this to the point where he's incapable of realizing a mistake on his part.

I'm convinced Jackie's appeal was based on his own feeling of infallibility. Whatever Jackie Stewart does, Stewart seemed to be saying, is safe and not a violation no matter the circumstances, since Jackie Stewart simply is incapable of being wrong.

I continue to support earnestly Jackie's view about racing conditions and circuit safety, but so far as complaints about other drivers within the confidential meetings of the Grand Prix Drivers' Association are concerned, I'm afraid I'm going to be very suspicious from now on.

Perhaps we've all been a little too friendly up to now. Perhaps a little resentment will make better competition from here on.

Mandel · Two

The driver is lying in some enormous bed that is swarming with naked women who are feeding him sugared grapes and cognac.

Any race team will do; any McLaren team will do better.

They dress alike, so you cannot tell the car designer from the coffee gofer; at McLaren their sentences begin, end, and are largely made up of "fuck" and its participle. They are young and their hair is long. At Indianapolis and Ontario, during the long days when they must be there but the cars are sitting ready in their stalls, or they are waiting for engines from Detroit, they play soccer in the garage area. The accents are South Island, New Zealand; New England; or Wales. Their scorn for the civilian world is palpable. They do not talk to strangers, but they are used to their stares, and when one or several of those barely tolerated intruders stop at the outside of the garage to peer at the cars or try to find a driver for an autograph, they return their looks with withering contempt. Worse, they pretend it is the passerby who is the animal in the zoo.

The McLaren Formula 1 team, and the Championship Car Team leave in the spring and return in the fall. The crews leave their wives and their families, they leave their homes in Australia or Ireland or Massachusetts to go to strange continents, among people who speak indecipherable languages and pursue daily routines that are simply out of phase and out of context to the team members. The team members drip with loathing for the everyday plodders who swarm around them in France and Sweden and Brazil. They envy them too, but the envy never comes out until the crews are exhausted from six months' travel and eighteen-hour days and bad food. Then they say this has been the last year for them, they quit. They will retire from racing. The next year, of course, they're back.

When the teams travel, they travel according to status. The car designer goes with the managing director, perhaps with the drivers. The crew chiefs go on the same plane, and if it's a Formula 1 charter, the crews as well. But, mostly, the crews drive the transporters with the cars aboard.

(On the long South African and American trips, the teams fly, with the flight paid for by the organizers. For diversion, the crews flip team decals through the aisles; mainly, though, the object is to stick a Yardley-McLaren or a John Player decal to the backside of a stewardess. The Lotus crew is far and away the best of the lot at this, and in their frustration, the other crews stick team decals to everything they see. Toilet-seat tops are favorite targets; if you board a plane with a flashy, multicolored decal in the W.C., the Formula 1 crews have been there.)

There is no glamour in clearing customs three times between sunset and dawn in a transporter filled with spares to be explained away, and driving through the night. It is almost impossible to tell a Canadian customs man, for example, why the Universal Oil Products Shadow has to have its own lead-free gasoline shipped in drums to Edmonton. He is a simple, straightforward official, and he cannot be expected to understand that a $500-million American company is locked in a vicious political struggle with another American giant, the Ethyl Corporation, to convince the public that a passenger car can or cannot run properly on lead-free gasoline and is using a race car to make its point. To a customs man, that's an abstraction, and what the hell are four drums of obviously contraband gasoline doing in the truck?

The high-rollers who came in by plane will already have been there when the truck arrives. And now, although the status differences remain, their outward manifestations totally disappear, to the outsider's eye.

The car designer and team manager are as likely as not to have swept out the garage or set up the ropes with the little oil-company flags on them that define the crews' working area. They have checked into the hotel or motel. They have gone to the registration people on the circuit or in the nearby town and signed in for their credentials. They have checked everywhere for the racing accessory people, the tire technicians and the fuel people, and they have misplaced them again this race.

With the McLaren championship car team the motor home that the team and the sponsor use for a combination hospitality suite/bedroom/loo/office has finally come into town. But its driver is checking out the porno movie houses and he has the key in his pocket. No lunch today unless the crew leaves the track.

Usually, with the Championship Trail team (which of course runs U.S. races only) the cars have been back at the engine shop in Michigan since the last race, and they have fresh engines in them when the team arrives. But there is setting up to do, and checking and rechecking. That is what the life of a race-car crew is all about. That and a lot of fixing what the sonofabitching driver has done to screw up the car.

The driver, of course, isn't within five hundred miles of the track. He's lying in some enormous round bed that is swarming with beautiful naked women who are feeding him sugared grapes and cognac. His eyes are bloodshot from a week of depravity since the last race, his hand is shaking, and from somewhere in the ceiling, a stream of gold coins is pouring on his head. Outside the room, patiently waiting, are the television people and the newspaper people who will record, when the driver gets around to telling them, how he either won the week before purely on his own merits, or how he would have won but for the fuck-ups of his crew.

At that very moment, the Welshman, who weighs about 130 and stands 5′6″, and the Irishman, who's an inch taller but ten pounds lighter, have to manhandle the back of the car three feet in the air so the jackstands can go under it.

This is the table of organization as well as the pecking order of the McLaren championship car team: Teddy Mayer is on top (he always is anyway). Teddy is the commissar for political affairs. He is the strategist in the winter and the tactician in the summer. During the racing season, at least when he is particularly persuasive, he tries to convince the drivers to relinquish what they feel is their God-given right to make their own decisions about how to run the race. Teddy deals with organizers and sponsors. He is the governess and the animal keeper to the drivers. Teddy passes along his wishes to Tyler Alexander, who, although almost autonomous on the rest of the championship-trail races, such as Phoenix and Trenton, defers to Teddy in matters of political importance and policy at the big 500-milers: Ontario, Pocono, and Indianapolis. Teddy also writes and delivers protests.

Tyler, like Teddy, is an American on a Commonwealth team. He began as a mechanic for Teddy's brother Timmy. He signed on with Bruce McLaren when Teddy joined forces with McLaren; he rose to demileader of the all-conquering CanAm team; he became a director and the engineering chief of McLaren Racing. Tyler does not have a lot of weight in decision-making, but he is enormously bright. More than that, he is canny. And as a result, he is listened to. Tyler has become a mediator more frequently than he wants to. He is quiet and amusing. Tyler's words cut like a prized, old straight razor. Tyler's attention, when it's drawn to something he disapproves of, is concentrated in a stare that burns holes in concrete. Tyler's nickname is The Laser.

If Teddy Mayer is the chairman of the joint chiefs and Tyler is the commander in the field, then Huey Absolom is Tyler's adjutant. Huey was Jim Clark's crew chief at the Speedway and can wear any one of the three jackets he has been given as the winner of the pole mechanics' award. Huey is a Welshman, small and quiet, but his accent is northern England and it has the sweetness of an old Stanley Holloway 78rpm recording. When Huey speaks, which is a rare event, almost everything he says sounds like the "legend" of The Lion and Albert. Huey's mild, soft words are as devastating as Tyler's glare. He is intolerant of laziness and incompetence and stupidity. He works (as does Tyler) with the crew until whatever hour of the night or morning is necessary and is back again at crack of sparrow's fart the next day. They work again that night and the next and the next. Huey's fingernails are dirty and he is said to be the best chassis man in racing. Huey is the superchief.

At the Speedway or at other races important enough to McLaren to run two cars in the United States Auto Club, there are two crew chiefs: Alec Greaves and Dennis Davis—each to a car, each to a driver, the whole season long. They are British, quiet, and, in the McLaren mold, amusing to listen to. Dennis is disturbed that his work takes him out where there are people. It would be nice for Dennis if races could be run with one car at an empty track; no crowds, no fanfare. When his driver, John Rutherford, put his car on the pole at the Speedway, and the Indianapolis 500 Festival Committee staged a banquet for two thousand people, with his fellow crew chiefs on the dais to pay him tribute; live television; and a special five-minute film of his life, his background, and his accomplishments as the highlights of the evening, Dennis could not bring himself to go.

Alec Greaves is the opposite. He is gregarious and lively. He feels at home among Americans; his wife is American. And he understands American curiosity and public folkways. Once, last year, Alec waved to a child at a race.

Each crew has a more or less rotating group of mechanics (two per car). The gofers are, recently, college men doing summer work. "They're a little more serious about it," says Tyler. "But *they're* not much good either." The mechanics come and go as well. The day after Indy, both Edgar The Incredible and John The Bewildered, who had come over from

England, were cast adrift. By Ontario, Peter, a New Zealand Formula 1 mechanic, had been added in desperation to Revson's USAC crew.

During the season, a crew member's life is incredibly demanding. He almost never sleeps; he is never in one place for more than seventy-two hours, and when he is, it's some god-awful place like Indianapolis, Indiana, for what seems a lifetime. He eats the same HoJo food for months on end, and he has to fight the team manager for a laundry allowance that he and his fellows thought they had wrung out of him as a concession once and for all at the beginning of the year. The McLaren crew is also badly paid.

A crew chief for McLaren can make about $175 a week plus his piece of the crew's winnings. A crew chief for a big American team (although McLaren insists *it's* an American team) can make almost twice that. In addition the McLaren people and the American team people get about the same per diem: sixteen dollars.

The crew member spends his life at Holiday Inns. If he's lucky, he sleeps with his wife from October til March. His insides are rotted from scummy motel buffets from Arizona to New Jersey and the foul liquor he pours into himself on the few nights a month he gets off. His hands are raw and bleeding and almost as red as his eyes, and nobody recognizes him when he takes off his sandwich-board team shirt and puts on decent clothes.

He loves it. Huey's fondest memory of all is of a night in Monza for the Italian GP when the team slid into the pension late at night. Three of them shared a room and, because it was dark, they grabbed what they could from the suitcases and left them open on the floor. It is hot in Italy in summer, so they left the door open. Huey was the only one who wasn't so exhausted that he dropped immediately off to sleep, and, to his horror, he heard a great clomping of steps outside, a pause, and then he could make out what he now describes as a bloodcurdling sight: an enormous figure which he took to be some upright animal framed in the light at the doorway. For an endless moment the figure stood there, and then, to Huey's increasing dismay it moved cautiously inside and stood, half sideways, by the wall near the suitcases. Shortly, Huey heard a rushing, hissing sound, and when he recognized it, he could barely stifle his laughter. He waited until it was over, and then awakened his crew chief, Alestair. "Hey, Alestair, wake up, some great bloody animal's just pissed in your suitcase." And in his shoes too. The great bloody animal turned out to be the motoring correspondent of a London newspaper, and now when Huey's asked to repeat the story of the Phantom Pisser of Monza, he ends the story with his upper lip curled in contempt: "A *journalist,* naturally."

As is true of the other mechanics on an international team, Huey's life has been touched by the colors of many countries. He has heard a variety of accents. He has dined off some very curious creatures. The result is a catholic approach to the language, drawing, as he is able to do, on expressions and experiences of every kind. When he first saw a kitchen trash compacter, he was fascinated by it as a device but quick-witted enough to give it the name it should have had in the first place: "Ah," said Huey, "that'll be an electric pig."

The crews form a team . . . and yet they do not. Racing is an individual sport. No one is so alone as a race driver. To the degree that the feeling is understood by the crews, it is shared. Graham Hill and Howden Ganley are two mechanics who became grand prix drivers, so some of the understanding, not to say the motivation, must be the same on the part of the crews as it is the drivers.

The crews are nomads. They travel across strange landscapes and among strange people, often not being able to read signs or understand the spoken language. That binds them together, and you can see it in the thin dawn of qualifying morning at Sambo's or the International House of Pancakes. The crews are together, bright lettered shirts circled around one table forming the only pool of warmth in the room.

Their jokes are private but loud, and they are clearly sharing the joy of mocking their surroundings. But when there are two cars on a team, the crews are often competitive. Tyler Alexander remembers the McLaren CanAm years with Bruce Mc-

Laren and Denny Hulme. Those days with McLaren, Bruce provided a sort of radiance. He was warm and understanding. He knew what effort was needed to make a car work week in and week out—the long nights, the longer hauls. Even so, the two crews were barely on speaking terms. The jokes had an unusually cruel edge to them: Huey was forced to apologize to keep a rival crew member with the team after he burned his sandals in the middle of the garage floor in contempt for the man's unwillingness to bathe.

And for all their independence, their free-lance ways, their commitment to the bravura life of the race track, for all that, the man about whom the crews feel the most dislike is their driver. There is a scene in a very funny racing novel called *Stand on It* that has an Indianapolis driver come walking in after smashing his car into the wall at a terrifying speed to be greeted in the pits by his crew chief. The two are surrounded by an enormous crowd of hangers-on, spectators, and journalists. Cameras are clicking and notebooks are being flipped out to open pages. The crew chief puts his arm around the driver, smiles, and whispers in his ear that he is a simple-minded motherfucker who has no right driving a farm tractor much less a race car. The driver smiles back (because, after all, the crowd is watching) and tells the crew chief *sotto voce* that if he knew the first fucking thing about setting up a race car, he, the driver, wouldn't have to risk his life in a shitbox like the one he just put into the wall.

It's no exaggeration. When Peter Revson hit the wall in practice before Indianapolis and came walking in, neither Tyler Alexander nor Huey Absolom had any thoughts but for the welfare of the car. It was the car they had built, slaved over, set up, tuned, retuned, reset up, and slaved over some more. The car was a perfect device. They knew it was. It was the product of their own endless hours of labor. It was the stupid son-of-a-bitch of a driver who ruined it all. "Shit," said Revson looking at Tyler hover over the wreck as it was being towed into the garage area. "That son-of-a-bitch could care less about me. He hasn't even looked inside to see if I got out." When Revson's teammate John Rutherford finished second in the next-to-last race of the season in Texas after his car stalled during a pit stop, Tyler was asked to what he attributed the failure to win. "What we need is somebody who knows how to drive . . . at least keep an engine running in the pits."

The crew has moments of searing hatred for its driver . . . but they're close to him too. And they are proud of him and defend him among themselves.

Peter Revson's crew never once, in the long summer I spent with them in their motels and in their garages, said openly that they felt proud to be working on his car. They didn't have to. They had taken on a Revson coloration. Revson is cool, all muted colors and understatement. His crew was the same. Their flattery by osmosis was obvious. They may have called his girl friends "drivers' stuff," with snorts of contempt, but it was plain they felt no other crew's driver could come up with anything close. They even toned their voices down in public; in their conversations they took up the scalpel in preference to the bludgeon. All of this, the herringbone quip instead of a hand-painted one-liner, Canadian ale rather than CC and Seven, may also have come from Bruce McLaren and certainly from Tyler Alexander. But much of it came from Revson, and in taking on Revson's cool manner, in smiling his sardonic smile, in repeating his latest put-down of Teddy Mayer (whom they also took to calling The Weener), they made it very clear that if Revson was capable of defeating all their labors by stuffing his race car into a wall, he was still a man to be admired and imitated.

The pervasiveness, the awful contagion, of Revson's manner and the manner of his crew washed over me like an enormous wave one morning before practice for the United States Grand Prix. I was standing with my back to the outside wall of the garage, and one of the crew members climbed into the tilt-bed transporter to maneuver it out toward the pits with some spares and some tires. He had to back it toward me and he came so close he almost touched my jacket. As the truck backed slowly into me I wondered whether I was going to be hit and crushed against the wall. It seemed a very real possibility. I was boxed in by a motor home and an engine stand, and

I couldn't move. All I was able to do was watch as the back of the truck came closer and closer, and it flashed through my mind just as the truck was about to hit me, in exactly these words, that the McLaren crew might think it very bad form on my part if, as I was being crushed against the garage, I screamed. When I told Tyler about it later, and told him what I had thought, asking him if indeed it would have had that reaction from him and from the crew, he didn't even laugh. "Yes," he said. But later on he smiled and said he wasn't absolutely sure, and would I like to try it and see?

Teddy is quiet too, but it isn't because he's cool. Teddy's deep, and all the way down you're bouncing against the walls of an emotional labyrinth.

The Teddy Mayer labyrinth should be no problem for the people who have known him since he began racing, as Revson has. But Revson roomed with him in New York, raced as a teammate with his brother Timmy, and still doesn't really understand Teddy.

Revson uses one of his favorite expressions to describe Teddy; he says he's a "street fighter." Tyler Alexander, who has had ample excuse for disloyalty, concedes that Teddy is "difficult" but refuses to abandon him to the whims of free-market judgment: He's a remarkable little man, says Tyler. He gets the job done. For Tyler, who would tend to be critical of a free lunch at the Côte Basque, that's high praise.

While it was Bruce McLaren who set the tone and determined the goals of McLaren Racing, since his death in a testing accident in 1972 Teddy Mayer has moved inexorably to the center of the operation. The company and the team have become Mayer-colored. These days, McLaren could properly be called Mayer Racing, which is not entirely pleasing to some long-time McLaren devotees. "They used to be the good guys of racing," says one English motorsports writer with a note of regret, "but they're rapidly squandering their reserves of good will."

That is moderately unfair to Teddy. He is not Mr. Charm, but nothing says he has to be.

On the other hand, Revson does like Mayer, and Mayer's

critics would be tempted to say that Revson has known him long enough to know better.

The Mayer/Revson relationship, which was to underlie everything that happened in 1973, began in Connecticut by the swimming pool belonging to the publisher of *Time* magazine, in 1958. Revson had gone to a deb party at the house the night before, had gotten drunk, and somehow found himself lying on top of a high stone wall. He remembers that, and he remembers that the next thing that happened was his discovery in the thicket beneath the wall by a grounds keeper, his dinner jacket in tatters, his co-ordination worse.

He was put to bed on a couch in a hallway and was awakened the next morning to his embarrassment with an invitation to join a party out by the pool. Luckily, Revson always tucked a pair of bright Hawaiian swimming trunks in his car wherever he went, so he was spared having to wear the battered dinner jacket to a brunch in the bright Connecticut sunlight. "I began to drink again, gin and tonic, and immediately felt better," he recalls, "but the trouble was that although gin makes me cheerful and gives me a sense of infallibility, after I drink any substantial amount, I can't stand up."

Revson remembers a good-looking young man smoking a pipe who was in the middle of a conversation about road racing. He asked him what he drove and the man answered, an Austin Healey. "Ah," said Revson, collecting his tongue and his teeth, "that's my model too." The young man, who turned out to be Timmy Mayer, described his plans to race the car between serious academic moments at Yale. Revson was aware of somebody by Timmy Mayer's side. Dimly, he thinks now, there registered an image of a little white-haired chap, but he isn't absolutely sure.

The little white-haired chap was the nephew of the governor of Pennsylvania and also Timmy Mayer's brother, and it may have been his ambition even then to make Timmy the world champion. That morning in Connecticut, Teddy Mayer had reason to expect his brother to be infinitely more successful as a racer than Revson. Timmy had run a couple of regional SCCA races and, as the drive home from the pool party was to suggest, his attitude was more serious than Revson's. Timmy started down the oiled road from the house with a ravishing lady friend by his side and the top down in his Healey 100, only to be passed in a flurry of opposite-lock driving by Revson, who was getting crossed up in every turn. Revson, busy as he was, waved casually to Mayer, thinking his display of bravado would more than make up for his less than elegant entrance at the party that morning. Two turns later the Revson Healey slid out from under him, spun, and ended up thoroughly bent against a huge rock that marked the outside entry to a driveway. Disgusted, Revson was still sitting in the car when Timmy and his lady came driving decorously by. "The son-of-a-bitch didn't even turn his head and look at me," Revson says now.

At the time Revson met him, Teddy was taking a few days off from Cornell Law School. Because he was gray-haired even then, he looked a lot older than twenty-three. But it wasn't only his gray hair; there was something unusual about Teddy Mayer. There still is. His legs and his thighs belong to a six-footer, but Teddy is only about 5'6". While this is distracting to see, it doesn't seem to inhibit Teddy much. He is an avid skier, swimmer, and jogger. He plays golf very well.

The Mayer family is old Scranton, which is also his mother's family name. William Scranton, a liberal Republican, finds himself at odds with his nephew at those times they are together; not often these days, since Teddy lives in London. Teddy is "very right wing."

While Revson was cutting a moderate swath in the East, Teddy was being properly conservative. "Teddy was not your college ass man," says Revson, who ought to know about such things.

Teddy Mayer is a realist if nothing else, and realizing he could never be a race driver, concentrated on making his brother Timmy the best driver in the world. Timmy left everything to his brother; Teddy managed Timmy's team and his car and him; he was responsible for preparation and he probably made himself responsible for everything else. Timmy, smoking his pipe, remained aloof.

Racing was a world that fascinated both Mayers as well as it fascinated both Peter and Douglas Revson. In a way, that was a shame, because the result was that Teddy never practiced law, and he might have become a brilliant lawyer. If Teddy *had* practiced, he would have been the kind of lawyer who would have been in a Washington law office, unknown to any but his colleagues but respected enormously by them. His conservatism would have served him well and his thoroughness too. Had he been a trial lawyer, it might have been advantageous that he was never convinced of any side of the argument but his own. But it could not have helped that he would rarely concede that there was another side to see. Teddy, according to Revson, is unsympathetic, insensitive, and demanding. In other words, a perfect political lawyer on the model of John Ehrlichman.

But he is demanding of himself as well, and if McLaren Racing is successful, it is because those demands are made and met.

After the morning at the pool in Connecticut and the incident on the oiled road, the next time Revson and Teddy Mayer met was at a local race in the East. Remembers Revson, "The Mayers were in their first year of Sports Car Club of America [amateur] racing, they felt they were very important and they were all business. I was on the outside looking in and they didn't know me."

To this day, Teddy's old friends and old associates can walk by him in the pits and he will not acknowledge their presence. Perhaps he really doesn't see them. Perhaps he is preoccupied. Whatever the reason, it doesn't make him widely loved. But Revson sidles to his defense, "That's just the way he is. He's absolutely dedicated. He's single minded. When you get him away from the race track he can be fairly sociable, but not at the track, not at all."

"If I had my choice," Teddy said to me wistfully one morning very early when there were only two of us in the garage area at Indianapolis, "I would chuck all this and go skiing. I prefer it and I wouldn't have to deal with all the people."

But before it was boring, before he knew better, Teddy was

ambitious to become a team manager, so obviously he needed a team to manage. Teddy was in New York studying tax law at NYU and he put a team together with Revson and his brother Timmy in small single-seater Formula Juniors. It made sense, since the two had to talk and travel to the race track together, to share an apartment as well. So they took a two-bedroom apartment on Thirteenth Street in Manhattan at $275 a month.

The apartment was stark and Teddy was neat and helped keep it that way. Revson remembers that he and Teddy would go up to Vermont skiing on the weekends in the winter, when there was no racing, and that when Teddy drove it was a harrowing experience. "He was a fairly good driver but he didn't anticipate. You got a lot of last-minute braking. He bought a police interceptor Galaxie with a special 390 interceptor engine. There were always unofficial records set on the way to Vermont."

Teddy was a reasonable roommate. He paid his share of the bills, he kept things neat, he didn't object to Revson's overnight guests, and he made a digestible beef Stroganoff.

Happily, his cost consciousness didn't surface until he began running a race team seriously. "In the early days there was nothing there to indicate that he was going to be a tough administrator. He was keen and aware of the way things in racing were being accomplished. He learned the hard way in racing but he learned very quickly," says Revson.

The third man on the team was Bill Smith, who just sort of showed up one day at a race with a Lincoln convertible painted green and a trailer with an open-wheeled Elva race car on it painted green and an absolutely stunning blonde. Smith was between marriages then; he was a car dealer from upstate New York. But what struck both Revson and Mayer about his equipe was that his name was painted in one-foot script across the side of his race car.

In those days, and especially in amateur circles, such things were never done. It was not only considered bad form, but it was actually outlawed to carry any lettering larger than the very modest prescribed size. To both Revson and Mayer, the sight of an obviously rebellious Smith, especially written in script on a race car, came as a considerable pleasure, chafing as they were under the ultrarestrictive gentlemen's rules of sports-car racing.

"There it was," recalls Revson about the name, "'Bill Smith' written right across the side! You couldn't miss it. The blonde, who had on a little jump suit, was his only pit crew, and while they were rolling the car off the trailer, everyone was standing around hitting each other in the ribs and laughing and asking 'who's this?'—all the time telling each other he couldn't drive and he was just a beginner. But he could, and he became a member of the team." Today Bill Smith and McLaren Racing are the majority stockholders in McLaren Engines, in Detroit.

Teddy set out to make Timmy the national champion in Formula Junior, only to see Timmy go into the service. But Teddy could solve that one too, and while Timmy was in the service, he was flying from Puerto Rico every weekend to national races on the mainland. Revson was in basic and couldn't fly anywhere on the weekends.

Somehow, when Timmy got out of the service, Teddy managed to arrange a ride with Ken Tyrrell, the legendary team manager who later took Jackie Stewart to the top of the profession.

Tyrrell had a factory Cooper Formula Junior team. Probably Teddy paid the cost of the car and its maintenance. In other words, although it was a factory team and supposedly underwritten by the factory, Timmy's was a bought-and-paid-for ride.

Revson went to Europe too, and while he was an independent, living out of a Thames bread truck, the Mayer brothers had taken a house. Timmy remained very detached. "He would smoke his pipe, put it aside, come in and drive a race."

That didn't mean he couldn't drive. "He was very good," says Revson. "But he seemed to have concentration lapses."

The next step up the ladder for Timmy was a ride in Formula 1 . . . and Teddy arranged that for the following year. But in the interim, the brothers went to New Zealand, where they got involved with Bruce McLaren.

They made a deal to build two Cooper-based Tasman cars, named for the series run in New Zealand and Australia, to be driven by McLaren and Timmy.

It was in one of those cars that Timmy was killed.

Certainly Timmy's death was a loss to Teddy. A brother dies, there's a void. But Timmy also defined Teddy's career at the moment he was killed. The racing people who are totally taken up with the sport don't blame racing for racing deaths. If they feel grief, they seem to recognize it is for themselves. Thus the appalling cliché about death that is racing's favorite phrase: He died the way he wanted to, in a race car. It's a way of justifying a terrible waste in selfish and human terms. It's a way also of making a mistake into a heroic act.

However Teddy handled the death of his brother, it was not by leaving racing. On the contrary, he went back to England with Bruce McLaren and they made a deal that turned Teddy into a participant in McLaren Racing.

Listening to Revson talk about meeting the Mayer brothers and racing with Timmy, their lives together, and Teddy's early ambitions, you cannot help but feel regard and affection for them all.

There is an air of World War I fighter-pilot exploits to the whole thing; they were all sure they would make it to the world championship. Nobody in World War I began to understand the awful majesty of what air warfare was to become, the tens of thousands of planes, the millions of tons of bombs, ultimately the mushroom cloud.

And Teddy and Timmy Mayer and Peter Revson, in those early days for all of them, had absolutely no understanding of the cruel and commercial world of international motorsports, which is a promotional battleground for auto manufacturers and cigarette companies. So they were not intimidated by it.

It was all terribly casual and offhand. The Mayers and the Revsons went into racing almost as a lark. It ended up with two of the brothers dead, one survivor the head of an enormously successful motor racing team, another a grand prix driver making $300,000 a year.

It's hard to say what transformed Teddy from the friendly

young man on Thirteenth Street into Teddy Mayer the managing director of McLaren, who threatens British sports publications with libel suits.

It began with Teddy's money underwriting the team. The shift of power and the shift of people surely affected it; Bruce's friend Phil Kerr began to gain influence and then to lose it after Bruce's death. Patty McLaren, Bruce's widow, was obviously unable to offer any kind of the help her husband provided. An early director, Eoin Young, left the firm, and although he did publicity for McLaren, his voice became dimmer and dimmer.

So what emerged through the years in which McLaren dominated the Canadian American Challenge series in the United States with its orange sports cars was the influence of Teddy Mayer. What McLaren needed, now that Bruce was dead, was an extremely efficient manager. The entry into Indianapolis-type racing by McLaren made Teddy even more prominent: a crisp, emotionless, staggeringly efficient man; just the thing that was needed to unravel the parochial, tightly guarded mysteries of the world's richest race, which, for all its bulging purse, was still held in an Indiana cornfield.

Something else had happened to McLaren Racing too. To some, it has seemed that Teddy substituted ruthlessness for Bruce McLaren's warmth, which made the teams efficient but impersonal.

Cold business decisions deprived Tyler of information he might have felt should be his, but Tyler is an operational man at McLaren. Sometimes it is not good that he have all the facts.

Still, Tyler worked enormously hard for ten years hoping for some equity in the company. He thought the time had come when an offer was made for most of Patty McLaren's shares. The refinancing, which had become critical, would have provided additional shares, some of which would have been Tyler's.

But Teddy and Bruce's friend Phil Kerr found themselves in disagreement. Both were directors and it took a year to sort matters out. By then the offer was withdrawn. By then, too,

McLaren had been forced to retreat, after 1972, from American sports-car racing, because the new Porsche, with factory backing, was proving invincible. There went an enormous part of McLaren Racing's income.

Not a word of the wrangle between the directors slipped out of the McLaren offices, nor a word about Tyler's disappointment or even a word about the company's money trouble. Tyler was as hard-working, as dedicated, and as happily acerbic as always.

But it hurt. And what hurt worst of all was the confrontation with an ugly truth: McLaren Racing was facing real money problems that Teddy had just proved he was unable to solve.

PART THREE

Mandel · Three

Indianapolis is a ceremonial gathering, a terrible kind of tithing, the biggest shuck in the hucksters' carnival.

Jackie Stewart to A. J. Foyt; Teddy Mayer at Kyalami, South Africa, to Teddy Mayer in Middle America; the transition is abrupt and frequently ugly. It goes from a polished and well-dressed grand prix world to the boots and Levi's of American championship racing; from the languid southern hemispheres to the rude immediacy of Speedway, Indiana. After South Africa comes Indianapolis.

You can run the Indy 500 in under four hours these days in a good championship car, providing the accidents are kept to a minimum and it doesn't rain. But the United States Auto Club, which sanctions the event, and the Indianapolis Motor Speedway, which runs it, open the track on the first of May, so a driver has little option but to spend the entire month in Indiana.

USAC and the Speedway want the cars and the drivers there all during May because by demonstrating they can hold fifty or more people in captivity every day, they are telling the world the race is important. *That it is, in fact, more than a race, that it is a ceremonial gathering.*

Think of it: grand prix drivers, champ car drivers, stock-car drivers, sports-car drivers . . . all of them must pause for a sixth of the working year, pass up all other activities, in order to stand in the rustic, dilapidated garage area at Indianapolis shuffling their feet while the self-important businessmen of the city take one and then another of them to Elks Club luncheons and YMCA dinners to reassure each other of their importance.

It's a terrible kind of tithing. And if the race were less important to the great American companies that sponsor the teams, the oil companies and the tire companies and the motor-home manufacturers, the people who pay the drivers their enormous retainers, they would no more say hello to the Indianapolis grocery storekeepers than allow themselves to be seen on the campaign trail with Bella Abzug.

Thirty Days in May. It would be ludicrous if it weren't for such high stakes. But the winning driver makes an immediate $100,000 or so and gains a financial cachet that doubles his endorsement earnings for years. His sponsor justifies everything spent on racing for all those years that were barren of success. The tire companies sell an extra five million tires. The oil companies' sales spurt. The Detroit manufacturer that supplies the pace car sees the sales graph shoot upward on the model he uses to lead the pack of race cars around for three laps. Indy is the biggest shuck in the hucksters' carnival; but the companies that spend millions there think it works, and whether it does or not, so long as the sponsors think it does, the drivers have to arrive at the Holiday Inn Northwest, the HoJo in Speedway, and the Speedway Motel at the end of April, and stay in one of those godforsaken places for thirty endless days.

That's the least of it. So long as Indianapolis can make a man rich or famous; so long as it can kill him or destroy his hopes, the thirty-day wait is like a month-long walk to the gas chamber; a four-week spin of a roulette wheel with everything you own sitting on the red. No matter how calm, relaxed, and friendly a man is on the thirtieth of April, by the end of May he is a snarling savage. Lifelong friendships are shattered in a brutal evening; sponsors lost, teams broken up.

We are all able to rise to an occasion, so long as the occasion is a weekend at most. The man doesn't live who can be graceful under pressure for thirty days.

The game at the Speedway is: What is it going to take to make the program? There are far more entries than there are open spots for cars in the race. The hopeless, the hopeful, the forlorn, and the bedraggled of racing somehow manage, each year, to gather together a car and a team and arrive in Indiana, praying that this year they'll fill one of the thirty-three positions and make the race. If you qualify, just qualify, as one of the thirty-three fastest cars, your reputation is made in Williams Grove, Pennsylvania, and at Ascot. From then on, you'll be able to be a draw at the little one fourth-mile speedway in your home town. You'll be sponsored by the local Chevy dealer, lionized by loyal fans, noticed by the one sportswriter (who doubles with the obits) on the weekly paper. That's all the drivers ask for, that and the fifteen thousand dollars or so they get for going even one lap, the people who tow from one thousand miles or more with their old and sagging race cars. They almost never achieve even that much.

A few years ago, an unknown by the name of Jigger Sirois drew the first qualifying position, which meant he was the first man to try to make the field. Sirois was an almost pathetic figure, aware the odds were astronomical against his being even the last man in the starting field, but hoping against hope. He took three of the four laps he was allowed to try to go fast enough to be among the thirty-three fastest, and then his crew chief, sighing an inevitable sigh, looked up from his stop watches and waved him into the pits, cutting short his qualifying run because he knew it wouldn't do. That is a crew chief's job in qualifying. If he thinks his driver isn't going fast enough, he aborts the run and then the driver's time is not official and he has another chance. But that year, with Sirois, even the fates were on the side of the big, rich, confident teams. No sooner did Sirois come into the pits than a rainstorm began. There was no qualifying that weekend at all, which meant that if Jigger Sirois had run one more lap, he would have been on the pole at Indianapolis . . . the first car in the field. He wouldn't have stayed there when the race started of course, the other thirty-two cars would have passed him in the first lap; but it would have been the realization of a wild fantasy for all the hopeless strays in the pits. One of them would not only have made the program; he would have led all the rest. And for the two weeks before qualifying and the race, Sirois would have been the toast of Indianapolis, where the pole sitter is royalty. Rags to riches, postman to President. Of course it didn't happen, because such things never happen. And there is no more sentiment, there are no more happy endings, in racing than in contemporary novels.

Last year, Jigger Sirois surfaced driving sports cars. It was the first time anyone had heard of him in years. He qualified last for his first and only race of the year.

If Indianapolis 1973 was different from an Indy 500 twenty years ago, it was only in detail. The cars looked different, they went faster, but the track had changed not at all. The greed of the promoters had prompted them to put what they called "luxury suites" outside of the second turn, but they had built the rows of seats down to the fence along the straightaway years before, and this time the people who sat in them got hurt. There was another disastrous start, for which the bumbling old men who run the race are notorious. The same inexorable pressures of the month were greater exactly in proportion to the increase in the purse and the value of commercial exploitation; there were about as many fights in about as many bars, as much fried chicken eaten in the infield per person/day, but there were three more days, because it rained and the race had to be postponed twice.

Art Pollard was killed in practice; Swede Savage was killed by fire in the race; Armando Teran, a crewman, was killed when a fire truck raced the wrong way down the pits to get to Savage's car; and the spectators mentioned above were injured in an accident on the first lap of the first start, which also injured driver Salt Walther.

There was a great scandal when a proper eastern road racer

was caught trying to substitute cars. The scandal made the local papers and the Los Angeles Times, *because the driver had moved to Southern California and was news. Besides which, his sponsor was a Los Angeles bomb manufacturer and worth tweaking.*

In every way, a mainstream Indianapolis 500. So representative, in fact, that STP made a movie of it, which they tastefully called "Fire and Rain."

Revson was the median Indianapolis man in 1973. He put his car into the wall before fifty miles were run and was back at the Howard Johnson's when they finally stopped the thing at 376 miles and declared a journeyman driver named Gordon Johncock the winner.

The bankruptcy court even let Johncock keep some of his purse.

Revson · Three

In this business, a mistake can ramify itself into something terminal.

An American driver of any stature doesn't have much of a choice about Indianapolis; he has to be there. Usually he has an American sponsor, and so far as the sponsor is concerned, Indianapolis is the most important race in the world in terms of promotion of his product.

I have done well at Indianapolis, although I have never won. But 1973 was the most frustrating for me since my first year there.

I was very confident about an improved version of last year's car, in which I did well although I did not finish the race. I was confident in this year's car; it was very quick.

For a grand prix or even one of the other 500-mile races in the United States, you can arrive a few days before the race, practice, qualify, race, and be on your way to the next event. At Indianapolis, however, you must spend the entire month of May. There is no particularly good reason for that except that it is the way it has evolved. The result is that it takes a big part out of the racing year and not a great deal is left to show for it.

But in terms of recognition, Indianapolis is the most important race in the United States; perhaps in the world. Next to becoming the world champion, being the Indianapolis winner is the single most significant accomplishment a driver can achieve. Of course, it pays a great deal of money to the winner as well.

I have always been extremely well treated at Indianapolis, and not only by the people at the Speedway. The city is entirely behind the event, and I have made friends there among the businessmen of the town.

This year I arrived at Indy, got into the car, and it was almost undrivable. There was much talk going around about the unsuitability of the Indy McLarens (the M16Cs), so much so that Roger Penske, the car owner who won last year with Mark Donohue driving a McLaren and who had ordered a new car from Teddy for 1973, decided to buy an Eagle as well. It turned out that the Eagle is the car Mark drove in the race.

McLarens had two cars at the Speedway, one for me and one for my teammate, John Rutherford. John was evidently more or less happy with his. Although the two cars were set up the same, mine had a handling problem we couldn't seem to solve. No matter how hard we tried, we seemed to be chasing that chassis problem from one end of the car to the other. I was still four or five miles off the pace due to that particular and annoying quirk in the handling characteristics.

It didn't seem to make any difference what setup Tyler and Huey and Alec put in the car, this quirk came through. The result was that after four or five days I thought I'd probably have to drive around the problem. That decision was made through sheer stubbornness.

So before the first qualifying weekend I finally got the car up to a speed higher than I'd achieved all month, 190, and on the very next lap I spun the car and hit the wall.

Now that I think about that spin, which was my first at Indianapolis, I look on the whole thing as brain fade, or brain fuck as they call it. I kick myself that I allowed myself to think it was driver error and my fault, to fall prey to the doubts that it was me and not the car and that I'd just have to press on and drive through the problem. In fact, I should have stuck to my guns about the car being wrong and persevered until we found the problem, which we partly did the day before I had to leave for the Belgian Grand Prix, which was the weekend after I qualified and the weekend before the race.

So long as I thought the problem might be my inability to get the car through the turns, it eroded my confidence. But once we isolated the chassis problem, it was clear that the car was the source of the difficulty and my confidence was restored. It wasn't I, after all, and so I ended up swearing at myself for having doubts about my ability.

A great deal of the month at Indy is spent in testing and in sorting out the car. At the speeds we are now going (and John Rutherford qualified at almost 200 mph, which represents the average for four laps), it does not make sense to allow yourself to drive a car in which you do not have complete confidence. The answer to that is to test. Teddy says that Denny Hulme is a better test driver than I am, but I don't agree. At any rate, Teddy does concede that I am willing to put forth more effort over an extended period during a race than Denny is.

That is an interesting point Teddy makes. It goes right to my motivations for being a race driver. At this point in my life, the reason I'm racing is to be a winner. And if I'm not going to be a winner this year or next, I'm going to quit. Finishing fourth or third or second is not worthwhile; I've done that. I don't want to go on as a journeyman. Racing won't accept me as that for much longer. Racing only accepts you if you're improving or if you're a winner. But if you've established that you're not going to be a winner, you're finished. People pay for winners or they pay for potential in this business.

About quitting: I'm still at an age at which I have a great deal of energy and enthusiasm. If I persist indefinitely in racing, eventually I won't have the energy to do anything else. The racing I do after the next few years will be anticlimactic.

Whatever I do, I want to be successful. While I've reached a modicum of success in racing, the point is I don't want to pursue it if I conclude I'm beating my head against the wall. It's a waste of precious time if I do that.

Time is certainly a determinant, but so is money. Beyond a

certain point, money is just a way of keeping score, but it is important for that purpose too. It is the evidence of success. Earning a lot of money in itself is no goal, but it represents being able to do what you want to do. In this day and age, to travel in the circles in which you wish to travel, to do what you want to do, takes money. The point is I don't want to work for the rest of my life. That's another point against belaboring the race thing too long. I want to be as creative with my life as possible, not burdened with the discipline of work after a certain age. The sooner I get to this point the better, but I see people around me who have set bad examples. They've gotten to the stage where they don't have to work, but they're bored. They've discovered that not having any responsibilities is not what they wanted after all.

Life is a journey whose meaning is as much *in* the journey as in its end. Jackie Stewart is here doing the color part of the telecast for ABC TV. My financial manager, Bud Stanner, is his also. Stanner is always making references to me in contrast to Jackie; I can't help but do the same.* I think Bud is wrong comparing me to Stewart, because I don't have the ego Stewart has. I don't push myself forward, as Stewart does continuously; I don't have his need to be the center of attention. I admit to having a large ego, but it doesn't manifest itself in the same way Stewart's does. With Stewart it's "me," "me," "me." I'm not as anxious as he is, and I think Jackie is a very anxious person about being number one all the time.

I take pleasure in being noticed, but I've been able to do it my way without being personally aggressive and pushy.

Stanner can't understand, for example, why I'm not aggressive with women. In fact, I'm shy with women and that's some-

* H. Kent Stanner, who manages all the McCormack motorsports people, is overseer to some very heavy hitters indeed. The Jackie Stewarts and the Peter Revsons are among the highest paid athletes in sports. As their manager, Stanner is privy to financial matters and to personal negotiations every bit as secret and as delicate as those of, say, Luxembourg or the State Department. Stanner's office is in Cleveland, and Stanner calls himself The Gnome of Cleveland, a not too modest comparison with the Swiss financial geniuses who manage the great private fortunes of the world. L.M.

thing he can't comprehend, perhaps because he's so much the other way. He has embarrassed me with girls. He takes so much for granted. He's so cocksure of himself in every situation, it's ludicrous. "Look at that girl on the barstool," he'll say; "she's wetting her pants to meet you." I find that really embarrassing.

Teddy compares my ego to Stewart's too. I think that's equally wrong. Teddy thinks certain things, and he's a very stubborn individual. He may have said something like that in a really casual way, but you begin to question him and all of a sudden he digs his heels into the ground.

I believe the reasons for the difference between Stewart and me is our backgrounds. I've had more all my life. Jackie comes from fairly meager circumstances, and owning things, having things, is a big deal to him. I've always had good clothes, for example, always been able to dress the way I've wanted to. I didn't have to go out, once I got money, and buy a huge wardrobe. I don't need to live in a big mansion.

To me, success is not measured by what material things you have but, rather, by what you're accomplishing. For some people, it's the result that counts; style means nothing.

But style is *very* important. It's the manner in which you conduct yourself, a means of achieving things, the way you handle your life. I would hope my style says I'm a gentleman; that's very important to me.

A French writer said a gentleman is someone who never undermines the self-respect of another; I think that's as good a definition as I've ever heard.

Now, by style I'm not talking about literal style: clothes, haircut, whatever. Style is important in the way you do everything. For example, here at Indy it is a matter of style the way you approach people at the fence around the garages. You can ignore them. You can be gruff with them. You don't have to acknowledge them at all. But they are sincere in their interest in you—although I don't understand the hero thing at all—and you must absolutely give them something in return.

I have a friend in Indianapolis named Danny Folsom, a businessman in town. He goes out of his way to be more than nice not only to me but the whole McLaren team. Now I first met him casually. He struck up a conversation while we were both sitting on the pit wall here one year, and I could easily have been abrupt or gotten up and walked away. But if I had done that, I would have missed out on a friendship that has been very valuable to me. Not only Danny's but his wife, Nancy's, too.

Danny almost adopts me during the month of May; he's like a Jewish mother. And while sometimes he seems as over-protective as a Jewish mother and I get a little annoyed, I shouldn't. Because spending a whole month here would be unbearable without all the things he does. He's very protective, and now that I've reached a certain stature here at the Speedway, he feels I'm a target for a lot of people he thinks are insincere. Any time I go to a party or spend some time with anyone else, he has to know the details, and when I tell him, he pauses and then says, well, that's O.K., as if I were waiting for him to give me his approval.

I don't understand the great awe men like Danny have of drivers. But I *do* understand the reaction of the women. And with me, it's mostly women. That's because I've been built up as a sex symbol, and that's how these people see me. I get the publicity, and I think it's amusing.

I'm not any different from anybody else, and every stud walking around here at Indy in two shoes is a sex symbol for that matter, except that some people get to play and others don't.

I stand back and look at the whole thing and sometimes I laugh. When *Pageant* magazine polled their readers and they voted me the sexiest athlete, I thought it was marvelous. *Every* stud thinks he's the sexiest guy in the world. Choosing me shows the American woman has good taste—or at least that the editors of *Pageant* do.

I like women and I don't use them. And I like the gals who go all googoo at the fence; I think it's marvelous. I like to give them something in return because maybe we dig each other for a minute.

Besides, women can offer a hell of a lot more to the world than men can. They add sensitivity and variety.

A woman doesn't have to be beautiful to appeal to me. She can be striking. If she's well groomed and possesses obvious female self-respect, she can be attractive to me. She has to be neat and tasteful. I'm concerned with the total effect.

She must have a kind of continuity and a sense of style. Young or old, it doesn't make that much difference so far as I'm concerned, although I'd prefer to stick to women my age or younger. A woman of thirty can have the understanding of a woman of forty, so older women have not had the particular appeal to me they seem to have for some men. But I want someone who is feminine, kind, sympathetic, who has strong feelings and good character.

It's obviously hard to tell about character on first meeting, although there are women who exude character immediately. But how can you tell if someone is honest or not? I don't know.

Usually when you meet a girl, you only meet her socially. You never meet her in a situation where there's a test of her character. Now if a girl I've just met begins to talk about people, and she obviously makes snap judgments before she knows what she's really saying, that tends to turn me off. As far as I'm concerned, there are the same criteria for men and women on that subject. A person is either tolerant or intolerant.

For a woman to be appealing, she must behave with style. I've been with a lot of beauty-contest winners and actresses and models; there's far more to appeal than looks.

A woman must not be too intense. Being too intense intimidates me. But someone who is intense enough to be thinking and obviously involved and concerned about things is ideal. It means she's an interested person and she's not bored with life. She's lively, and that's important.

The Penske team is garaged at the end of the same row of garages we're in. They have three cars, a McLaren each for Bobby Allison and Gary Bettenhausen and Mark Donohue's Eagle. When I compare my record with Mark's it's definitely inferior. I realize this; I'm aware of it. If I were as single-minded as Mark, in the same way that he is, maybe I would have achieved the same things. I would have had to make the same sacrifices. But I haven't been willing to live in the garage. I haven't been willing to live between races the way Mark has lived: to engineer, to test, to fly across the Atlantic ocean twice a week, to live with his team, to sleep with them . . . to do all that to the exclusion of everything else. I have not been willing to make those sacrifices.

When I get in a race car I'm going to give 100 per cent, and I'm going to give 100 per cent to a certain amount of preparation leading up to my getting into the car. But I guess I've never gotten involved to the degree that Mark has because there are other things I'm interested in, other things I've wanted to do. I have my business partnership with Peyton Cramer, I like other sports, I like to fish.

When I'm going fishing, Mark is underneath the car. There are times when I ask myself if it isn't important enough to me to stop all those things and concentrate on racing. I certainly want to be as successful in racing as Mark has been. But to be well balanced, to be accepted as a man of many interests and thoughts beyond the race track is more important to me.

There is a great deal of indecision in my mind about this, about how much sacrifice I'm actually willing to make, and I'm sure that part of the indecision is due to my feeling that a racing career is nothing but a stepping stone to something else. Which I didn't realize when I started.

I was impressed with Eddie Rickenbacker's story. Racing occupied only the early part of his life. After that, he achieved much greater things.

Whatever happens, I want to be able to make the transition from racing with a certain amount of style and to know where I'm going. I like the automobile business, and our Lincoln-Mercury dealership in Harbor City and our sports-car store in San Pedro are profitable. But even that is just a foundation. I'd like to do something more challenging individually than just selling cars.

John DeLorean, who was a vice-president of General Motors, is an example of a man in the automobile business who represented a new kind of automobile executive in Detroit. He was able to work at General Motors and still go where he wanted to go. But he was a swinger, and he evidently felt tied down to his job, so he quit. Perhaps it was a matter of personal problems. The point is, he made his mark.

I don't think DeLorean left General Motors because of any feeling of being uneasy with a big corporation, at least so far as its ethics were concerned. I think American corporations are probably ethical. Some are better than others, which is certainly the consequence of some people being more ethical than others. I've been disappointed with the President, with Nixon. People have argued to me that you have to make compromises. Evidently, some people have to make ethical compromises.†

Perhaps emotional compromises are necessary too. Perhaps it's my idealism that has kept me a bachelor. Some gal said to me, you're not going to be able to be ideally romantic, you're going to have to make compromises. I asked her what she meant and she said I'd never find what I was looking for. Well, I told her, if that time comes, if I have to do that, O.K. But I'm not ready to do it right now.

Right now I'm not willing to accept things about a woman I might have to accept in a marriage partner. When I get married, I would hope it would simplify my life to a certain extent. If in any way I looked at a potential marriage partner and saw that she was going to complicate my life, it would turn me right off. It's sometimes taken me a year to find that out, sometimes two years.

† Revson does not often talk about anything controversial; when he does he frequently defers to the judgments of others. But during the particularly difficult summer of 1973, Revson was obviously disturbed by the political atmosphere. The motor-racing community is conservative. Before the 1972 election, a petition in support of Richard Nixon circulated at Ontario Motor Speedway was signed by all but five of the people in racing who were asked to sign it. Even during the next summer, the racing people were staunch Nixonites—particularly in the Indianapolis area, a Republican stronghold. Although in May Revson's views, his moderately Republican opinions, were unshaken, by the end of the summer he was troubled and actively questioned the ethical flexibility of the Administration. But not in public. L.M.

But no matter how long it takes, there is one thing I know I have to be sure of: I don't want to marry someone and find that I have to keep cleaning up her mess. Someone once said to me, quoting someone else I guess, "Don't marry a girl who has more problems than you have." That's what I'm talking about.

I'm not sure why these thoughts occur to me here. Indianapolis wouldn't seem to be the place for examining your personal philosophy, but it is. Perhaps it's because of the nature of the race, the sudden things that happen. Perhaps it's because of the sharp contrasts with the rest of the races I go to; the different people, the different scene.

I know, for example, that I am inhibited with my teammate, John Rutherford. Because we're rivals, I feel inhibited. In most circles, I would be completely at ease. But I'm more deliberate in the way I act with John.

I could care less about the events leading up to this race. So far as I'm concerned, I wish it was all done in four days. Two days' practice, qualifying, and then the race. The results would be just about the same. The attrition rate would be no worse; the race would be just as good and just as interesting.

But John takes everything very seriously. Every year, the Indianapolis Symphony has a guest conductor, and when they can manage it, he comes from the racing people. This year it's John Rutherford, and so far as John is concerned, that means a great deal.

Because I like John, who has great style, I don't want to give him the impression that I don't take all this as seriously as he does. Because I appreciate the fact that these are his friends, this is his life, and he does take it seriously.

Still, although everyone here calls him "Johnny," I can't bring myself to do the same, although I do it to his face. He has "Johnny" written on his helmet and his trucks and even his goddamn car, so obviously he prefers to be known as that. But I think of him as a man, not a boy, and not as a character on the race track. John is a man's name, a gentleman's name, and John is a gentleman.‡

When I look back on this year's race, I know what word will occur to me. The whole month has been a struggle. We couldn't find the problem with the car, we couldn't make it work. I'll accept a lot of that responsibility; but John's car was working a lot better than mine. Since both cars were supposed to be identical, except for individual preferences, I couldn't help but feel there was experimentation going on with my car at my expense.

I know John's engine was stronger than mine for qualifying. They dialed in a lot more turbocharging boost, so much that Roger Bailey, who is the assistant engineman in the McLaren engine shop in Detroit, said he was scared to stay in the dyno room when they were running the engine.

I made a mistake driving around the handling problem my car had. When I spun, and the car went into the wall a couple of days before qualifying, it was the first time I had anything of the kind happen to me at Indianapolis. It reinforced my feelings that I should not drive a car hard unless I am absolutely satisfied with it. My principal feeling was one of disgust with myself.

After my spin, when I got back to the motel the phone started ringing. There were some old friends who called me. And my partner Peyton Cramer called from California to find out if I was all right and to tell me it wasn't that important that I race at Indianapolis. I think he knew it was a hopeless call in terms of convincing me otherwise. But Peyton is not a fan of Indy. He thinks it is overly dangerous. He would be just as happy if I didn't drive there. Evidently my little excursion made the front pages of the sports sections and the evening television news in a lot of places in the United States—because people I hadn't heard from in years were trying to get in touch with me.* I know it was the big news of the day in

‡ If Revson is particularly sensitive about this, it's because he detests being called "Pete." Teddy Mayer and Eoin Young call him "Revvie," which he doesn't mind, but his preference is really for "Peter." L.M.

* No matter how unconcerned Revson pretended to be about this long-distance attention, no matter how disgusted he was with having spun, as

Indianapolis. They have thirty days' worth of Speedway action to report on; it is traditional. The trouble is that not that much happens. So the writers and the broadcasters are almost grateful when they have something they can actually write about, and I certainly provided them with that.

Sam Posey also spun his car and hit the wall earlier in the week, and some of the stories compared my spin to his, since he is also primarily a road racer. But at least I hit the wall about 20 mph faster than he did.

The time between the beginning of the month and the race itself did not go entirely to waste. Of course, I was busy trying to get the car to work before qualifying. And after the first qualifying weekend, Teddy and I took a flight to New York, and from there to London on our way to the Belgian Grand Prix. For a while, we didn't know if the Belgian GP would be run at all, because the surface at the track at Zolder had been criticized by the Grand Prix Drivers' Association. In fact, at a sedan race on the new surface, several cars had lost their windshields because of rocks being thrown up from the cars ahead. At any rate, nobody seemed to know if the race was going to be held or not, right up until the last moment.

Qualifying for Indianapolis is held the two weekends prior to the race, and the pole position is determined on the first day of the first weekend. You pick your place in line to qualify out of a hat, and as it turned out, mine was to be the first contending car out on the track. I was not unhappy about the qualifying number, since the month had been windy and cold and the morning is usually a time when the wind is at a minimum. At the speeds we go, a wind can make a great deal of difference, so it seemed to me the cars that drew the late numbers were at something of a disadvantage.

The night before qualifying, I acted as I do the night before a race. Eat lightly and go to bed early. And no sex. At Indianapolis, there is the added problem of trying to find a restaurant

---

the calls began to back up at the motel switchboard and the afternoon papers were delivered, he brightened considerably and, when I told him my wife had called from California asking if he was all right, he wanted me to repeat her conversation word for word. L.M.

where you can get served. You don't even try to get a decent meal. The people come to the qualifying weekend almost in the same number that they come to the race, and although the track never gives out the actual attendance, it has to be close to 200,000. As a result, all the restaurants are jammed and they go on a kind of race-weekend basis, on which they stay open twenty-four hours a day and serve a limited menu. The waitresses get awfully tired and very surly and the food is extremely bad.

Before qualifying this year, I walked over to the Howard Johnson's restaurant next to the motel and had a light supper with Leon. Behind us were Joe Leonard, the 1972 United States Auto Club Champion, and his wife. Although Joe is a fine driver, he is not a very good qualifier, as he will be the first to admit. He was particularly worried about his car and admitted to me he was having some of the same organizational problems with his team, Vel's Parnelli, as I seemed to be having with McLaren. He did not think his new Parnelli was as good as the cars of his teammates, Al Unser and Mario Andretti. He had been having trouble all month getting up to speed, and had yet to go 190.

A lot of the talk, most of it in fact, in the month preceding the race is about what speed it will take to get into the program—that is to say, to be one of the thirty-three fastest qualifiers, in order to make the race. This year, the consensus seems to be 190 mph, and so Joe is right to be concerned.

But I don't know if his worry is really about his car—although it is interesting that ours is not the only team with evidently unequal cars—or whether it is about himself as a qualifier.

Qualifying is a different art from racing. Only Bobby Unser has been better over the past three years in the USAC 500-milers than I have been.†

Without intending criticism of Joe Leonard, it's my feeling

† By the end of the year, the comparison favored Revson. Revson had taken the pole in the other two 500s, Pocono and Ontario. As a result, Revson had three pole positions in three years and he had taken the front spot at each of the major tracks. L.M.

that qualifying has always been a true test of a man's mastery of his machine. In a fine profile of the great stock-car driver Junior Johnson, Tom Wolfe says it well: "[So] qualifying becomes a test of raw nerve—of how fast a man is willing to take a curve. Many of the top drivers in competition are poor at qualifying. In effect, they are willing to calculate their risks only against the risks the other drivers are taking. Junior takes the pure risk as no other driver has ever taken it."

Perhaps qualifying *is* what Wolfe says it is, a test of raw nerve. Regardless, I like what he says about qualifying being the "pure" risk.

At supper, Leon asked me if the death of Art Pollard, an Indy veteran, in practice late in the week was going to have an effect on me when I qualified. My answer was that it's a matter of concentration. Concentration is important above all things. Pollard's death, or the death of anyone, does not break my concentration. As far as I'm concerned, I'm not indestructible, but there just isn't anything short of not racing at all that I can do to make the odds any better for me even after seeing Pollard's accident. I'm taking the precautions necessary. I'm not taking any more risks than I would have, had I known this was going to happen.

So I told Leon that as far as any driver with any sense is concerned, there's more at stake than our pride and our reputations, our standing in our sport and the money. There's more than that. We all have the pressure of keeping our necks connected to our spines. If we make a mistake it's not a question of striking out or losing fifteen yards. It's not a matter of losing or even making an ass of yourself in front of a great number of people. It's more than that.

In this business, a mistake can ramify itself into something terminal.

In other words, Pollard's death doesn't change my game plan at all. The only way it could really affect me would be if it prompted me to quit racing.

At the same time, there are people who think this kind of thing, at least the possibility of its happening, adds a kind of spice.

I don't think that's true. Mind you, I like an element of risk. But an element of risk can be a lot of things. It doesn't have to be a risk that you will kill yourself.

Only gamblers take complete chances. Nothing was ever accomplished without taking some sort of chance, though. There's nothing risk free. But I try to minimize the risks of race driving. I'm said to be a conservative driver. I don't know why people say that; maybe it's true. I look at other drivers and at times I think they drive beyond their ability. They drive with wild abandon, and I ask myself if that's why I'm not winning more races.

I don't get the Triple High that some drivers seem to need.‡

The Triple High seems to help some people qualify. But to me it's the simple challenge, the pure risk, and the opportunity, at least at Indianapolis, to demonstrate the mastery of the machine all by myself on the track.

I hoped for 192 mph or slightly more, and when the average of four laps was taken for me, it turned out to be 192.606. There was much speculation about the 200-mph qualifying speed this year. A lot of people didn't think it was going to happen. In my opinion, the conditions had to be exactly right, and the likely man to do it would be Bobby Unser.

Gary Bettenhausen, driving for Roger Penske, went out right after I did in Roger's new McLaren, the same model as mine, and did 195.5, and then A. J. Foyt went 188.9. So although I was not ecstatic about my speed, my number was second on the big pylon in the infield that indicated positions in the field, and I didn't feel too bad.

Jerry Grant, who led the race last year in the so-called Mystery Eagle and who is a very good qualifier, could not get

‡ This is a reference to one of the bizarre cryptocultists in racing who claims that only when his psychological, emotional, and physical wavelengths (whose durations were once and for all determined at the moment of his conception) coincide at their highest points will he race. At those times, he claims, he is absolutely invincible. Those are the moments he is on a Triple High. Curiously, even then he rarely wins. I have spoken to a variety of people about this man, and some whom I respect absolutely agree with him. They cite BOAC as a corporate believer in this method, and the Japanese railroads. Maybe the cryptocultist should give up racing and become a locomotive engineer. L.M.

13. Alec Greaves, Peter Revson's Indianapolis crew chief.

4. From the left: Revson in his Peter Revson Autograph Model Sunglasses, Roger "Boost" Bailey, the deputy chief engine man from McLaren's Detroit engine shop, and Gordon Coppuck, designer of all McLaren race cars and one of the secret men of motor racing.

5. Revson, the first American to campaign full time for the world championship since Dan Gurney, makes his announcement in a 1971 conference in Akron, Ohio, with the Goodyear racing chief, Larry Truesdale, at his side.

16. Early in Peter Revson's CanAm career, there were times when things plain didn't work. Here he barely contains his disappointment after his car wouldn't start from the grid. The rest of the field is long gone.

17. The cool-off lap after winning the CanAm at Laguna Seca in 1971, the year he became champion for McLaren.

8. Drivers spend thirty days or more at Indianapolis, very little of it racing. The lucky ones have motor homes parked in back of the garage area, the luckier ones have blondes to sleep on their shoulders. Marji Wallace with Revson.

9. Just prior to the 500, Revson made a promotional tour for RevUp vitamins. His audience was appreciative but the product was being marketed as The Vitamin for Men.

10. Revson may be distant with adults, but he is particularly warm with children. He has also been known to talk to good-looking ladies. The picture shows a technique George Lysle calls "working the fences."

21. Three of the top drivers in the United States, (from left) Bobby Allison, Ma[rk] Donohue, and John Rutherford—Revson's '73 McLaren teammate at Indianapolis— still laughing and smiling as they wait for a drivers' meeting before the second Ind[y] start. They weren't laughing much after the meeting, which was filled with acrimon[y]

According to a story in *Good Food* magazine, Revson is a chef of *cordon bleu* quality —up to and including peanut-butter-and-jelly sandwiches.

23. There are grim reminders everywhere of what can happen in racing. On the pit waiting for Indianapolis to start.

any faster than 190.2 in his factory Eagle, and another good driver, Bill Vukovich, was slower than I was, at 191.1.

So it came as a surprise when Steve Krisiloff, who is a relatively new driver, from Parsippany, New Jersey, went 194.93 in Grant King's Eagle copy. Although I was not overly distressed, it made me less optimistic.

There were some real contenders coming up, but the wind was increasing and that improved my chances for staying high up in the field. In fairly quick succession, Gordon Johncock went 192.55 in his Patrick Eagle; then his teammate, Swede Savage, a very good qualifier, went 196.58. Since Swede was one of the people who many felt had a good chance at the 200-mph mark, it didn't seem that it would be reached, but he was still considerably faster than I had been.

Thus far it was Eagle (Savage), McLaren (Bettenhausen), Eagle copy (Krisiloff), Eagle (Johncock), and McLaren (I), but then Al Unser of the Super Team went out in his Parnelli and did 194.8 and the next contender to qualify was his teammate, Mario Andretti, who did 195.05.

That left at least three very fast drivers to come: Bobby Unser, Mark Donohue, and my teammate, John Rutherford.

Mark was first and went 197.066, which I thought would be far and away fast enough. But after Wally Dallenbach, John went out and did 198.415.

I went down to the pits to stand by the team as John qualified, and Gary Knudsen, who heads McLaren Engines, was so nervous as he watched John in his four laps, he had to walk away from the pit wall and into the crowds in front of the tower-terrace grandstands. He couldn't stand to watch. Gary, or, as he is known, The Hippie, had dialed in so much boost in John's engine he was afraid it would blow at any minute.

The crowds really liked John, and the fact that he was on the pole brought them up cheering when they announced his four-lap average.

Bobby Unser's late-afternoon 198.183 was an anticlimax, although Teddy, Tyler, and John were nervous until after Bobby's run.

I ended up starting on the inside of the fourth row, which is not the best place in the world, but, as it turned out, had some advantages.

After qualifying, I walked back to the garages and then to the Starcraft motor home we had arranged to park for the month just behind the pits, to make myself some tea. In the garage there were eight telegrams for John and one for me. In 1971, when I won the pole here, Denny Hulme, my McLaren teammate, must have felt as I felt now. Then I was the star.

But you've got to be flexible in this business. One day you're a star, the next you're making your own tea.

The race in Belgium was not calculated to improve my frame of mind. As I've said, nobody knew for sure until the week of the race whether or not it would be held. They had resurfaced the track and received tentative approval from the Grand Prix Drivers' Association, so we arrived there and began to practice.

But by Saturday the track was breaking up once more.* The drivers all got together to talk matters over in the Texaco trailer parked in the pits. A message was sent to the organizers about our feelings of risking our equipment and ourselves on what we considered a very dangerous surface. The organizers sent a deputation in to us. We sent word back to them. That was about the time of the Wounded Knee confrontation in the Dakotas and it occurred to me, while all this was going on, that we were enacting the same drama here in Belgium that the Indians were involved in in the States. Although that

---

* One little pothole is nothing more than an annoyance on a freeway. Why should the very best drivers in the world think of canceling a race because of a break in the track's surface? In the first place, it wasn't only one pothole, it was a lot of them. Part of the surface was disintegrating near the edges of the track. So the deterioration was major. Then, too, you have to understand that to be successful in this league, you have to be driving at the very edge of control all the time. An unexpected puff of wind or an apple core thrown on the track can mean disaster when you're that close to the limit. A pothole, let alone ten or forty of them, on the surface of a Grand Prix track is like Grand Canyon in the middle of the New Jersey Turnpike. L.M.

was an amusing thought, the problem itself was anything but funny.

Eventually, we reached a solution and the organizers fixed the worst parts of the track.

In the race itself, I was running third when I came to the particular corner where four cars had spun before I arrived, and two were still sitting there, off the track. The surface on the apex of the turn was very bad and I got caught out by it. So I joined the other two cars parked off the road, which was the end of the Belgian Grand Prix for me.

When I returned to Indianapolis, I had a busy schedule facing me. Not only did I have certain awards dinners to attend, including the Jim Clark affair, which, as the previous year's winner, I had to go to in order to present the 1973 award, but a YMCA dinner was arranged at which I was to be the guest speaker. Then there was a dinner Boyd Jefferies gave for all the McLaren people, and the pole mechanics' dinner as well.

I also had a fairly heavy schedule of promotions for RevUp, which was going to be introduced in Indianapolis to coincide with this year's running of the race.

After the promotion was over at Haag's drugstore, where they had a disc jockey broadcasting for several hours, security guards, and the whole thing, Danny Folsom, Leon, and I were walking out to the car, when out of the corner of my eye I saw that Danny was talking to a very good-looking girl. I didn't pay that much attention until she got in the car and Leon said she was joining us for a sandwich. When I think back on it, I'm not sure I was particularly pleased about that, because although I'm always happy to be in the company of a beautiful woman, I also value my privacy and the whole day had been spent talking to strangers in drugstores. I had been looking forward to relaxing, taking off my public face.

I must say I thought Leon was a little rough on the girl in the car on the way to the restaurant. She was, after all, in a strange situation with people she had never met before, and it didn't seem quite right that he should immediately begin to subject her to the same kind of "stress interview" (as he calls his small talk) as he did regularly with me.

Anyway, at the restaurant, she seemed a little shy, which I liked, but very self-possessed. Danny was impressed with her looks and offered to sponsor her in 1974 for queen of the Indianapolis 500 Festival. I'm certain he was absolutely sincere in that, but I'm afraid the girl thought it was probably just talk.

Her name was Marji Wallace and she was a model who lived in Indianapolis. I found out that evening, when I took her to dinner, that she lived with a girlfriend, that she had been an age-group swimmer, and that she had just turned nineteen.

That surprised me, because she was extremely mature. The more time I spent with her, the more surprised I was at her age, because she seemed to be able to deal with any kind of situation. She was not at all affected. She was very straightforward.

I invited her to be my guest at the race, and Eoin Young, the press-relations man for Gulf, our sponsors, gave her a Gulf racing jacket and found her a credential. I became more and more impressed with the way Marji handled herself in new situations, particularly with my family, who had flown in from New York. Many of the other drivers, particularly Jackie Stewart, were taken with her, and Bob Jones, who was covering the 500 for *Sports Illustrated,* told me that at luncheon at the Speedway Motel Stewart had gotten up from his table and come over to talk to her three separate times.

Jones also told me that, in the last effort to impress Marji, Jackie offered her a complete set of the women's underwear that is marketed with his endorsement in Europe. It didn't seem to work very well.

Marji and I spent considerable time together, and I continued to find her a delightful companion. When Leon asked me what I thought of her, I answered facetiously that I wouldn't be a bit surprised if she made the traveling squad—a remark I'm afraid he took seriously. When I saw his reaction, I hastened to tell him all I really meant was that I'd probably be seeing a lot of her in the months to come.

A couple of months later, at the U.S. GP, at Watkins Glen, it was my turn to misunderstand. It was after the race, in the Kendall Service Center. The weekend had been long and difficult, and Leon, Marji, and I were talking about his research. He told me he had it handled. Ever since Indianapolis, he said, Marji had had a micro tape recorder surgically implanted, and for just a second I thought he was serious. That it was a crazy idea didn't even occur to me. All I could think of was what might have been on those tapes. Then I saw the big grin on his face. It was something of a relief.

At Indianapolis, they should postpone the race to a pre-arranged date when it rains. By waiting day after day until the weather permits, they are making it too hard on the drivers.

This year, the pressure kept building and building, because nobody knew when the race was going to start. Usually, when you know when a race is going to be, you can prepare yourself psychologically. You peak for the race.

But at Indianapolis, we were all standing around waiting for the thing to start. Since I did not have the greatest confidence in my car anyway, that just made things worse.

I was fined on the day after the first start, the start that involved Salt Walther in his accident. But it turned out the USAC stewards did that just for form's sake. They officially penalized me for moving up at the start before I should have, and they put out a statement that I had been fined. But, privately, they told me to forget paying the fine.

The first few laps at Indianapolis are potentially the most dangerous a driver will ever face. You are going very fast and you are in close quarters. Coming down the straightaway for the start, there is a great deal of turbulence from the other cars, and since you are not in the racing groove, there is a lot of dust kicked up and it is very difficult to see.

I probably think too much at Indianapolis anyway. The things that are instinctive to the people who race there all the time are not so instinctive to me.

So I see and I think about how dangerous it is. I know that in those close quarters, for that matter anytime there, you can't avoid a car when it spins, as you can on a road course. A car will spin and there's no place he can go. That means there's no place you can go to avoid him.

I think it was the English motoring writer Dennis Jenkinson who first talked about good drivers always trying to drive at ten tenths of their ability and the car's potential. He said that nobody could maintain that all the time; it was a matter of intensity and concentration. He used it as a measure of a man's commitment to racing. In those terms, I guess when I qualify I'm driving at ten tenths. But during the race at Indianapolis I suppose I'm driving nine tenths.

From the start, the third and real start, the car was a handful. I had to fight it from the very beginning.

Somewhere during the early laps, I was getting ready to overtake the eleventh-place car, fighting the turbulence and drafting him on the backstraight. Having to pull out of the draft to pass meant having to enter the turbulent air outside the draft just when we came through the fourth turn entering the start-and-finish straightaway.

There were other people who confirmed afterward that the fourth turn was more slippery than the others, especially in the early laps, before a lot of rubber was put down. At any rate, I went to make the pass when the tail swung out and the car got loose out toward the wall. I controlled it, but it began to swing in the other direction, toward the inside, and it started to fishtail. I delicately backed off the throttle to regain stability, and then the car swung once too often.

With the power off, I did not have the instantaneous throttle response to be able to correct, and the car began a slow spin.

On its second complete spin I caught it going in the right direction, but it was too late. The car hit the inside retaining wall, crushing its left front suspension, and I was out of the race.

That was bad enough. But then the bastards in the tow truck who lifted the car to get it over the wall, dropped it right on the retaining wall, totaling it. So what was only a case of some bent suspension pieces turned into a completely ruined race car.

I left that night in a Lear Jet that Skip Scott's executive-aircraft-leasing company sent up, making the New York connection for Monte Carlo, where I arrived in time to get in exactly one day's practice for the Grand Prix of Monaco.

I had seen the end of the race on television before I left, including Swede Savage's accident. Thinking about how dangerous the start is in the 500, and how dangerous the track really is, I kept coming back to one of my impressions when I first drove there. When cars start spinning and crashing, there's no place to hide at Indianapolis.

Mandel · Three Continued

As Revson walks by, he whispers, "A hawk has very stiff lips." Revson's lips are pretty stiff, too.

Everyone goes back to Indy, although without exception they have sworn after the race the year before it has been their last. Edwin Ingalls is a photographer who was standing on a photo platform in 1971 that was hit by the pace car as it pulled into the pits. The pace car was going at a lunatic speed and was being driven by a local Dodge dealer who had no more business driving it than he had performing open-heart surgery. When the pace car hit the platform, it knocked it down and sent the photographers tumbling. One man on the platform was paralyzed for a year. Another will never walk properly again, and Ingalls had to be evacuated to Methodist Hospital in Indianapolis by helicoptor. "Just replace my cameras," he told the Speedway management later, and they were soothing and very reassuring about it all. Cameras, hospital bills, anything he thought proper.

Last year, the bills still unpaid, Ingalls brought suit. They run the Speedway on a tight budget, because although its owner, Tony Hulman, is a man beloved the length and breadth of Indiana, he is also a businessman. A businessman has to be careful about spurious claims and rip-off artists, right?

Ingalls belongs in the middle circle of racing; he is not only a photographer but an illustrator, but you can't actually support yourself taking photos of race cars.

So, in 1973, Edwin Ingalls, who was no longer limping and who had bought some new cameras, flew over the flooded Mississippi Valley to Indianapolis to stay for the month. Even though he didn't exactly have a place to stay and he didn't exactly have a car lined up to get him around and he didn't exactly have any idea what kind of assignment he might have to pay for his month, Ingalls went back to Indy anyway, just like everybody else.

It can't be because of the town. Indianapolis has a nice zoo, and there are some friendly people there as well as the Indianapolis Pacers of the ABA. But still, Indianapolis is the place that wouldn't rent its community center to the ACLU during the McCarthy days because the ACLU was some kind of radical organization and if there's one thing Indianapolis is, it's careful. So it isn't charm that pulls people back to Indy. It isn't weather either. May is tornado month in Indiana, and when it isn't tornadoing, it's hot and muggy. It's also flat as far as the eye can see, and the restaurants in town are bad and expensive.

All those people don't go to Indiana in May for the scenery. They don't go for a vacation. But somehow they behave like spawning salmon; their instincts tell them they have no choice. Very much against their will they find themselves on TWA from the West Coast, or Eastern or Allegheny from the East, sitting near bulky men with crewcuts who chew cigars the whole trip long—the crew chiefs and the owners.

All those people know that when they get to the Speedway there's going to be a hassle about credentials—the creaking security guards employed by the Speedway won't let them go where their passes say they can go. They know that the motel clerks that have held their reservations for six months will look blank when they give their names at the desk, even though they've been staying at those same motels for ten years or more. They all know that. And they also know that by the end of the month their nerves will be strung tight enough to snap and they'll have run out of money. Most of all, they know they're going to see an artistically abysmal race.

But there's something else they know. They know that for the rest of the year, wherever else they go, people are going to ask whether they were at the Speedway this year. They'll ask at Talladega and Daytona in the heat of midsummer, and they'll ask in the pits at the Edmonton CanAm in September. To say no is to admit to being an outsider. To say yes means being a part of a nomad band, part of the racing tribe that wanders across the summer face of the country.

Spending a month at the Speedway, even if you have no reason, means you have paid your dues for the year. "Yeah, four fucking weeks in that place," they can answer with the same weariness in their voices that is reflected when John Rutherford speaks. Small enough price to pay for acceptance.

In the hierarchy of hangers-on, status depends on where you've managed to get a room. There are only three places that count. The big-shooter car owners, the Parnelli Joneses and the Roger Penskes, are put up at the Speedway Motel, which is a part of the track complex and requires only a two-minute drive to the pits or a one-minute walk to the suites overlooking the second turn. The freebie affairs are held at the Speedway Motel: the Goodyear cocktail party, the *Car and Driver* postqualifying dinner, the American Auto Racing Writers and Broadcasters breakfast. *Sports Illustrated* staffers and photographers take up almost a whole wing at the Speedway along with the ABC-TV crew: Jim McKay, Jackie Stewart, and retinue. If you're at the Speedway, and you're only at the Speedway if you've been going to the race for fifteen years as an owner or if you're on a Very Important Media list, you walk with your head held high waiting for someone to ask the standard opening question of every race weekend in every country in the world: "Where you staying?" And the answer confirms your place in the racing community as much as though you had a caste mark on your forehead. The people who are at the

Speedway walk around with a kind of quizzical look on their faces, an invitation, a plea, for someone to ask The Question.

A. J. Foyt and a lot of the senior members of the herd stay at the Holiday Inn Speedway. It's a worn sort of place, but the bar is always good for a fight and it's across the street from the track. Down Sixteenth Street, out toward the airport, is the Howard Johnson's; new, comfortable, and inexpensive. It's ten minutes from the track all month long until race day, when it's an hour and a half away. Team McLaren stays at the HoJo's. Everywhere else is nowhere.

The people of Indianapolis, like the people who live in all towns where there's a race track, can't make up their minds whether to say hello in the supermarkets to the racers and their wives who have stopped in to shop and save a little money on the track food prices, or whether to boot them through the plate-glass windows.

Of course the laundromats and the markets and the movie theaters and the restaurants profit; but there *you* are, living in a neat, cultivated brick house near the track. You've spent a year on the lawn and the flowers are just coming up. You're close enough to the high school so your daughter can walk in the morning. Suddenly, a horde of barbarians descend. They crush your flowers, they park on your lawn. You can't even understand what your daughter is saying about what happened to her on her way home this afternoon because she is hiccuping through her tears. When you go to the supermarket you have to wait in the checkout line for twenty minutes. They've run out of orange juice again, and there's no point in trying to go around the corner to the Bonanza steak house for dinner because *their* line stretches into your driveway. And Christ! the place is filthy. The whole town is strewn with hot-dog wrappers and chicken bones and drunks.

So far as the racing community is concerned, Indianapolis in its best seasons hasn't much to offer. In May, it's overstocked on hostility.

But, for the people who live there and are part of the race, it's a month-long carnival. The circus has come to town. No more endless, bleak days ahead; instead, all those wonderful people, a festival of lunches and dinners and parades. Work in the morning, spend the afternoon at the track. School buses by the hundreds take fifth-graders out in the sun in the grandstands, courtesy of Tony Hulman, and the YMCA has a fund-raising dinner at the Hilton downtown, and the Elks and everyone else registered as a non-profit corporation with the state of Indiana has something going on as well.

Think of it! There is Indianapolis, condemned to dreariness and midwestern routine until the end of time. Bleak gray days in winter, hot wet days in summer, and the same awful office routines that Santa Cruz has but without an ocean to splash in. Just . . . Indianapolis. Then, suddenly, it's May. And all the puritan rules are suspended. Every day's a vacation. Nobody minds if his wife drinks too much or if he gains weight. After all, it's Mardi Gras.

If you lived in Indianapolis, you'd hold your breath until Magic May too.

Danny Folsom does.

Danny Folsom is a middleman between the great chicken manufacturers of the South and the Colonel Sanders' chain in and around Indianapolis. He also sells to supermarkets. What he delivers are plucked and eviscerated chicken corpses. To the McLaren mechanics, he is known as The Chicken Plucker.

All year long, except for the fall, when he goes to every one of the Detroit Lions home football games and also when he goes up to his hunting camp in Michigan, and except for the month of May, which he spends at the Speedway, Folsom gets up at 5 A.M. to go out to the chicken pens and sort over his inventory. He gets his chickens in salable order, counting and packaging them for delivery. It is hard and unpleasant work. But the business has been profitable. Danny Folsom is a respected member of the Indianapolis business community—a man of dignity, some wealth, and considerable standing.

But, in the fall, when Danny goes up to Tiger Stadium to see the Lions, and during May, when he takes his days out in the sprawling, enormous Speedway, Danny assumes an entirely different personality. It is not complimentary but it fits.

Danny Folsom becomes the king of Indianapolis. The superfan.

If May is carnival to the rest of the city, it is fulfillment, transport to a magic world, the moment of highest calling, to Danny Folsom. It's for the *others* to watch NBC Nightly News and see their very own neighborhoods and even for just that moment feel some warm identification. Danny Folsom is *there*. With Peter Revson. Wearing a McLaren team jacket. Inside the garage when Tyler is telling Teddy what's really wrong with the car, not what he's told Ray Marquette of the Indianapolis *Star;* not what everyone else reads the next morning in the paper. But the real thing! Danny can swagger through the opening in the cyclone fence around the garage area and get a nod of recognition from the old men on guard who look with their rheumy eyes to make out the silver badge pinned to his jacket. It's not for Danny to hang by his fingers on the fence, pushing up through three, five, sometimes eight rows of people straining to get the quickest glimpse of Bentley Warren or Jigger Sirois—maybe even Lloyd Ruby or Roger McCluskey. Danny Folsom is right there with Peter Revson and Johnny Rutherford, talking to them in warm intimacy. Certainly the people along the fences look at his big, chunky figure in the blue kapok jacket with "McLaren" printed on the back in orange and his name in elegant script on the left pocket and think he's one of *them*. Not a driver, of course, but perhaps a mysteriously talented car designer? O.K., a fabulously rich owner.

No, a superfan. However much the name might derogate him in the world of professional football, Folsom is a genuine part of the racing troupe. Not because he bribes his way in with food for the McLaren refrigerator and his annual mechanics' party, but because he seems to understand. And with the racers and the crews who live on the frontier, who travel forever, never seeing home and deprived of any trace of permanence, the people who come and stick even for a month are welcomed. In a tribe that is filled with transients, permanence is measured in minutes.

It's measured in devotion, too, and in an unwillingness to

be critical; the threads that hold the racing people together are too fragile to withstand the pull of diverse opinion. If there is one thing Danny Folsom understands, it's how to ease the strain.

Even in his language. When he is with the football people, he uses football jargon: "spit" for "vomit." When he is with the racing people, with Revson, his language is filled with racing euphemisms. So Art Pollard didn't crash and kill himself, he "eased his car into the wall."

Maybe it's because Revson was brought up in New York that he so well understands the superfan phenomenon—the remora who swim around the shark. Joe Namath has his clique, so do Willis Reed and Dr. J. If Revson is to be a superstar, he needs one too. Of course, it wouldn't be stylish to seek them out, to actually encourage them. But if Danny Folsom presents himself, isn't Revson acting according to old New York tradition in accepting him? Of course he is.

Revson's view of Folsom is filled with—astonishingly—affection. Revson, whose background has given him a rich interest in sports anyway, knows that Folsom is to be worn in his buttonhole—almost a part of himself; and Revson is nothing if not self-approving. In turn, Folsom thrives on the nourishment of Revson's affection.

He is Revson's one-man Praetorian Guard, his nanny, his executive secretary, his Elsa Maxwell.

I was not at first accepted by Folsom. I knocked on the Revson door the evening of his encounter with the wall at the Speedway and, not actually believing that a bright star like Revson would be contained in an ordinary room at an ordinary motel, inquired if it was indeed Peter Revson's room. "I'll see if he's here," said Folsom, who answered and who had spent the past three hours closeted in a 14x12 room with his charge. Although the door was left open, it was very clear that I was not to come in, so I wandered back across the hall to the room Revson had reserved for me. ("Be sure they give you the right rate," Revson had said, ever mindful of a world that waits to ambush the profligate.) About ten minutes later, Revson came sauntering in with the newspaper, amazed at the fact that his afternoon's achievement had rated a 36-point skyline banner. The whole episode took about fifteen minutes, but when we went back across the hall to Revson's room, Folsom had clearly made up his mind about me. It was an opinion fixed not by his own feelings, but by Revson's. During May, at least, it's not what Folsom thinks that counts, it's what Revson thinks. And not only was I accepted, but I was accepted at the same level as Revson. So it was much like being confronted by a guard dog, facing his public snarls, and then meeting him again in the company of his master.

During the rest of the month, Folsom was as solicitous of my welfare as he was of Revson's. The days were filled with What can I get you's and Can I bring you something tomorrow's. And it was not a matter of my status or my achievements or that Revson and I were writing a book together. It was entirely fixed by Folsom's perception of Revson's judgment of my worth.

Thus, when Neil Leifer, a well-known *Sports Illustrated* photographer, spent several days shooting Revson for an *SI* piece, Folsom was guarded with him, jealous, and almost inhospitable.

Curiously, since Indianapolis in 1973, Danny Folsom and I have spoken frequently on the telephone. He calls to ask me about my family with very real interest. He tells me about his vacations; he shares his successes and his jokes. They are warm and valuable conversations, and I begin to understand Revson's affection for Folsom, who may be ingenuous but who is, just the same, a genuinely nice man.

Everywhere Danny Folsom follows Revson at the Speedway, he sees someone he knows. Indianapolis, at least in that sense, is a small town. And everywhere he goes, he very likely takes reassurance from what he sees: the massive grandstands, the infield golf course, the Art Deco dining room of the Speedway Motel. But there is a feeling to Indianapolis, which is really imparted only by successive layers of perception over the course of a whole month, that even Folsom can't understand.

It is made up, like an exposed sedimentary section, or a Dobos torte, of slice upon slice of sensory experience.

At the back of the tower-terrace grandstands, which line the inside of the front straight and define the back line of the racing pits, at the back of those stands and on their ground floor, is the racers' cafeteria. A guard stands at the door. (There is a guard everywhere at Indianapolis, except on the third race day in 1973, when most of them had used up all their vacation or sick time and had to go back to work.) It is actually two cafeterias, joined at the middle, Siameselike, by a double cashier's counter. The public is allowed in the far area and they can look over the cashier's shoulder and see the drivers and the crewmen and the old-timers eating the same simple food they buy.

The food is unremarkable, although the iced tea will rot your bowels, but the people are extraordinary. It is not the museum near the Speedway's main entrance that marks the history of this race, it is the cafeteria. Here are the elder statesmen of racing. Everyone has gathered again this year during May. Everyone who has ever raced here, who has ever crewed here, who has had anything to do with the sport. The men are old. If you are deeply woven into the fabric of the 500 yourself, you might recognize the faces. To everyone else, the press people, the new drivers, the brash young owners, they are anonymous people, these old men who made screaming headlines twenty-five years ago and became instantly rich while the whole country stopped, for the briefest second, to recognize their accomplishments.

Now they are obstacles in the line on the way to the franks and the instant mashed potatoes.

The old men are there and so are the maimed young ones. It's not only in the cafeteria that you see racing's failures. Up and down the walkway at the back of the tower-terrace grandstands they hobble. One-legged, noseless, horrible burn scars on their short-sleeved arms; racing's cost is high, and these are the ones who have paid the bills.

On the sidewalks of their home towns, people turn their faces away in horror from these men, or stare at them in fascination. Here, at the shrine of racing, they are not only accepted, they are heroic commonplace. For one month a year, these men live as normal humans, even as distinguished ones. No wonder they come back.

From Sixteenth Street, the track looks unremarkable, it just seems to happen. It does not rise suddenly from the countryside like Ontario Motor Speedway. It hasn't even the grace to shine in ancient white contrast to its surroundings, as Yankee Stadium does. It's simply a continuation of the dreadful blight that runs along the road, a huge photography studio perhaps. Maybe somebody's idea of a monumental auto-club headquarters.

But, inside, it is stunning.

The track is two and a half miles around. Two and a half miles! So enormous that from the grandstands on either straight, you can almost not make out the color of the cars on the opposite straightaway. So enormous that the space inside the oval seems to stretch the size of a small nation. The nine-hole golf course is tucked away near the back straight with ease. There are picnicking areas and rest areas and parking lots and roads. There are roads that would serve a city; as well they should, since perhaps a third of the 300,000 crowd parks its cars inside the track on race day. And in the center of the infield, perched cozily at the back of the front straight, are the pits, the tower-terrace stands, and Gasoline Alley.

From the pits, you cannot really make anyone out in the endless, great grandstands that circle half the track and hold almost 200,000 people. That is just as well, because it also means they cannot see you.

Gasoline Alley is enclosed by a fence perhaps a couple of city blocks square, and it is as squalid as anything in Appalachia. The garages burned down some years back, and they must have been rebuilt by an antiquarian. But that is not the point.

The point is that it is an island. All around it, outside the fence, on race day the crowd seethes. Each year, Tony Hulman returns the fondness his neighbors have for him by inviting them all inside the Speedway for his big party. Capris and beehives, Levi's and beer bellies, bawling babies and shrieking teen-agers—sullen, cheering, weeping, drunken, shouting, vomiting, pushing, trampling; the whole state of Indiana seems to pack the four sides of the garages, dangerously buckling the fences and posing an almost insurmountable human wall to the drivers, who have to make their way from the garages, through the walkway, and to the protection of the racing-pit fences, where they are safe again.

And their cars have to be pushed through the mobs as well. So the tactic the crews have taken is to hook up the cars to the Wheel Horse tractors provided by the Speedway, jump in the tractor seats, and shove the throttle ahead. The tractor-race car parade lurches forward, and it will not stop for anything.

The old-men guards blow their whistles frantically, grab arms, push against shoulders; haul and shove. Every year there are Hoosiers who bear proud scars from the Speedway they earned by nothing more than being in the way.

Danny Folsom knows those sights, but he rarely sees them any more. He is too drunk by the headiness of being inside it all.

Bud Stanner is drunk at Indianapolis too. But his trip is of a very different sort.

Stanner comes down from his windy office at One Erieview Plaza, in Cleveland, to scatter his own stardust on Gasoline Alley. You would think that, as a modern American marketeer, he would be very much in the background, hustling deals for Jackie Stewart, huddling with ITT on behalf of Peter Revson, haggling over a multimillion-dollar endorsement for Bobby Allison. And, in a way, that is almost what he does. But something has happened to Stanner during the years he's spent lurking in the background and watching the coronas around his clients. He has become almost envious. He is no less beautiful than Allison, rounder maybe and older, but his Prince Valiant haircut is every bit as chic. Stewart has a lovely Scots burr that Stanner can't match with his own Midwest-flattened vowels, but Stanner's turns of phrase are as nicely formed and the words themselves come tumbling out like a flood, more than making up in volume what they lack in musicality. And if Stanner is not so measured in his judgments as Revson, not nearly so tolerant, so stylish, or so mannerly, what difference should that make? Isn't wicked sarcasm, piquant gossip, and abrupt scatology just as good? Of course it is, and Stanner knows it.

With Stanner you can catch up on this morning's happenings in the world of scandal, framed in this week's trendy words. Stanner cocks his hairsprayed head to the side and spits out more dirt than a road grader. He knows when to flatter and when to shock. He can't help but be amusing. To Stanner, a client has two reasons for being: He must be exploitable of course, but he is there to provide Stanner with delicious secrets to be doled out over the french toast. It all makes Stanner feel very important. It also makes him a delightful breakfast partner.

So think of Indianapolis as having perhaps twenty top drivers, each with a Danny Folsom, each with a Bud Stanner, each with a Teddy Mayer, each with a Tyler Alexander. It is a rich, deep river that swirls around the garages at the Speedway, marked with currents and countercurrents, whirlpools and rapids.

The drivers are there to work.

Here are two days' schedule for Revson picked at random during May 1973.

On a day close to qualifying, Revson awakens at seven-thirty, breakfasts at Howard Johnson's (grapefruit, toast, soft-boiled eggs), and is at the track by nine. The car still had not been made to work, which will mean all day sorting it again. Revson has borrowed a Mercury Marquis Brougham from the Cincinnati zone office of Lincoln-Mercury, which he drives to the track and parks behind his motor home in the large parking area behind the garages. It is cool and windy, but the sun is out for the first time in a week. In the infield stands, the bottom rows and the top rows are filling with school children (admitted free) and some groups of visiting businessmen.

Revson walks toward his garage, where Alec Greaves and Huey are refitting body panels that had been taken off the car the previous afternoon so the crew could work on the suspension.

Somebody recognizes Revson on his way into Gasoline Alley, despite his being dressed in a blue sports shirt, blue sweater, jeans, and Gucci loafers, and asks for an autograph. Expressionless, he signs a notebook, then turns and smiles as he hands it back. Danny Folsom waits at the garage entrance, and taking Revson by the arm, leads him around to the alley between the second row of garages, where a television crew is working. Gathered around the crew is a crowd of drivers, mechanics, and officials. Jim McKay is there with Chris Economaki, and they are asking Jackie Stewart about the United States Auto Club's morning announcement of its withdrawal from international racing. They all play-act the scene as spotlights focus on Stewart and Economaki and the TV crew hold up bright reflectors on either side. Revson pauses on the outside of the circle until McKay motions him inside, where he poses self-consciously. Just then, just as the cameras turn on him and Economaki starts to ask him a question, Johnny Parsons, Jr., a young driver, sneaks underneath the crowd and gooses him. Revson doesn't drop a syllable.

Back at the garage, driver Salt Walther has just walked by. Walther, who had bought a last year's McLaren from Roger Penske, had gone 192 mph in it the day before, far faster than Revson has been able to go thus far in the *new* car. Noticing that Teddy Mayer has seen Walther, Revson yells across the garage to Mayer, "Hey, Teddy, did you at least find out what *his* setup was?" That breaks up John Rutherford, who has been watching the whole thing with amusement in the next stall. Teddy grins and tells Revson that maybe he'll buy last year's car back.

As the Wheel Horse tractor tows Revson's car out to the track, the yellow light on the infield pylon blinks on, indicating some sort of trouble. "Somebody threw a beer bottle on the track," explains an official hurrying by. "That's just lovely," says Rutherford, who is walking alongside the car. "I can't for the life of me understand why someone would do a thing like that. Lovely, just Lovely."

A journalist known for his blunt, rude, direct questions confronts Revson at the pit gate, notebook in hand. The car goes on without its driver as Revson pauses to talk. Five minutes later, he rejoins his crew and his car. "He never ceases to ask me stupid questions," Revson marvels to no one in particular.

The sorting session begins with very slow laps. Revson, who has changed into his Gulf McLaren uniform in his garage, is recognizable in the bright-orange car only by his helmet, which has pastel-colored lollipop shapes painted along its sides in a kind of rain-swept torrent of candy drops.

It takes forty-five seconds to circle Indianapolis if you're averaging 200 mph. The four cars that are out keeping Revson company are all in the low fifties.

Since it's only a few days before qualifying and the sun is out for the first time in a long while, the crowd grows. By now it's as large as a good turnout at almost any other track in the country. But here the people seem lost in the sweep of the stands and the immensity of the infield.

Revson is out on the track for four laps, into the pits for ten minutes. Back out and back in. Twice the car is taken back to the garage. By now Rutherford is out in his car too. Just before the car is towed back out to the racing pits for the last time, Revson walks by swinging his helmet and saying out of the side of his mouth, "Remember, a hawk has very stiff lips." Revson's lips are pretty stiff by now, too.

The testing goes on through the afternoon, with Revson pausing only for a short while to go to his motor home for some tea and a sandwich made of cold cuts and whole-wheat bread that Danny Folsom has put in the refrigerator the day before.

With the wind dying down in the late afternoon, most of the cars that can make it are out testing.

5:02 P.M.: Revson goes out on the track again. Suddenly, behind the pit fence that separates the stands from the racing area, a man appears in full flight, his hands holding his trousers, which are split wide down the back. He has no underwear on. His nose is bloody. There seems to be no cause, and no explanation is ever forthcoming.

5:03: The track is on yellow and the pace car goes out. Neil Leifer, the photographer for *Sports Illustrated*, pops up in the pits like a leaping trout. He makes a perfect ball, red hair, orange shirt, green jacket; one hand is stuffing an apple in his pocket, the other is holding his camera. Then he begins to focus his camera, and he shoots everything he sees.

5:05: Revson is in. As he stops, the crew folds in around the car protectively. Tyler has a foot up on one wheel, the Goodyear tire technicians are probing the tire treads with short, sharpish instruments with gauges on top of them. Teddy is crouched next to the cockpit, facing the rear of the car. Revson takes off his gloves and crosses his forearms over the top of the steering wheel.

5:07: The track is open for practice again. Nobody knows why it was closed; nobody seems to care. Revson is the first of the drivers who pitted to go back out. Foyt is next. Two laps later, Foyt turns a 192.184.

5:11: Revson comes back in. Rutherford is sitting in his car, which is parked against the wall behind Revson. He is wearing his helmet backwards and talking to John Cooper, who used to run Ontario Motor Speedway. "I'm going to wear it this way in the race," he tells Cooper. Cooper turns to a bystander and says, "There's been something wrong with these cars since February, when they arrived. John put the first one into the wall and, right afterwards, Mark had Roger get him an Eagle."

5:13: Revson goes back out; Tyler joins Teddy, who is sitting on the inside pit wall.

5:16: The yellow comes on, the ambulance is dispatched. Ambulances and fire trucks only roll at the Speedway when someone has hit the wall or when there is a fire. As a result, when the crews see them roll out down the track, there is an involuntary clenching of fists, an almost inaudible grunt.

5:17+: Graham McRae's car appears and rolls into the pit lane; so does Foyt's, then Andretti's. Rutherford's car has been sitting in the pits, but John has been back in the garages. Now he strolls out into the racing pits. Teddy turns to him and tells him to get in his car and warm it up slowly out on the track while the yellow is on. Teddy has no idea who hit the wall or who is on fire. Revson hasn't come into sight. For all anyone knows, Revson could be out there in a burning car.

5:18+: Revson comes in. It's Sam Posey who has spun and hit the wall; Posey is not hurt. While the track crews clear the wreckage, the drivers walk up and down the pits visiting. As they see their favorites, the crowds in the stands behind the pits shout to them, "Give 'em Hell, A.J.!" and "Give 'em Hell, Roger," and "Give 'em Hell, Mario." Indianapolis crowds are not inventive.

5:33: The track is on green.

5:36: Rutherford goes out.

5:38: Revson goes out, with Lloyd Ruby and Al Unser right behind him. A lap later, Unser turns a 191.

5:39: The track is on yellow.

5:42: The track is back on green.

5:46: Revson comes in and sends someone for his sunglasses, although the sun is well down on the horizon. Obviously he isn't going to use them in his car; he has a tinted visor for that. It's just that Revson likes to anticipate, and there's that walk back through the still-large crowd to the garage. Revson's sunglasses are particularly stylish. They are made in France and have his endorsement, for which he is paid handsomely. But he isn't sure he wants to continue with the sunglasses program. The manufacturer seems to have been careless lately about workmanship, and Revson genuinely does not want his name on anything that is not first-rate.

5:48: Revson is back out.

5:51: The track is on yellow.

5:54: The track is on green.

5:59: With one minute to go before the track closes for the day, Revson comes in, takes off his gloves and helmet, and sits in his car on the line for ten minutes. Tyler walks over, and slowly, very slowly, Revson raises his head and speaks to him. Tyler's expression is sad and his answer floats clearly over the pit wall. "Please don't ask me those kinds of questions, because there's no answer for them." Then Tyler turns to the crew and yells to them, "Let's get this shitbox out of here."

By now it's clear Revson is going to have to drive around the problem or not drive at all.

Revson has practiced, hit the wall, qualified, flown to Belgium to race against Stewart and Hulme, Cevert and Peterson and Fittipaldi in the Belgian Grand Prix, flown back to Indianapolis, and now awaits the day of the race.

This morning he slept late and went to breakfast at the house of a man he had met several years before and with whom he plays tennis when he is here. There would be time for only two sets, because at 11 A.M. he is due first at Hook's and then at Haag's drugstores to promote RevUp.

Revson, who always argues heatedly that he does indeed have a deeply ingrained sense of time, is late. The man from Commerce Drug, which makes RevUps, has come down from Chicago and is nervously pacing the Kleenex aisle at Hook's. There are signs on the window announcing Revson's exclusive appearance and the introduction of RevUp, The Vitamin for Men. The crowd waiting is small and is made up of housewives and their teen-aged daughters.

The Commerce man looks as though he would be vastly more comfortable in the frantic traffic of Seventh Avenue, New York's garment district, but he is gamely swallowing his impatience while reciting a litany that seems to soothe him. "Besides RevUp, we make a lot of things, a lot of well-known household names," he says. "For instance Commerce also makes Ora Gel, which is in the toothache field." His voice drones on and he seems unaware that every time he flourishes a Commerce household name, it is a signal to him to look at his watch.

. . . Tan-Ac, cold sores, mouth sores, and fever blisters (by now Revson is ten minutes late, according to the Commerce man's watch);

. . . B.BD.B, a wart remover (twelve minutes);

. . . Oro Ear Drops;

. . . Boil Ease, for boils;

. . . Stye, an ophthalmic ointment (fifteen minutes);

. . . Trip Tone, for motion sickness;

. . . Staze, a denture adhesive;

. . . *Baby* Ora Gel, a teething lotion;

. . . Viganic, "Natural Vitamins";

. . . Detain, "which is advertised in *Penthouse* and *Gallery*, for reasons I don't have to tell you . . . and (his voice rises in triumph, Revson is almost twenty minutes late but he has finally walked in the door);

"RECOVER! A COVER-UP LEG CREAM FOR VARICOSE VEINS AND FACIAL SCARS, PETER, HOWAREYA?"

The Commerce man is joined by the store manager, who walks over beaming and offers chairs, Cokes, anything, anything at all. Would this table be handy for the stack of 8x10 glossies of Revson with his CanAm medals around his neck? Perfect. The people start to line up, and the Commerce man and the manager slip into the background, like parents at an eighth-grade harpsichord recital.

I have seen these women in the late afternoon on my television set: They are the audience of the Mike Douglas Show. I have heard them say about Merv Griffin off camera what they are now saying about Revson: "Gee, you're *too* handsome" and "This one's not for *me*, it's for my son, who's just *furious* he couldn't be here himself," and "I promised I'd get your autograph for the girl I work with," and, "Sign it 'for Connie with love.'"

By now it's lunch period at the local high school, and Hook's begins to swarm with teen-aged girls. One of them, the one with *Sara* written on her blouse collar, asks Revson to sign her photo "To David," and he tells her he'll be glad to write David's name, but in return she has to promise to give it to David and not sell it to him.

A fat girl wants an autographed photo and she proffers her notebook as a writing desk. The notebook has Al Unser's name written on it.

An old man, looking very out of place, wanders up and asks if he can get Mel Kenyon's autograph. The fat girl comes back to tell Revson to take it easy; "I'll be watching you in the third turn," she says. A middle-aged lady with a beehive hairdo walks by haughtily. She is wearing a Leader Card Racer's team jacket. The man from Commerce has an idea. "Let's have some Cokes," he says to the store manager. "I'll tell you what: I'll give you a damaged-goods report and that'll pay for them."

Not only the teen-agers, but the adults as well are wearing sweat shirts and jackets proclaiming their prejudices and their loyalties. HONDA, says one. GREAT SMOKEY MOUNTAINS is written on another. And INDIANA, NATIONAL RIFLE ASSOCIATION, CANDY SPECIALIST, MARY O, FUN LOVERS CLUB, and BEEP, BEEP YOUR ASS, say some others.

A young housewife introduces herself as a former "Miss Grapefruit" and it's time to move on to Haag's across town.

At Haag's the crowd is bigger, the signs gaudier. HERE IN PERSON, PETER REVSON, says one; PETER REVSON, SPOKESMAN FOR REVUP, and, to Revson's total embarrassment, PETER REVSON, ADMIRED BY MEN, ADORED BY WOMEN, ONE OF TODAY'S OUTSTANDING PERSONALITIES. In an obvious reference to Stanner, Revson looks at the sign and at the women and says quietly and with sarcasm, "A Budley Stud Horse Production."

Here the women are in curlers, the young girls in braces; it's a far more fashion-conscious neighborhood. The store is newer and larger. A man walks up and introduces himself as the director of a private security firm; Revson seems puzzled, as though he expects a pitch for mutual funds. But there are guards all around. A local disc jockey is doing a live broadcast, interspersed with RevUp commercials, and pitching Haag's RevUp contest. The store is giving away Peter Revson sunglasses, Peter Revson racing jackets, Peter Revson driving suits, Peter Revson racing patches . . . "nothing to do, nothing to buy."

There are lots of people, but the bottles of RevUp in the pyramid display are not moving well at all.

Danny Folsom arrives wearing his McLaren team jacket with news of his preparation for Charles Revson's arrival. Folsom tells Revson that when his uncle's private jet arrives at the Indianapolis airport, a driver in a limousine will be waiting. "Jim will be driving," says Danny; "Jim said he'd be properly dressed." Jim is the young college boy who delivers Folsom's dead chickens to the Colonel Sanders' stores in Indianapolis. "He told me he's going to change," says Danny about his early-morning conversation with Jim as the driver was about to start on his deliveries. "He said he'd change. And

I said, 'What'd you think, that Peter expects you'll be delivering chickens in a tuxedo?'"

The store P.A. system comes on to ask someone named Debby where the Pretty Feet is, and the disc jockey looks up furious from his live microphone. "All Peter has to learn to do now," says Danny, leaning back in a green-and-white deck chair in the patio-furniture display and looking at Revson surrounded by schoolgirls, "is to sing and play the guitar." He says it with great pride in his voice.

At the end of the two-hour session, a young girl who has been waiting patiently approaches Revson, identifying herself as being from the Middlebury, Ohio, newspaper and asking for just ten minutes. Revson sighs and takes her over to the patio-furniture display. She flips open her notebook, opens her eyes wide, takes a deep breath, and asks Revson, "How do you feel about the ever-present danger?"

Revson's head drops to his chest in despair, and very much under his breath so the girl can't hear him he murmurs, "Fuck me."

When Marji Wallace heard the disc jockey at Haag's on her car radio and, noticing she was almost in the same block as the drugstore, decided to stop and wander inside, she was an unknown and frequently unnoticed nineteen-year-old model living in Indianapolis. At that very moment, there were probably fifty thousand girls much like her scattered from Des Moines to Memphis; fresh young good looks had given them all the same amorphous ambitions, prompted the same fantasies.

Within six months, Marji Wallace's fantasies would have become the realities of her everyday life. Nor, really, was Marji Wallace in any way like any other nineteen-year-old in Des Moines, Memphis, or any other town in any other country in the world. She was entirely her own woman: independent and self-confident. Nor were her ambitions amorphous. In fact, they prodded her days with outlines as sharp as a square-cut diamond.

Peter Revson, leaving Haag's with Danny Folsom at his side, could scarcely be expected to understand that the graceful blonde swinging across the parking lot was any more important to him than any of the housewives to whom he had given a moment of grave courtesy or smiling attention during the day. In fact, it is unlikely that he noticed Marji Wallace at all. Perhaps he saw her, and it registered that she was an uncommonly good-looking young woman. But there are a lot of uncommonly good-looking young women in Revson's life, and if he notices any one in particular, it is in much the same way as a vacationing ornithologist notices a felicitously formed pigeon in Central Park, or a bus driver on a holiday unconsciously remarks to himself on a shiny Mercedes 0-309D shuttling around an airport.

In fact, it was Danny Folsom, with the longing eyes of middle age, who saw her first, and it was Danny Folsom who waited until she was almost by Revson's side and then took her by the arm, and with an understanding smile, told her she would be coming along with them both for a late lunch.

Of course, that is exactly what Marji had in mind when she stopped her car, but she hardly expected to accomplish it without having spoken a word.

Claudette Colbert would have known exactly how to cope with George Brent, but when Revson was obviously annoyed by the sudden materialization of an unexpected luncheon guest, Marji Wallace, for all her poise and self-assurance, was intimidated. She had not yet said a word, and for the next half hour she would utter only a half dozen. She said "Yes" and "No" several times, told Revson and Folsom her name, and in the restaurant said, "Herring," to the waiter. A moment later she remembered her manners and added, ". . . please."

Considered or not, here are some of Marji Wallace's thoughts after having spent four days with Revson prior to the race. She had been taken to a crew party given by McLaren's patron, Boyd Jefferies, probably fairly impressive to a nineteen-year-old from Indianapolis. She had also gone to the pole mechanics' dinner, an enormous affair at which she had stood by Revson as almost everyone in the place came up to genuflect, and Revson had introduced her on every occasion. He had deferred to her wishes about where to sit, how long to spend at what was actually a professional obligation for him, escorted her gallantly to a frozen-custard stand on the way home. Marji's first encounter with Revson was over a sandwich; food would continue to punctuate their relationship. Anyway, here are some of Marji's reflections:

. . . A man's looks attract me. And his attitude toward women in general. Women are just as good as men; they should be treated on the same level. All men don't do that, but Peter does. When men joke and kid around about women, women seem to feel they should keep quiet. I don't like to do that. I was quiet at first, but that was natural.

. . . I want to know in advance what kind of relationship a man's interested in. It makes a difference, because I like different sorts of relationships with men: platonic, sexual, long-lasting. I wouldn't particularly want it put to me bluntly, but if a man and a woman are communicating, they should be able to know what each other wants. That kind of communication was easy with Peter because he's sensitive.

. . . I may be complicated, I don't know. I can be devious and calculating. So far as meeting Peter was concerned I don't know if I was devious, but I was calculating. I was driving down the street and I had the radio on. I heard Peter's voice. I thought to myself, "I'd like to meet him." I'd seen pictures of him and I knew he was a bachelor, that means a potential. At least I could meet him and I wouldn't feel guilty about it. It wasn't a matter of having sexual fantasies about him though. I was hoping that he would like to meet me too.

. . . Well, I got out of my car and I saw a couple of men standing near the drugstore and then I saw Peter and I thought, "Oh, God, this is going to be good." So when Danny took me by the arm and I didn't have to go myself, he helped me out. I didn't have to be too bold. I can be aggressive if I need be, but in this case I was a little inhibited. I figured, maybe I shouldn't even be here, this is stupid. I was nervous and I was excited. I expected that after we ate I'd just go back to my car and it would have been interesting and fun and nothing more.

. . . At dinner that evening, and I was surprised at the invitation, he made me feel completely at ease. He was fun. I don't know whether he considered me just an ornament, but I don't think he did. It's hard to say, but he seemed to be really interested in *me* and what I had to say. Were we both collecting each other? That's probably as good a way of putting it as anything else.*

... By the second evening I wasn't thinking of him as Peter Revson any longer. He was Peter, a new person. He was very nice and polite and very good-looking. Everywhere we went, the photographer from *Sports Illustrated* followed us. I'd never known anybody who had so famous a name, who was so well recognized. I noticed that he didn't think about his name; he didn't seem to be affected by it. He didn't act like an extremely well-known person. If you just walked up and met him and didn't know who he was, he wouldn't tell you. The last thing he'd do is to make it obvious. I thought to myself, he's really a genuine person. And I was amazed by that. I really had thought he'd be above it all, but he can deal with people on any level necessary.

... I think, now that I know him, the things most women see aren't the things he really is. They see that combination

---

* It was this admission, freely given, along with Marji's long blond hair, that immediately earned her the name: "The Golden Retriever." Nicknames are common in racing, but they are closely guarded secrets. John Wyer, the English team manager, is known for his intense stares of disapproval, hence "Death Ray." Jim Travers, of the engine-building firm Travers & Coon (Traco) is not even tempered. He is called "Crabby." Roger Penske is "The Captain." Tony Hernandez is a cheerful, high living racing P.R. man called "The Puerto Rican Rum Runner." Stu Hillborn, who lives in Laguna Beach, California, makes injectors, which determine the richness of the fuel mixture in racing engines. Hillborn is "Laguna Leanout." Danny Folsom, of course, is "The Chicken Plucker," but Fred Bartlett, his best Colonel Sanders' customer, who also times and scores for Team McLaren, is "Chicken Freddie." The Gulf liaison with McLaren in 1973 was Chick Creazzi. It was all very confusing. The Goodyear engine man, Herb Porter, is "Herbie Horsepower"; George Lysle is, reasonably, "Big Time"; and Jody Scheckter, who crashed a lot in 1973, is named "Fletch," after Fletcher, the novice bird in *Jonathan Livingston Seagull* who was forever easing himself into a cliff. Edwin Ingalls, the photographer who was knocked off the platform by the pace car in 1971, is "The Buffalo Hunter," because he spent the month of May trying to find a bearded man nicknamed "Buffalo." Revson himself eventually came to be known, for simple enough reasons, as "Redondo RevUp." L.M.

of things: looks, name, money. That combination means a lot to most women and they just automatically think they're in love. That's my ideal man, they think. Now they wouldn't be disappointed in Peter. He's a good person; in fact, I'm amazed that he's as good a person as he is.

. . . It doesn't make a bit of difference to me that I might be one of fifty women in Peter's life right now. He doesn't owe me anything. All I want is that whatever happens between us be mutual. I want it just to come the way it'll come. I don't expect anything, I'm not looking for anything. . . . I have a friend named Helen, and I told her about meeting Peter, the way we met and what happened. I said to her, "I'm going out with him and I just can't believe it." Her answer was "*I* believe it. You deserve it."

When Marji Wallace became Miss World, in London last November, the first American to win the title, there were people who claimed to have predicted she would be the first woman in history to become a greater box-office draw than John Wayne. Maybe even than Richard Barthelmess. She became a property of Mecca Productions, moved to London, and was earning twenty-five hundred dollars for a weekend's appearance. She wasn't absolutely sure she should have signed the Mecca contract, because it meant she might not be able to travel with Peter on the Continent when the Grand Prix season started again. But Revson convinced her the time had come for her to be selfish. She flew to Chub Cay to spend Christmas with Revson, and when a fading English soccer star named George Best allegedly broke into her apartment and found himself on the front page of every paper in London as a result, she fled to Florida to spend a week with Peter in Fort Lauderdale.

But all that was six months away, and in the meanwhile, if Marji Wallace had not been with Revson during the three terrible rainy days in which they tried to run the 1973 race at Indianapolis, it would have been an even more hideously difficult interlude for Revson than it was.

It may even have been sprinkling on the back straight when they started the 500. It was certainly threatening to. Championship cars are not meant to run on a wet surface. It is suicide to try it. The great, wide, 15-inch-section tires have no tread. The slightest film of moisture will lift them up and they will aquaplane. If you imagine a 1000-hp car that weighs half as much as a Chevrolet Vega, its driver encased in bags of fuel because it is only around the cockpit that some of the fuel can be distributed evenly; if you imagine such a fierce, hostile environment for a human and then try to think of not one but thirty-three of those lethal, vicious projectiles flagged off with rain threatening, almost without traction, without enough bite for the front wheels to be able to steer, three rows of eleven cars, each within five feet of the other, at 100 mph plus, you begin to get an idea of the homicidal stupidity of the old men who tried to start the 1973 Indianapolis 500 in the face of the weather.

With about $1 million at stake, the results were predictable. In the blue-gray darkness of the sky, there was a bright puff of flame; a moment's horrible confusion of tangled cars and wheels flying high in the air; the ugly *whomp* of car hitting car, a rolling scream from the crowds in the stands along the straight and through it all the calm voice of The Greatest Spectacle in Racing telling his radio audience of 100 million that there seemed to be some confusion down there, several cars were involved, but he was sure everything would be all right.

Everything would not be all right. Somebody deep in the pack of cars had shoved his way through the field when the green flag fell, hitting somebody else, who hit somebody else, who hit Salt Walther in the car that Teddy had joked about buying back. The impact sent Walther high in the air and into the cyclone fence that separates the spectators in the rows at trackside from the cars. Burning fuel sloshed in a stream across the seats and on the spectators, some of whom were eating lunch. Walther's car took out two hefty steel fence supports and bent the fence far back.

Walther was not dead, but he was terribly burned, and he spent two months in the burn units at Indianapolis and Ann Arbor hospitals before the doctors concluded he would live.

No other driver was hurt, but they took twelve spectators to the hospital, at least two with burns on their eyeballs. One of those was George Lysle's sister. Nine cars were damaged.

Revson spent the rest of the day in the back of the motor home with Marji and Danny Folsom's family.

The next morning, the track called a closely guarded drivers' meeting and penalized or warned four competitors for driving infractions. Revson was one of them, but no one accused him of having anything to do with the accident. The meeting was bitter, with one driver the object of the thinly veiled hostility of the others. He reacted as he always does, and threatened to take on anybody or everybody who thought he was at fault. Since drivers are no better at keeping secrets than secretaries, the incident was soon familiar in every detail to racing insiders. A man from one of the Indianapolis dailies not only heard the story from a number of drivers, he was shown a stop-action sequence of the crash.

His paper reported baldly that there had been a drivers' meeting and that four drivers had been disciplined.

That afternoon, after postponing the second start for hours, track officials started the race again. This time there was no question in anyone's mind at all that it was raining. Two laps later they stopped it.

By now the infield was a quagmire. "The Indy infield is like the inside of a pig's stomach," say the race's detractors. In normal years that may be hyperbole; in 1973 it was understatement. For two days, several hundred thousand people had tramped, trompled, drunk, evacuated, slept, and generally behaved in a very human and therefore very dirty fashion in that infield; and the infield showed it. The portajohns were overflowing. The streams of water were running everywhere, and they carried unimaginable filth. Cars were parked hub deep in mud; some seemed as though they couldn't ever be gotten out. Food had run out in the concession stands.

Given all this, it was understandable, in a way, that the men who make such decisions felt the pressure and started the race on the second day in the rain. Understandable in their aging minds perhaps, but not to the young drivers.

Certainly, by the third day, the officials were right to be desperate.

The weather was still cold and it still threatened rain, but that was not the reason for the great patches of empty seats, like lichen on a rain-splotched cliff, in the grandstands. The enormous wave of people that had flooded into Indianapolis had washed through the town for three days now. It could not sustain its level. Most people had to go home to the little Indiana and Ohio and Illinois and Kentucky towns from which they made their annual trip to the Speedway.

The track was operating with a dangerously small crew too, and even some of the ones who were able to stay and work the race another day were growing jittery.

When the race started for the third time, the tension had reached an ominous level. Revson didn't stay on the track long enough to suffer the consequences.

Whether he was still trying to drive around the problem, whether he simply made a mistake in the wrong place at the wrong time, whether the track was still far slippier than it should have been, he still does not know. It's likely it was a combination of all three. In any case, he was in traffic and doing well when he felt the car go out from under him, and then he spun and hit the wall in seconds.

There were not very many people around the Gasoline Alley fence when he came walking in, and those who were there were either on their way to the toilets or craning to glimpse if the cars were on the back straight. There were fewer people inside the fence, around the garages themselves. Even so, Revson shut the door of his garage behind him. He got out of his drivers' suit with resignation, clearly unhappy with himself, and then walked over to turn on the radio to the station that was carrying the race. Marji Wallace sat by herself in the corner, crying.

The door opened; Neil Leifer walked in and immediately began shooting pictures of Revson and of Marji sobbing in the corner.

Suddenly there was an unearthly wail, then screams. And then there came a babble of excitement from the radio. Revson rushed outside to see a billow of smoke rising from the top of the front straightaway. He waited only long enough to be sure it was smoke from an alcohol fire, watched it turn white as the fire crews turned their equipment on the flames, dropped his head, and walked wearily back into the garage to slump up against the far-end benches near the radio. He held up his hand as Leifer began to ask questions, until he heard his teammate's name mentioned as not having been involved, and then began slowly, dispiritedly packing his helmet bag.

Only half an hour later did he learn that the wail he had heard came from a section of the stands immediately in front of the spot where Patrick Racing crew member Armando Teran was run over and killed by a fire truck racing the wrong way down the pits.

It was Swede Savage who was killed by the fire, but not immediately. He lingered in Methodist Hospital burn unit, from which Salt Walther was transferred to Michigan, for more than a month before he died.

In January, two months after Marji Wallace's coronation as Miss World, Walther lowered himself painfully into an Indianapolis car at Ontario Motor Speedway, clenched his teeth in agony as he tried to grip the steering wheel with his desperately tender hands, went out on the track, and turned 180 mph to prove to himself he was still alive.

PART FOUR

Revson · Four

I had won my first grand prix. I was earning better than $300,000 a year, and there I was looking at the unemployment line.

It's probably natural that I'm partial to Pete Lyons' race reporting. Pete is a very fine journalist who goes to all the grands prix, the only American who does so. His reports appear in *Autosport* in England and in *Autoweek* in the United States. I kid Leon, who is the publisher of *Autoweek*, about its generally friendly attitude toward me and it never fails to get a rise out of him. He thinks he's impartial, and although *Autoweek* takes some pretty strong stands, it upsets Leon to think his publication's position might be influenced by the fact that he and I are writing this book.

Since Monaco was not one of my greater triumphs, maybe I'd better use a couple of paragraphs from Pete Lyons' story to describe what happened.

"Monaco is more than a race," Pete wrote. "It's a game. You don't just go, you *appear*. The streets are packed with the most calculatedly exotic automobiles; you'll probably see your first Lamborghini Countach there by the Casino. In the harbor, the trick is to have a finer boat than anyone else. The sponsors, many of them, hire yachts to act as refined hospitality centers.

"The streets of the city are an insane place to stage a modern motor race, but to give it up would be unthinkable. It's too pleasant to be there.

"Jackie Stewart won. He drove around on his cooloff lap . . . came slowly up again by the pits and parked [his] Tyrrell in front of the Royal couple. It was his third audience before [Prince Rainier and Princess Grace], and his 25th time to wear the wreath of a Grand Prix victory—one more time than [Juan Manuel] Fangio and as many as his friend Jim Clark. He'd done it in the most car-killing race on the calendar, on the circuit he enjoys above all others."

In particular, the things Pete says about enjoying Monaco are absolutely true, although this year was not the best one for me. I had arrived late from Indianapolis and only gotten in one day of practice, so I started sixteenth on the grid. After a number of failures in cars on the track, and I hope some determined driving on my part, I managed to finish fifth, which placed me fourth in the world driving championship, behind Emerson Fittipaldi, Jackie Stewart, and Jackie's teammate, François Cevert.

I have always considered Monte Carlo the most enjoyable race of the year if only because it is traditional and because the surroundings are so civilized. Nowhere else on the circuit do we find better accommodations, better food, or better wine. The women are probably better-looking in Monte Carlo as well.

But none of those things matter very much when you do not do as well as you could.

Although Sweden was the next race, it was the French Grand Prix I was concerned with, because it conflicted with a 500-miler at Pocono, Pennsylvania. Teddy wanted me to run Pocono because of his contract with Gulf. I told him that if I was going to race at Pocono, I would have to take out a United States Auto Club license. Besides, his major sponsor, who was also mine—Goodyear—would prefer that I run in France.

There were not enough engines to run three cars in France, according to Teddy, but I think the real reasons for his stand were that he had no replacement for me at Pocono and that he didn't want to have to make excuses to Gulf. I approached Teddy originally on this matter, confidentially and as a friend, telling him I would prefer to race the French Grand Prix if at all possible in order to make points for the championship. If I want to win I can't afford to miss even one race. With a strong finishing position in the championship, I'm in a good bargaining position for next year no matter what happens with Team McLaren. The handwriting on the wall as of now seems to be that Jody Scheckter is going to replace Denny or me for 1974 with McLaren's.

I approached Teddy as a friend because we'd been friends long before I ever drove for him and I hope we'll be friends long after I stop. I hoped he'd do something for me on this basis.

It was an awkward situation. I also had a contract with Alfa Romeo in sports cars, and the position there was that there was a race with them the week before Pocono. Originally that date was open, but in making our contract with Alfa, Bud Stanner and I simply forgot that that was the qualifying weekend for Pocono. So what Teddy was now claiming, was that the only reason I had for wanting to run in France was being able to meet my commitment in Europe the weekend before to Alfa. He knew that would be the first race for which Alfa would have both its cars available and in which I'd be able to drive, the first four races having been passed by Alfa because of trouble with car development and strikes.

Teddy said if I did that race for Alfa, I would be in violation of the McLaren contract, because originally that date was committed to him and he would hold me to it. I answered that it would be a pretty shitty thing to do on his part, especially since, although I would not be at Pocono for McLaren, I *would* be driving a McLaren in the French Grand Prix.

There were a lot of reasons for me to conclude that Teddy had not been completely square with me. It seemed to me he obviously was making things as convenient for himself as he could—at my expense.

So there was pressure on me because of Scheckter, and I knew that if I did race the French GP Teddy would probably tell me I was in violation of the contract and terminate it. He told me so. As I had predicted, Gulf was amenable to my racing in France instead of at Pocono; all they wanted was for the second car to be driven. But after looking around, it seemed there was no driver available who was acceptable to McLaren. So I was back where I started. Doing Pocono. The course is the most interesting of the 500-milers. There are three turns, and each one is different from the others, so in that sense it represents variety.

In every other way, it's The Mickey Mouse 500.

Begrudgingly, I airmail-special-deliveried my USAC license application, to be sure to get my license in time for the race.

With some time to go before Sweden, I went back to California. One of the reasons was my need to buy clothes. Somehow, in my two-month trip away from home, what seemed to be sufficient in the way of clothes had suddenly become totally insufficient. I never know what happens to clothes, but when I send them to laundries all over the world, their quantity somehow diminishes. A sock here, a pair of shorts there, a pullover some other place. When I get home, the suitcase that was so full when I left is suddenly about half empty.

I went to Van Cleef and Arpels in Beverly Hills to buy a piece of jewelry for a friend. I expected to spend maybe fifteen minutes in the store, but I was fascinated by their workrooms and by what they could do, and the time suddenly stretched to over an hour. But I thought it would be worth it to the lady.

On Tuesday I flew to New York and stayed with a friend. That night we went to hear Buddy Rich, who is one of my favorite musicians—a swinging evening. Next morning I left on a day flight to London on TWA.

In keeping with this day and age of inflation and currency devaluations, it seems to me the meals on the airplanes are getting slightly smaller. Somehow that annoys me and it keeps running through my mind.

In the three or four days I was at home, I got a sharp view of the gasoline situation. On Sunday I had to drive seventy miles, and I had to stop twice for gas because each gas station would give me only five gallons.

I arrived in London Wednesday night and went straight to Teddy Mayer's. The next morning we went to Luton airport, about an hour north of London, to take a BAC-111 charter to Sweden.

We landed in a town about forty miles from the race track, where we rented a Saab. Along with Gordon Coppuck, the car designer; chief mechanic Alestair; my chief, Davey; and Patty McLaren, we drove to the track, and believe me, the track was in the boondocks.

We found the track with no trouble, but finding the hotel was more difficult. We had to negotiate a series of unmarked turns, dirt roads, etc., until finally we arrived at an establishment called, believe it or not, the High Chaparral. It looked like an 1860s cavalry post. It had stake fences all around and was covered with wagon wheels, stirrups, saddles, old hatchets, and frontier gear of all kinds.

Once inside, the motif ran a little thin, and the rooms looked like the room in my dormitory when I was a freshman in college, only more Spartan. We had two bunks, one small dresser, a small desk, a sink in the corner, and a closet without any crossbars and with the hangers sitting on the floor.

They said the place was just completed in time for the Grand Prix and built especially for it because there weren't accommodations enough in the area. I believe it. The surrounding countryside was said to be a semipopular summertime resort, there was some camping by the lakes, but it was basically a farming district. We were out in the middle of nowhere.

The first night, we had a fairly amusing dinner at the High Chaparral, where the food wasn't too bad. The only alcoholic beverage, though, was beer. But that didn't particularly bother me because I was drinking Coke, which was not exactly Coke either but something local the Swedish called Cuban Cola.

The track seemed very tight and had a fairly lengthy straightaway. I doubted if we'd get into third gear on the rest of the course; there were a lot of 180s and very tight 90s. But, interestingly enough, many of the turns were banked, so they're faster than they looked. Practice was very early in the morning. There was only one, common bathroom at the end of the corridor at the hotel, and even though it had only one stall shower without a door—a phone-handle-type shower with a flexible tube—there was still sure to be a mad dash to shower . . . especially considering the hot-water situation, which was bad.

After the first practice, we had dinner *al fresco* in the compound; barbecued pig, potato salad, wine, and orange juice. Very authentic western surroundings. I suppose the party was a great success. In contemplating why this sort of thing doesn't happen more often on the circuit, I think one of the reasons is that Marlboro's presence looms too large. They seem to sponsor about five times more cars than anyone else, so they seem to take over the races. The people connected with Marlboro are quite nice and quite civil and very professional. But when you go to a party or a press conference during a race weekend, it always somehow seems to turn into a Marlboro function. That's probably to their credit, but since I am with Yardley, which is a part of British America Tobacco, the last thing I want to do is have it thought I might be a Marlboro driver.*

Practice went fairly well. I was the sixth-quickest. I hoped to have a more effective time on the track the next day—but that's not the way it turned out. Ronnie Peterson, in the Lotus, who was literally at home on the track, was quickest. He seemed to be making a habit of that. He wanted very much to win in Sweden, and I was sure he'd do everything he could to get out front and stay there. But, to win, his luck was going to have to change. He'd yet to establish himself as a finisher. Up until Sweden he hadn't done much at all beyond a third-place finish at Monte Carlo.

The next night, we changed gears and roll bars. I looked forward to improving from my 24.9 to perhaps a 24 flat. I felt I had a handle on the course. It was not particularly hard, so

---

* Was this prescience? Were there stirrings and forebodings at work in Revson's mind when he wrote this fairly snippish commentary on Marlboro's tendency to take over? After the last grand prix of 1973, Teddy Mayer announced his sponsorship by Marlboro for the coming season, and only after considerable anguish and much negotiation was Yardley included too. By then, of course, Revson was long gone from McLaren. L.M.

it became just a question of driving it particularly well and getting the car set up right. We would have another three hours the next day and we intended to take full advantage of them.

Even though I went to bed that night at about a quarter to eleven, I wound up waking at 3:15 A.M. I grabbed for my watch thinking it was at least 6 A.M. because it was light out and the birds were chirping. That always happens when I fly east from California or New York. Of course, I do lose time, but my body clock gets screwed up too, so by the second or the third night the time change really catches up with me.

The next day, we did a little experimenting: going back and forth trying different front tires. As a result, we never did get down to the previous day's time and I dropped from sixth to seventh on the grid for the race.

The weather had been good. Warm in the morning with an afternoon breeze. This place reminded me of Donnybrook, in Minnesota, or Kent, in Washington. It was very American, the atmosphere a bit clubby and very nice. That morning, I noticed how many tents there were. It promised a good crowd despite the track's being far away from a metropolis.

The next day, race day, we intended to make some more changes. The brakes seemed to get very spongy after about thirty or forty laps. So we were going to put in a new set of pads in the morning. We were going to even stiffer roll bars front and rear, and back to the first set of tires we started running earlier in the week. A lot to check out in half an hour. Either it was going to feel right or it was not.

Denny won the race and I was seventh after a very frustrating ride. I should have recognized in practice that, after four or five laps, the car's tendency to understeer got progressively worse. Race morning, in warm-ups, I was quite slow and went to a smaller front roll bar. After a few more laps, I thought I had something to stand pat on.

When the race started I was fairly competitive for two or three laps, but after that the car just went off progressively. The front end seemed to be floating. I seemed to get a tremendous amount of steering-wheel vibration. I didn't think it was imbalance in the front tires, and I was right. After the race we rebalanced the tires and found only an ounce and a half out in one wheel. I think the handling problem was due to bad shock absorbers, which I didn't recognize or identify during the practice sessions. I didn't get it sorted out and I was kicking myself.

My fastest lap in the race was a second and a half slower than Denny's. I was particularly off the pace in one big loop where I couldn't put the power on without the front end's just washing out. I was also slow in several other turns, where the front end would just search.

It was an unhappy race for me but a good day for the team. It put the team back on a winning track, since it represented the first grand prix win since last year in South Africa, a race that Denny also won. Things were looking up for the French Grand Prix, which came next. But not for me; I was off to Pocono instead.

I had a conversation with Don Nichols in Sweden. His Shadow team, which is sponsored lavishly by Universal Oil Products, had a bad race. Jackie Oliver broke a suspension part and spun. George Follmer lost a gear, though he finished the race. This is the first year for the Shadows. Don is an American; UOP is an American company. It's a good effort, and he should not be too disappointed, because it is asking almost too much to start out brand new in this league and hope to win. Next year he wants his team to be all American. He wants to hire me. I told him I wasn't in any position to make any decisions and probably wouldn't be until September.

On my way to Pocono I thought that, when I got back, I'd be able to stay in Europe for four or five weeks and perhaps establish some continuity.

For now, though, it was report to practice in Pennsylvania.

I've just pulled into the parking lot at Pocono and the place looks as unfinished as ever. The parking area is unpaved, there seem to be endless mounds of dirt dug up. After two years of building, this place is still under construction.

It was foggy here this morning, and now it's overcast. The track is still slightly damp and practice is supposed to start at noon. After we finish today, we'll only have Thursday and Friday, during which we'll practice, and then we'll qualify on Saturday and Sunday. The next Sunday is race day. A good setup. I don't have to go through the long-drawn-out process of Indianapolis, even though this race is billed as one of the Triple Crown 500s, along with Ontario and Indy. But here the prize money is only about a third as much as it is at Indy; so I suppose that means we can be spared spending a month in Pennsylvania. I'm grateful. It's been a long week.

The constructor's charter from Sweden connected to the 3:35 P.M. PanAm flight at Heathrow. I'm always suspicious of that flight because it's been canceled twice when I've been booked on it, for what I suspect is lack of passengers. PanAm is the only airline with a midafternoon flight, and it seems to me that unless they have a reasonable load, they'll cancel and combine with their Flight One, which leaves at six. Last night (having spent one night in New York) I came up to Stroudsburg and stayed at the Holiday Inn with the team.

It was a longish trip and it gave me some time to contemplate the results of Sweden. I was not happy, but the more I thought about it the more I realized I at least contributed something.

At around fifty laps, François Cevert, in the Tyrrell, was running fourth and Denny was fifth. Denny evidently couldn't get by François. They both came up on me and I got a signal from the pits that said "Plus Hulme," which meant that Denny was behind about to lap me. I saw what the problem was and it looked to me as though François was holding Denny up. Regardless, he was certainly impeding Denny's progress at that point anyway.

They were both about eight and a half seconds back from the leaders. As François came up on me, I put out an extra effort and made it quite difficult for him to get by. When we got to a spot where I was going slowly, it was easy to frustrate François, allowing Denny to catch up. In that way, Denny managed to get by François and then I let Denny by me while keeping François behind me for a couple of laps more. The point was that I did spring Denny loose from François, and he went on to win the race.

Coming back to the United States to race reminds me that we have no organization here to compare with the Grand Prix Drivers' Association. The GPDA performs some really important functions, and it seems to me that drivers who race here all the time would do well to think about some similar group.

For example, after Saturday's final practice for the Swedish Grand Prix, we had a meeting in which we graded the two preceding races: Monte Carlo and Belgium. The Belgian race scored low in most areas, including the condition of the track.

The GPDA meetings are like a United Nations General Assembly session. This time, three French drivers were sitting in one area and they were scoring in half points. We score in whole numbers on a 1–10 scale. But, for this race, the French, who have diplomatic skills the rest of us just weren't born with, came up with the idea of initiating the half-point score. It was something new and it provoked more than normal discussion on a number of points. Ronnie Peterson, who was in a pretty good frame of mind after getting the pole for his own grand prix, just shook his head and mumbled to himself, "Fucking frogs."

Jackie was his usual loquacious self, and much as I tend to agree with him, he does go on. While he was in full flight I got a little bored, and being caught up in Ronnie's mood, I slipped one of those nice Texaco wooden matches into his shoe and lit it. He was concentrating so hard on what he was talking about, he never did feel the flame against his foot.

Now that I think about it, that level of humor could be taken straight from the GPDA and used by the USAC and NASCAR drivers in this country.

Although I'm in Pocono, there's no rule that says I have to like being here. But I *am* here and I'm determined to give a good performance. In the first day's practice, the car was not what it should have been; but now that we have sorted it out somewhat, adding new shock absorbers and so on, it's gotten better, and I wound up third-fastest on the day. It turns out this is a different car from the one I drove at Indianapolis. This is the car John drove at Trenton. He touched the wall with it, so it has been rebuilt.

Mike Moseley was quickest, with a 185.5; Bobby Unser was second, with a 184.8; and I was third, with 184.4, but I was running a race boost, so we were certainly not extending ourselves.†

Now it's Monday after qualifying at Pocono. It was probably my best weekend in a long, long time. The car was going well from the first. During the rain on Thursday we didn't get in much practice, but on Friday I was second-fastest to Lloyd Ruby. So, going into qualifying on Saturday, I knew I had an excellent chance of being on the pole. Certainly of getting on the front row.

As qualifying unfolded, most of the big Firestone guns—Al Unser, Mario Andretti, etc.—got out first and they went surprisingly quick. It began to look like the Firestone cars as a group were quicker than the Goodyear cars. But the Firestone cars' qualifying laps were characterized by their progressively going slower, while mine kept getting faster. This may mean that their tires will go off in the race, but it's mere speculation at this point.

At any rate, when I went out, I went fast enough to get the pole. It was heartening to know that a lot of people weren't too surprised to see me do so well. Although it may not have been absolutely expected, it was no surprise either. If it hadn't been for my time, the front row would have been all Firestone; so I've struck a blow there too.

On Sunday we practiced to determine how powerful an engine setup we could run and still have enough fuel to complete the race, the amount of boost versus the total amount of

† Until 1974, the amount of turbocharging pressure used for qualifying was much higher than that used in the race itself. With a lot of boost, an engine won't live very long. But since a car has only to go four laps to qualify, it doesn't have to have long life. Thus, some teams were dialing in "three digits" (or 100-plus inches of manifold pressure) for their try to make good grid positions, but they backed way off for the race. This is at least one explanation why race speeds were significantly lower than qualifying speeds. L.M.

fuel allowed us being the critical equation. We discovered the McLarens did very well, and although we had only 340 gallons of fuel (thirty-five gallons less than last year) we were not pessimistic. We got 1.65, 1.62, and 1.65 miles to the gallon on the three different tests, and that's reportedly better than the Eagle—which I attribute to the better McLaren aerodynamics. Even at that, we were able to run enough boost to go 185.5 mph, which is as fast as anybody could run in practice.

Today, my friend and I tried to drive back from Pocono but we ran into a lot of resort traffic on the way to New York City. When we got there, we intended to hop a light plane to my father's house in Easthampton, on Long Island, but evidently Easthampton had a lot of fog, so we drove all the way.

We used to race at the Bridgehampton race track, not far from my father's house, but the track has been all but abandoned. I miss it. Not so much the track, but not being able to go, at least twice a year, and spend some time on the beach at Easthampton. This is a beautiful house. It's right on the beach, and the crashing of the waves on the shore is a tonic to me. It is very soothing. I enjoy the nights, the breeze, and the sound of the surf. It's just very restful. Now that there is no Bridgehampton, to all intents and purposes, the races don't bring me out here. All I am able to squeeze in these days is one weekend a year between trips to Europe on my way to or from California. So just having this Monday and Tuesday means a good deal. It's something I will savor. Besides the beach and the pool, there's great fishing, which I love. Looking at the sea, I conclude for maybe the ten thousandth time that if I didn't live on the ocean in California, I would miss it terribly. There are times I take the sea for granted, living by it as I do. I grew up on the water in the East, so it was just natural for me to choose to live on the beach by the Pacific. By now, I don't think I could tolerate anything else.

Of course, the sun didn't come out until we were ready to leave. The whole place changes character when the sun shines. And though there wasn't much time before I had to go back to Stroudsburg, there was enough so that I ended up feeling better and more relaxed than I have for about four months, ever since I caught a lingering bronchitis. I played tennis both days and swam also. As a result, I feel rather fit.

When I got back to the motel in Stroudsburg, there was a telegram from our sponsor, Gulf, that read, HOW SWEET IT IS THAT THE RELUCTANT DRAGON SHOULD GO SO FAST. They know as well as Teddy does that I really didn't want to run here. But I hope they also know that whatever my initial feelings about France vs. Pocono, they will have no effect on my attitude or my performance.

Last Monday, Cindy Adams, the wife of comedian Joey Adams, called me to ask if I wanted to be a judge for the Miss Universe Pageant in Athens in July. It would mean leaving England right after the British GP, spending six days in Greece with all my expenses paid, and doing almost nothing except going to one party and looking at a lot of good-looking women. Life can be extremely demanding.

If I do it, I'll be able to go to Greece despite a Makes race scheduled for Watkins Glen, because Alfa Romeo is still not ready. The chassis seems fine, but they are having engine problems. On top of that, they're plagued with strikes. Thus far, they have canceled out of four races; I have canceled out of one. Now they're canceling the sixth. Zero for six. I'm being paid for not driving, so I can't complain.

During the traditional front-row photo session at Pocono, both Mario, who is on the front row too, and Al Unser came over to congratulate me. That was extremely nice of them, because I know how hard they tried for the pole. To come over and concede in such a gentlemanly way was gratifying to me and did them great credit, particularly in Mario's case. He and I are not that friendly, although we talk whenever the opportunity seems right.

But I remember his visiting me in the hospital after my testing crash at Daytona and being considerate enough then to investigate my habits and discover it would mean something extra to me if he brought cigars. That was particularly nice. The man is a gentleman.

Carburetion day went well, although the new engine does not seem as loose as the qualifying engine. In fact, it seems a little tight. Our engine reliability has improved, because the qualifying engine was the same engine we used to qualify at Indianapolis, with no rebuilding in between. When they took it out, it had over seven hundred miles on it. But the new one doesn't seem to respond to the throttle quite so well. It seems to labor more. The new engine is not getting quite the fuel mileage the old one got, so maybe we're going to have to run less boost.

Back to New York on Wednesday to try to make a jazz concert on the Staten Island Ferry. Didn't manage to. Dinner with my friend, and then lunch, the next day, with the editor of our book at Doubleday. He is not up on motor racing, although he professes to be a sports fan. He asked me about safety in racing, though, which is a good question. In Europe we have the GPDA, here we have nothing.

Now it's Friday and back to Pocono for pit practice. Pit practice is particularly important since, with the reduction in allowable total and on-board fuel as a result of the furor over Indianapolis, there are going to be perhaps double the number of pit stops than there have been in the past. We're going to try to get everything sorted out now. Huey is quietly confident about it, as Huey always is. But I think Huey is running out of steam, being away from home for all these races. It's a hardship for him, and I think this may very well be his last year. Huey probably wants to win as much as anyone else on the team. Maybe more. He's running out of time. He's put in a lot of years of hard, solid work and he's a very important cog in the McLaren Indy organization. If anyone deserves to win, Huey does.

Tyler, as usual, works continuously. All during the last couple of months, it's been a rare hour during the day when he hasn't been on the job, and that includes every day of the week from sunrise to sunset. Even though he is always talking about going somewhere for a vacation, he takes almost no time off. He is as loyal to the team as anyone on it. He's so conscientious that his job comes before his own personal considerations—no matter how important they might be. I think Teddy is really lucky to have Tyler. He's particularly lucky to have

Tyler in charge of the USAC program, because it frees him completely to do Formula 1. At most, Teddy has to jump between the two just to oversee and make managing-director noises. I appreciate Tyler as much as or more than anyone else on the team. I'm sure Tyler appreciates my contribution. He doesn't make any bones about my value to McLaren. When I do a good job he lets me know it, despite his reputation as a curmudgeon. At Indy, where I had a bad race, he disregarded it entirely. Obviously I appreciated that. He looks at the over-all picture. He considers one bad race to be just one of those things, whereas some other people on this team figure one bad race means you're on your way downhill. I *do* appreciate Tyler.

The Mickey Mouse 500 was a bad race for me. We dropped a valve at about the seventy-second lap. At the beginning of the race, I got jumped by Mario, so again after winning the pole I ended up following somebody on the first lap. I've never been first in the first turn starting from the front row and I'm beginning to wonder about it. John Rutherford had to spin to avoid another car on the first lap; and then, after a few more laps, Al Unser hit the wall in the first turn. Finally they had to put out the red flag to stop the race, because the retaining wall caved in where Al had hit it. I had made a pit stop under the yellow for fuel, so on the restart I was down to sixteenth.

By the time I retired, I had gotten within 4.5 seconds of the leader and was gaining. I really felt confident about the car. But they say if you're running good, that's when the car breaks; when you're running lousy, you run all day.

The Pocono 500 was a disaster.

We're in Connecticut, and yesterday we got out on my old friend Matt Forelli's boat. We did some fishing, and as usual when Matt and I fish together, we caught some worthwhile fish, including a twenty-pound striped bass. When I go fishing alone I get skunked more often than not; when Matt goes fishing alone he gets skunked; but when we go together, we do well. Last night, we went into the city for a jazz concert at Carnegie Hall featuring the current Count Basie band. There was a tribute to the members of the band who are no longer with it. Joe Williams was there and I enjoyed it very much. This week in New York, they're having what was once the Newport Jazz Festival. I don't know if I'll get down. I'm torn between going down to the city and listening to the music or just staying out here and relaxing.‡ I think it would be wise to relax, because next week I'm going on a four-race tour in Europe.

It's going to be a critical four weeks. Jody Scheckter is definitely going to be included on the Formula 1 team next year, which means that one of us is going to have to go. I have every intention of keeping my job, so for the next month I'm going to have to produce and that's all there is to it.

I hated to see the stay in the country come to an end. On Monday we took a light plane back to New York, had lunch with my dad, whom I hadn't seen in a while, and took the 10 P.M. night flight for London. I didn't leave any too soon. As I've long since discovered, it takes me two nights to get over the time change; and now, on Wednesday, it's time to go out to Silverstone to begin practice for the British Grand Prix.

I had been feeling pretty good about Silverstone because our cars are especially suited to the track. I had a pretty good test there last April. But things seem to have changed. The Goodyear engineer this year claimed my left front tire was rolling, so we went to a harder compound. That slowed me down at least six-tenths of a second. But we persevered and finally got down to fifth-fastest time. Denny wound up on the pole for today.

Nobody seems to be using the tire I had decided on at the

‡ Curious that the fresh air should have won out. Revson is a confirmed jazz fanatic. If he weren't a race driver, he'd be a musician. His favorite instrument is the alto sax. When he was a child he wanted to be a drummer but his mother insisted that, before he take up any other instrument, he'd have to take six months of piano. The intensity of his ambition was such even then that he endured the six months of piano and got his drums only to find that his brother Douglas was given a set of drums at the same time. Revson speculates that his mother gave Douglas the drums in the hopes that since Peter was going to be beating on drums, Douglas might do the same and both would refrain from beating on each other. It didn't work. L.M.

end of the day yesterday. We might have to use it in the race. The grid position is too important here to experiment a lot. But I, at least, have a lot of time with that tire, so if we have to change back from the tire we have gone to, the tire that Denny used, I know where to start. This is a high-speed circuit. The car's very sensitive to wing changes. We did change roll bars because of wheel-spin problems. We stiffened the car up and that seemed to help.

I've been staying at Teddy Mayer's house, where I always stay in preparation for a race in England. The house is very comfortable, and Sally Mayer's hospitality is first-rate, the ice box always being very full.

After Saturday's practice, Denny and I had identical times. Until fifteen minutes before the end of the session, McLarens were sitting one-two on the grid. But, about forty-five minutes from the end of practice, Team McLaren decided to quit running and concentrate on setting up the cars for the race, inasmuch as Goodyear informed us we could not run the tires we had qualified on. It seems the qualifying tires just wouldn't stand up to the pace. They were having trouble with the left side, which is the heavily loaded side at Silverstone. Goodyear took the qualifying tires away from everyone, except Lotus, which wasn't joining into the spirit of the thing. In the last few minutes, Lotus let Ronnie go out and he got a time two-tenths quicker than Denny, to take the pole. Big deal. We were still on the front row and I was quite happy about that.

The big sweat toward the end of practice was getting the car well balanced on the hard, left-side tires, which made the car considerably looser. I managed to do this as a result of having run on the tires in the first day, so I set a time in unofficial practice before the race at least equal to the fastest time posted, which was by Emerson Fittipaldi, I think. But the car didn't have the adhesion, particularly in the back, that it had with the sticky tires.

When the race started, I got a pretty bad line into the first turn, because Denny, who had a new set of tires on, was a little hesitant. As a result, I got blocked out of a line into the first turn and about three or four cars got underneath me. At the end of the first lap, Jody Scheckter, who was driving the third of our cars, lost it coming through Woodcote and crashed into the inside retaining wall, blocking half the track to the inside. I just managed to squeeze through alongside Cevert, only knocking off a chip of metal out of my rear wing, which was no problem at that point.

But nine cars were in the resulting accident, and the race was stopped and not restarted for more than an hour. The marshals and the stewards were very careful to be sure the track was clear of debris before restarting the race; and the restart was a completely new one, using the original grid positions.

On the restart, I did somewhat better, but again I was blocked out. Emerson somehow got through ahead of Denny and me and as we came out of the first lap, Denny was fifth and I was sixth.

I got by Denny quickly to a position behind Emerson. We were some seven seconds back of Ronnie Peterson, who was the leader at that point. From then on, for a large part of the race, all I did was stay very close to Emerson. I wasn't able to get by him comfortably and I didn't want to use the motor until I absolutely had to, perhaps toward the end of the race.

Still, we were catching Ronnie steadily. Then Emerson broke his drive shaft, and I moved up quickly behind Ronnie. With a few sprinkles of rain coming down, I was able to move by Ronnie and take the lead. Behind me, Wilson Fittipaldi's Brabham blew its motor and dropped oil all the way from the entrance to Woodcote through Copse.

While the oil was on the track, I managed to maintain my five-second lead easily. I think being able to do that lulled me into a feeling of security. Even after the oil dried up, I was still maintaining a very careful pace until I realized that Ronnie was in hot pursuit—very closely pushed by Denny. In turn, Denny was being pushed by a new fellow, James Hunt, in a March, on Firestone tires. I'd driven against Hunt at Monte Carlo. He was good and coming along very rapidly. The three of them were making time on me and I began to feel the pressure. But I was able to open a bit and maintain the interval. I crossed the finish line .8 second ahead.

I'd won my first grand prix.

It had been a long time. Thirteen-plus years. One of my great ambitions was to win the world championship, and to win the first grand prix was the initial step. It was probably the hardest thing I'd done, the hardest thing to accomplish, that first one. I'd worked for it harder than anything else. I'd say that, even if I had won the Indy 500. They say the first GP is the hardest, and the rest of them come easier.

After the last lap, they took us around the race track on a farm wagon towed by a tractor, with the first four finishers and the press on it. Behind the wagon was my crew with the race car. They had the biggest crowd ever at Silverstone, and the British race fans were extremely polite and very appreciative. They all clapped as we passed them. I have never seen an American crowd so enthusiastic. Most American crowds are almost gone by the time the victory lap takes place. This crowd stayed even though it rained quite hard for ten minutes. They stood out in the rain and waited for us to come by. It was gratifying.

We had dinner at the race track, catered for Yardley's. They had a tent set up, and by the time dinner was over it was 10 P.M. It was a great day and I was looking forward to the next race.

A friend of my family's called the next day and told me an interesting story. He said he was watching the race and he got a view of the accident involving Jody Scheckter. You know, he said, I saw your teammate after he crashed. It was just like he had the plague. Nobody would talk to him. He was just allowed to sit and sulk on his own.

Looking at Jody, he said, he realized how cruel the sport is. He said over and over again that the winner is the winner but he is only one man; the losers are everybody else and nobody wants to know about them. He found it remarkable that there sat Jody Scheckter, who had been touted as the next great ace, and he had this first-lap shunt at Silverstone and suddenly he was discarded.

Even though my family's friend found that hard to understand, that's the way it is in racing.*

In the last month and a half, three of the races I'd started had been red-flagged shortly after the start. Yesterday, on the BBC, Raymond Baxter, the commentator, asked me if the nine-car pileup and the starting and stopping and restarting of the race had shaken me up. I told him I'd gotten used to that kind of thing.

It's after the race and I've moved to the Carlton Towers, in London, where I'm going to savor life for three or four days. In the morning I run in the park, and later in the day play a little tennis. The area around the hotel is very nice, it's sort of near Belgravia, close to Chelsea and the Kings Road, and yet not too far from the West End. London is a more swinging place than it was when I first came here, in 1963. Then, the sidewalks literally folded at 11 P.M. Now it's a late town, with a lot of clubs open until all hours. It's my second-favorite city to New York. As a place to live, it's probably better than New York.

The press in London is being very kind about my victory in the British Grand Prix. This was my twentieth grand prix, but even at that the win came quicker than it has to others. Chris Amon is getting near the 100 mark and still hasn't won.

As a side note, but a very pleasant one at this moment, the bookmakers' odds on me were 14–1 before the race. Betting is quite legal here, so I took advantage of it and put 150 pounds down. I have to confess, though, that it wasn't 150 on the nose, but fifty each way, which is the English way of saying across the board. So instead of making fourteen hundred pounds, I made 875, which was still not bad.

I'm going to use the money to take a little vacation with a friend in Sardinia. I don't know anything about the hotel

* Later that month, I was interviewing Scheckter for a profile that *Car and Driver* had commissioned. I was particularly interested in Jody's assessment of how the Silverstone accident might affect his vigorous, on-the-edge driving style. "Not much," he said. "Somebody else is going to be at fault the next time, and I'll probably have to pay for it then." Racers seem to be able to feel remorse, but they don't seem to be able to feel it very strongly. L.M.

there, so we'll be taking a chance. Alfa very generously is going to lend me a Montreal for a month. I'll drive it to Zandvoort, in Holland, for the next race.

In Sardinia, the sun was shining brilliantly and there wasn't even a breeze. The airline we took is owned by the Aga Khan, who started developing Sardinia about five years ago. We finally got a rental car to go to Porto Rotunda, which is very Italian. It's only recently been built up and there is a nice beach, but too much congestion in the small yacht harbor. They've allowed too many boats to come in and make permanent moorings. The food's good, the people are nice, and for the three or four days I have here, it's going to be great.

When I was younger, I used to agree with everyone who said racing is living and the time in between is just waiting. Since then, I've certainly learned how to wait a lot more graciously. We went to a party given by Lady Anne Ovv-Lewis, which was held in a great setting. Her house is up in the rocks, and the surrounding terrain reminds one of New Mexico or Arizona. There is some vegetation, but mostly it's rocks and jagged peaks. The incongruity is that the sea lies just below.

We flew to Italy and picked up the Alfa Montreal. For the first time, I stayed at the Villa d'Este, at Lake Como. Everything I've heard about it is true. It's an absolutely beautiful place, with gardens and shrines and fancy tile patios. It was a beautiful night on the lake. For the first time in a long while, I didn't mind putting on a tie. The setting was so elegant it seemed appropriate; and we dined on the terrace overlooking the lake to the music of a trio.

We drove the next day to Bernard Cahier's place, in France. Bernard is the acknowledged king of the continental motoring press and its unchallenged best host. His family's estate is right on a big lake and, as usual, Bernard entertained in fine fashion. Bernard has a friend who is one of the growing number of European dune-buggy enthusiasts. He has one built around a Porsche engine that is phenomenal, according to Bernard. It weighs about thirteen hundred pounds, has a 911S engine, and gets to sixty in about four seconds.

Off for Holland in the rain.

The first practice for the Dutch GP was held in the rain. There's no point in wearing out the car with too much driving when the weather's this bad. The accommodations here are in one of the two high-rises in Zandvoort; I checked in after dropping my friend at the airport. The view is breath-taking. Below is a raging North Sea being driven by high winds.

The sea is as bleak as I've ever seen it. I wonder how this can be considered a summer resort, with the sea being as cold as it is and the weather so frequently chilly.

Roger Williamson was killed in the Dutch Grand Prix. About ten laps into the race, he lost control of his car at the new tunnel right-hand bend. He got upside down and hit the inside guardrail. That touched off a fire, and Williamson was pinned in the car while it blazed. David Purley, who was following closely, saw his dilemma, stopped, and tried to get Williamson out. But the marshals on the corner refused to help. They even refused to let Purley get near the fire. There was some fire apparatus just a hundred yards down the road. Admittedly it would have been something of a problem backing up to the fire. But had the clerk of the course reacted quickly and correctly and red-flagged the race, Williamson might be alive. Instead, the fire equipment just sat there while his car, with him in it, burned.

It was beyond comprehension. When some equipment did get there it was too late, but the equipment and the debris made it a single-file lane near the wreck. For four laps we went through a cloud of smoke that completely blocked vision on a track with rises and drops that make turns come up suddenly anyway.

More high-speed understeer for me. The same problem, the same symptoms as Sweden. The steering was so bad the front end would just wash out across the road. I knew I wouldn't be in the hunt, so I settled down, compensated for the problem, drove my own race, and finished fourth.

A disappointing day, with the problem from Sweden coming back again. We must find it in time for the next race and cure it once and for all. It's on to the Nurburgring, and after the German Grand Prix there, testing in Austria. I'm looking forward to that. Austria is another high-speed track, made to order for us.

In the pits at Zandvoort, Denny asked me if I'd heard about Jacky Ickx. I said what about him, and he said, well, Ickx might drive at the Nurburgring. Denny said not to worry, though; it would never happen, that we had enough problems with two of us that we didn't need a third added.

The morning I left Zandvoort, I awoke fairly late and had a leisurely breakfast, then wandered over to a nearby hotel to have one last smoked herring before I left. Their lightly smoked herring is the best part of their town.

I was following Bernard Cahier, and he suggested we stop at a country inn near the old Spa/Francorchamps race track, probably the most beautiful track in Europe. I remember liking the track very much when I raced there in the '60s, but unfortunately it's so very fast that you can't race there unless it's absolutely dry. It's very, very dangerous even then. The countryside around the track is fabulous. It's a forest with rolling terrain. Bernard and I stopped overnight in a superb inn. My room was on the top floor overlooking the Ardennes Forest, which appeared a myriad of pines.

The food was excellent. If anything, I find Belgian food even better than French. The Belgians truly appreciate what they are served. Bernard ordered a particular burgundy that turned out to be extraordinary. Bernard said it's the best he'd ever tasted. He said the Belgians like burgundy more even than the French do. This was a superb example. It was the smoothest wine I'd tasted in a long time. It didn't even have baby teeth in it.

I left the inn, picked up my friend at the airport, and drove to the Nurburgring, hoping to refamiliarize myself with the circuit. That is not the easiest thing in the world to do. During the whole of practice you might get in only fifteen laps or so, because the course is fourteen miles long and has a seemingly infinite number of turns. When I got to the Nurburgring I discovered that Jacky Ickx had been signed to drive there for McLaren.

My crew chief, Davey, confirmed that the Zandvoort problem was a bad shock absorber in the front. It may not have been really bad, but the point was that the valving was imprecise. He had gone from Konis to Armstrongs. In Germany we were going to try the Armstrongs again and hope they would maintain their valving, as they were supposed to do.

Since I've been in Europe this time, I've really begun to notice the prices. Yesterday the mark was 2.25 to the dollar. When I was here racing in the '60s, it was four. I bought six tennis balls in Germany at a price that worked out to be about ten dollars.

Hotel rooms are expensive too. At the hotel it cost about twenty dollars a day for two with breakfast but no bath and of course no toilet. That's a bit much.

After practice, during which it rained most of the time, I ended up starting seventh. Denny started eighth, and the Ringmeister, Mr. Ickx, started fourth.

The weather was good for the German Grand Prix, but the race was not. I've certainly done a lot better and I can't think of too many times I've done worse. I came around in the first lap in sixth position, right behind a bunch headed by Ickx, Niki Lauda, and Carlos Reutemann. Just as we started through the first ess section, I hit the curb and it bounced me back across the road. I hit the guardrail very hard at the inside of the race track. By the time I got it gathered up, I was next to last. I motored on, but the impact had bent a wheel and that made the car very hard to drive. I finished ninth. Mr. Ickx finished third. His best lap was a 7:16 or thereabouts, which is good but not that good. Even with the bent wheel, I managed a 7:18.

We flew back to England from Cologne on a push/pull Cessna and arrived at Teddy's house just after midnight. That meant a full day in London before going off to Zeltweg for the Austrian tests, and a busy day it was going to be.

In the office of McLaren in Colnbrook, we discussed some of the problems of the car, particularly the slow-speed turns, where we seemed to be at a disadvantage. I tried to be as graphic as possible about the problem, and Gordon Coppuck, the designer, seemed to understand. The problem seems to be in the front suspension. We expected that the Austrian testing would go a long way toward solution. Any time I go testing, it always improves my performance for the race. Last fall, I went testing at Mosport and was on the pole. I went testing at Watkins Glen for a day and was second-fastest. At Kyalami, in South Africa, this year, I was a strong second after tests. After testing at Silverstone, I won the race.

These are facts Teddy seems to forget. I'm sure if he considered them as I do, he'd schedule a lot more testing.

My room in Austria was in the Leibensteiner Cafe, the only singles bar in town. Unfortunately it was also across from the railroad station, which made it noisy. The rooms were typically Spartan, but the beds were comfortable.

The test went well. We ran about three hundred miles until the engine began acting up. We got down to a 1:37, which didn't compare with last year's pole speed of 1:36, but there was no rubber on the race track and we had a bad motor.

I returned the Alfa, after the tests, to Autodelta in Milan after having used it for three weeks. Part of the trip was on the autostrada, where you find one sixty-kilometer truck and then a space and then another sixty-kilometer truck. You can average very high speeds, but if your car has any brake deficiency, you'll notice it right away, because you come up on those trucks at maybe 110 mph. The little Alfa was a very smooth car. It rode well at high speeds. It was very stable, but it *did* have some deficiencies in the braking department.

After I got back to England, I had a long conversation with Gordon Coppuck, trying to give him as much information as I could. The car just plain wasn't as good as it should have been. The rear end was all right. It had the adhesion and it could get the power down. But the car didn't point that well. The car understeered too much under light load conditions.

Zeltweg is a pretty track. It's a high-speed course, and it's one I like to drive. But it certainly is out of the way. We had to take a charter flight from Luton, then a bus for two hours, and once we got to Zeltweg we had to rent cars. All in all, about an eight-hour trip from Colnbrook.

On the flight, someone mentioned with sarcasm the supposed glamour of racing and the travel involved with it. I must say I see racing from the inside out, and for me it's not so glamorous—especially in these days of big money and high-pressure commercial involvement. Racing is an interesting job; it's adventurous, at best. But the glamour lies in the people who come to watch. The glamour is in the crowds, not behind the scenes. Behind the scenes, the pressure to win is too great.

In practice, I discovered that the training car was faster than mine, so I thought I ought to take it over. Teddy said no, they'd try to fix mine so it would be as fast. That didn't make sense to me. There are times when Teddy seems to be stubborn just for the sake of being stubborn. I kept saying that I was the one in the car, that the training car was faster, and that we should put another engine in it and run it in the race. Teddy would have none of it and once again showed his blind side. He's a great man for being right after the fact. It's exasperating.

In June I was told my car was absolutely the same as the others. Now Teddy has admitted to me it isn't. But he says he intends to find out what the problems have been. The season is flying by and I've decided I won't stand for it any longer. In the past four or five races I've run unsatisfactorily, and I think I'm right in attributing at least part of that to the car.

So they measured everything on my car and everything on the training car and there were discrepancies. That was no surprise. They found at the Nurburgring that the holes that determine the wing angles on my car did not correspond to the placement on the other cars. We discovered my car had 2.5 degrees more wing angle with a correspondingly numbered hole than the others did. When I questioned that, and some other things, I was told, no, everything's the same.

Nice.

In unofficial practice on Saturday, with a full fuel load, I was fastest. I was really looking forward to the race.

Then more disaster. We got the signal to come off the dummy grid after our motors had been running for thirty seconds and move up to the actual grid. I felt my clutch failing to disengage. The only thing I could do was to put it in neutral and try to anticipate the flag by a second or two, jam it into first, and go.

Well, I got into first, but the guy just wouldn't drop the flag. So I had to hold my foot on the brake for maybe ten seconds. That was too long. Holding the car in gear on the brake without having the clutch in fried it, and when the flag finally did drop I didn't go anywhere. I was very lucky not to get hit from behind and just coasted to the end of the pit wall, parked it at the exit to the pits, and got out.

The month in Europe, which had started out well at Silverstone, turned glum very quickly. And even the very real problems with the car were not the principal cause. I had tried very hard. Despite the problems and despite the failure on all our parts to solve the problems, I hoped I had maintained my enthusiasm and my interest. It was important for me to persevere. But it was difficult.

The most dispiriting thing about it traced back to the day of the Dutch GP. It was then that Teddy chose to tell me I didn't figure in McLaren's grand prix plans for 1974.

I had known there was a likelihood of that happening. But I didn't exactly expect to be told after I won my first grand prix. It seemed to me that Teddy's sensitivity index was particularly bad, and more than that, he might have been considerably premature in his decision.

His reasoning, though, as I discovered during that swing through Europe, was complicated. To explain it, I have to go back.

At the Dutch Grand Prix, Teddy said that I would not be on the Formula 1 team for McLaren during the following year. By then I had come to realize there was an unnamed driver, a Mr. X, who had seemingly made an offer to go to McLaren with sponsorship. I knew as well that Teddy had been complaining about his deal with Yardley, his Formula 1 sponsor. Teddy had been saying for some while that if they didn't come up with more money, he would have to disqualify them as continuing sponsors, although they still had a contract. Teddy claimed, though, that it was merely an option.

In Holland also, Don Nichols, from Shadow, talked to me

again about joining his team for the following year. I told him I'd think about it, particularly since he offered me a retainer that was larger than the one Teddy was paying. I told him to send me a written offer to my office in California for consideration.

In thinking about that, it occurred to me that Don was subsidized by Goodyear and that, since I was a Goodyear driver, he would very likely be talking to Larry Truesdale, the Goodyear racing chief, about my signing with him for 1974.

In order that Goodyear not have the wrong impression, and in order to discover what Larry thought would be best for me —because I have faith in his judgment and he has been very helpful—I placed a call to him in Akron.

I assured Larry that I had not signed with Shadow, but I was contemplating it. That's as far as the negotiations had gone. It turned out that Larry was convinced that the way for me to go was Formula 1; and since Teddy had offered me a place on the USAC and Formula 5000 teams only for next year, it meant that Larry was telling me I had his blessings to turn down USAC in favor of grand prix racing.

I told him what Teddy's situation was, that he would almost certainly claim hardship and refuse the Yardley sponsorship— and then I discovered who Mr. X was. It seems that, early in July, Emerson Fittipaldi, who was evidently upset that he had to share star billing with Ronnie Peterson at Lotus, had approached Teddy with the offer of Marlboro and Texaco sponsorship money, which he evidently controlled. That amount represented about four times what Yardley had been paying, and Teddy jumped at the chance.

That made me odd pig in the litter. Ironically, it did the same to Jody Scheckter, because Denny remained the favorite son as an old friend of Bruce's and an original member of the McLaren team.

So all this went a long way toward explaining some of the problems I had from Holland to Austria. I'm sure Teddy's attitude affected the attitudes of some of the people on the team. I tried my best to ignore that. I tried my best to ignore my own feelings of disappointment.

It's always the same way in racing. No matter how well you're doing, it seems you're always on tenterhooks. I had won my first grand prix, I was well placed in the point standings, and I was earning better than $300,000 a year as a racing driver. And there I was looking at the unemployment line.

Mandel · Four

Sentiment greases the economic wheels of racing. Sentiment and large inheritances.

The Teddy Mayers of racing ultimately justify whatever they do in terms of money. They are businessmen, they say, and therefore they are simply acting as businessmen should act. The implication is clear: In racing, there is no room for personalities, sentiment, friendships, or charity. It's a tough world out there. It's hard enough to be a survivor without the burden of decency to weigh them down.

So they say. Oddly though, the more you examine the economic foundation blocks of motor racing, the more you become convinced they are made of whipped cream. Racing is a very curious structure, seen in the terms of Teddy Mayers.

For instance, of the hundreds of teams racing in the United States I have never been able to find anyone who could name more than seven that are making money.*

There are probably three, maybe four road-racing tracks in this country that show a profit.†

* The consensus seven: All American Racers (Dan Gurney) and Team McLaren are barely making it; Vels-Parnelli is definitely making it. The others are Penske Racing, Petty Enterprises, either Bobby Allison or the Wood brothers but not both, and Don Garlits.   L.M.
† Mid-Ohio and Road America (Elkhart Lake) are certainly profitable. Laguna Seca might be making money too, but nobody knows for sure

Atlanta International Raceway, an oval track on which National Association for Stock Car Racing late-model Grand National cars compete—the most financially successful kind of racing in the nation—has just gone through bankruptcy for the umpteenth time. Atlanta, of course, is right in the middle of stock-car country.

Gulf Oil Company dropped its sponsorship of Team McLaren on the Championship Trail (which includes Indianapolis) because it could no longer justify the expense. Teddy Mayer himself hasn't been able to find another sponsor of any kind to replace them. Worse than that, Teddy had to close the books in early 1974 on a single-seater road-race program for the United States because, although McLaren had built a car especially for the series, he couldn't find even a small sponsor to underwrite the costs of that either. McLaren didn't have a chance to race the car, called the M25, even once. To make things more depressing, not a single competitor in the series, called Formula 5000, was willing to buy a brand-new, built-for-the-factory-to-race-itself car. It was sold to a South American nobody, and it will probably never be seen again.

Businessmen?

If racing's financial statesmen are not prudent and profit-making, they share at least one quality with their real-world counterparts. They are certainly rapacious, as the following stories show.

There once was a sponsor that supported a number of teams by direct subsidy and had one man in over-all charge of the racing program. On a morning during the season, one of the car owners his company was sponsoring called from the West Coast to say that, finally, one of the only competitive cars running that season had become available for sale in rolling-chassis (without engine) form. He said he needed twenty-five thousand dollars. The sponsoring company's man knew how desperate his car owner had been, trying to buy a car

---

since it's run by a non-profit, charitable group. The fourth track *might* be Lime Rock, in Connecticut, which is operated in very-low-profile style by Jim Haynes. Haynes, despite his great fondness for racing, is an extremely effective promoter. L.M.

that could stay up with the leaders. He also knew how short the supply was. So he answered that he would fly out that day with the cash. But it wouldn't be twenty-five thousand dollars, it would be thirty thousand dollars. He thought it would be nice, when he arrived, if the car owner would sit down with him and play a little gin rummy. Say five thousand dollars worth. The car owner was agreeable and agreeably lost the five thousand dollars. The next day he bought his rolling chassis. That very afternoon, he sold it for almost double the price he paid, having never intended to race it in the first place. (This story is probably—but not certainly—apocryphal.)

Mark McCormack's organization was retained by the Sports Car Club of America to find an over-all sponsor for its prestige series, the Canadian American Challenge Cup. One of the car owners in the CanAm had been sponsored to a very small extent the year before by a toiletries and drug company that was introducing a new line of men's toiletries called Roman Brio. The McCormack group persuaded the Roman Brio people that a $750,000 investment in the CanAm would pay handsome dividends in terms of promotion. There was a handshake agreement. But before the contracts could be signed, word got out. Almost immediately, car owners and team managers, some of them from the CanAm itself, who would have profited by the enormous increase in purses the Roman Brio sponsorship would have insured, approached the company directly with the argument that individual sponsorship of them would be far more valuable than series sponsorship. The Roman Brio people were new at racing and became terribly confused by the diverse stories and conflicting arguments of all those people streaming into their offices. All those stories and all those arguments producing all that confusion convinced Roman Brio it was in over its head. The company never signed the contract and shortly pulled out of racing entirely.

A race-sanctioning body recommended a particular reporter to a racing publication for an area of racing the publication was just beginning to cover. The correspondent was hired. For the next six months, the sanctioning body wrote letters and made phone calls complaining that not enough coverage was being given. Finally, in an excess of annoyance, the executive director wrote the publication saying that perhaps the reason coverage of his events by that correspondent was not as complete as coverage of other kinds of racing was because he, the executive director, might not have been paying the correspondent enough for each story. A phone call revealed that the sanctioning body was paying the reporter fifty dollars every time one of his stories appeared in the publication. The executive director saw nothing at all wrong with that. He was only curious about how much the other race groups were paying for *their* stories. When he was told, nothing, he was skeptical. When the reporter was forthwith fired for being on the take from the sanctioning body, he reacted with indignation and even had a number of the publication's advertisers write attesting to his good character.

None of this kind of thing is particularly pretty. But none of it is particularly criminal either.‡ It is all by way of saying that the team owners and managers in racing are well within the ethical mainstream of American (and British and French and Luxemburgian) business.

The problems of Team McLaren began when Teddy Mayer decided racing could be a profitable, businesslike venture. It couldn't, of course. That's a denial of its definition. Racing is a rich man's sport. Nobody but the drivers make money. Sometimes the drivers make a *lot* of money and become rich. Then, occasionally, they become car owners or promoters and they lose a lot of it back, which bewilders them. They have gone into the "business" end of racing convinced that it's where the real money is. Finally, sadder and poorer, they understand that sentiment greases the economic wheels of racing. That and large inheritances.

Of course it isn't all that cut and dried. There *are*, after all, those seven teams (maybe even a couple more) in the United States that make money. And in Formula 1, the possibilities

‡ There have been criminal involvements in racing, but compared to some more prominent institutions, the federal government, say, they are fifth-rate. For instance, one Andy Porterfield raced a Corvette in the early '60s on the proceeds from a hot-parts ring. He went to jail. L.M.

of showing a profit are definitely there, definitely tantalizing.

In Formula 1, until 1974 at least, there were probably two teams making money: Lotus and Tyrrell. But the black ink came not as a result of winnings but of sponsorship.

It costs about $500,000 to field a grand prix team for a season: two cars, a backup, engines, rebuilds, mechanics, expenses, and bonuses.

Any of the top teams budgets almost $150,000 for drivers. McLaren got a very good deal on Revson and Hulme. Retainers for both probably didn't exceed $100,000. Most drivers are on a bonus system when it comes to division of purses won. The bonuses range from 10 to 50 per cent. (Revson's contract called for 40 per cent of the purse to go to him.) The lesser teams give more because their retainers are so small. Ten per cent of the whole purse is distributed to the mechanics on a point basis, with the superchiefs and the chiefs getting a proportionately larger share than the mechanics. At McLaren, Tyler Alexander was on a bonus system too, but when he was put in over-all charge of racing in the United States, he may well have forfeited his proceeds from Formula 1 in exchange for a disproportionately large bonus from championship-car racing. Teddy Mayer probably ended up paying about 15 per cent of the purse to the men who worked on the cars. Of that, it is likely the Formula 1 superchief, Alestair, got almost a third.

So far as driver expenses are concerned, they are spelled out in the driver's contract. (The crews get a rather limited per diem.) Revson's contract specified that he travel first class on domestic flights, tourist across the Atlantic. Not only was all air fare and the cost of all rental cars reimbursable, but he was also allowed thirty-five dollars a day for room and incidentals.

Costs are high, therefore, and racing revenue does not come close to matching them.

In Europe, the race car constructors have banded together to negotiate with the organizers about "appearance money." That is a strange and terrible phrase in this country, where even thinking of actually paying a team or a driver to appear

24. When it rains at Indianapolis, it's bleak even for a superstar.

25. With friend and benefactor Boyd Jefferies.

26. Peter Revson is a walking conglomerate, with some twenty-five companies and business deals under his name. Wherever he goes, the phone rings. This in the McLaren Indy garage.

27. Except on race day, a speedway can be the emptiest place in the world. The McLaren superchief, Huey Absolom, checks the fuel tank in the racing pits the day before the California 500.

28. During practice week for the California 500, at Ontario, Roger Penske invit[ed] Revson to come out and try his 40-foot ocean racer. But when Revson got to [the] dock, the two 495-cubic-inch MerCruiser engines wouldn't fire up. Revson w[as] convinced Penske never intended to let him run the boat, particularly since Pens[ke] seemed to be having such a good time trying to fix it.

29. Taking the checkered flag at Silverstone to win the British Grand Prix for his f
Formula 1 win. After the race, Teddy Mayer told him he didn't figure in McLare
grand prix plans any more.

30. The organizers held up the results of the Canadian Grand Prix for an hour and
half while they tried to decide who won it. Among the candidates were Revson a
with his UOP Shadowed back to the camera, Jackie Oliver. Revson was sure
along that he had won, and this is his patronizing smile.

1. Revson on his way to winning the Canadian Grand Prix in the Yardley-McLaren M23.

32. There is a section in the Watkins Glen spectator area known as The Bog. Y[ou] venture there during Grand Prix weekend at your peril. In '73, Bog denizens burn[ed] twelve cars that got too close.

33. Three of the dreaded Bog People at the U.S. Grand Prix.

The Golden Retriever. Marji Wallace two weeks before she became Miss World, at her first grand prix, Watkins Glen, New York.

at an event is considered a mortal sin. That, of course, is promoter puritanism. The drivers and the teams in the United States would like to be paid to appear as much as the Europeans like it, and that's very much indeed. Anyway, the constructors in Formula 1, who are also obviously the team owners and managers, got together a while back and negotiated en bloc with the individual track owners and promoters at the tracks where the races are held. Since each country is given one and only one grand prix, it is not surprising that the track owners and promoters of Germany, France, Sweden, Spain, etc. had no more success in presenting their own united front than the Common Market people have had in reaching *their* goals. So the Grand Prix Constructors Association was very successful. Their negotiation devices were not subtle. They told each track in turn that if their demands were not met, they simply wouldn't appear.

Teddy was a prime mover in the constructors organization and he is thankful that he was. The association as a whole gets about $165,000 a race for European grands prix, to be divided among its members. Any car qualifying in the top twenty, therefore, gets about four thousand dollars. That money goes to the team.

Purses used to be small in Europe, because everyone was using the appearance-money system as the principal channel for payment and revenue. But now that the constructors have gotten together, the teams are getting larger purses too. The average first place is worth between sixteen and twenty thousand dollars.

In addition there is "contingency" money. If, for example, your car is using NGK spark plugs, you might win the five thousand dollar bonus that NGK has posted for the winner. It's worth a lot of money to NGK to be able to advertise that the winner of the Turkish Grand Prix was using its plugs. But you only get the money if you win *and* if you are using NGK's spark plugs. Contingency money is frequently offered by oil companies and engine-accessory companies. Makers of brakes will also offer contingency money. A grand prix win in Europe can mean as much as five to ten thousand dollars in contingencies to the winner.

A top team enters seventeen races, say. It averages four thousand dollars per race per car in appearance money; that's about $135,000. It makes perhaps another $150,000 in prize and contingency money.

But we said it costs $500,000 to field a team. So where does the rest, let alone the profit, come from? Sponsorship.

There are usually two major sponsors of a top-flight team: the so-called primary sponsor and a tire company. In the case of Elf Team Tyrrell, the primary sponsor is a French oil company, Elf. Because Jackie Stewart and François Cevert were the two championship-caliber men on the team, and because the team manager and car owner was one of the two or three best in the business, Ken Tyrrell, the sponsorship was large—perhaps the entire $500,000 cost of fielding the team for the year. Maybe even more. Lotus, the other money-making team in Formula 1, had Texaco and Player's Cigarettes. Its total sponsorship revenue—including the tire-company affiliation, which was worth another $100,000—probably also paid the entire cost of running for the year.*

Teddy's problems were not so easily solved. Since McLaren was not a contender when Yardley signed as its sponsor, the amount the company agreed to underwrite was not nearly so large. The total in 1973 contributed by Yardley was perhaps $100,000.

That is why, when Peter Revson called Larry Truesdale in

---

* Wait a minute; doesn't that mean that Lotus and Tyrrell are making about $300,000 a year? No, it doesn't. Say the total sponsorship *is* $500,000. The team gets $135,000 in appearance money and wins another $150,000. That's $785,000. But that's also gross revenue. The team still hasn't paid the drivers their retainers or their shares of the purse. If Tyrrell and Lotus have budgeted $150,000 in retainers, which is likely, they are back down to $635,000. The drivers' share of the prize money is about fifty-five thousand dollars, so now they are at $580,000. There are wrecked cars to replace and the crew's share to pay and a lot of "miscellaneous" expenses that soon eat up the other eighty thousand dollars. In only one case is Formula 1 a real business, and that is with Lotus. Colin Chapman builds road cars, and the glamour of his racing effort rubs off in marketing advantage. Everybody else, even tough-minded Ken Tyrrell, is what is usually described as a "sportsman." L.M.

Akron to tell him he had not signed with Shadow, and Truesdale identified Mr. X as Emerson Fittipaldi, a great light dawned.

If Fittipaldi could bring Texaco and Marlboro to Teddy, it would mean about the same amount of money to McLaren as Tyrrell and Lotus were getting. Of course, it would be awkward for Teddy to have to tell Yardley it was no longer needed, but no such awkwardness prevented Teddy from letting Revson know, within days of his winning the British Grand Prix, that he no longer figured in McLaren's Formula 1 plans.

At that moment, though, Revson did not know about Fittipaldi, and Teddy did not know the rocky road that lay ahead of *him*.

All Revson knew was that racing was providing him with a fine living and that he was accepted in the Formula 1 world as one of its premier drivers.

Revson's retainer from McLaren was apportioned between the USAC (the American 500-milers) and the Formula 1 programs. It totaled about seventy-five thousand dollars (although Revson himself was very tight-lipped about his own contract specifics), and this figure, as well as the ones that follow, are educated guesses.

Revson's contract called for 40 per cent of the Formula 1 and USAC purses, which probably amounted in 1973 to about fifty thousand dollars. He had personal contracts with a variety of sponsors, which added up to another fifty thousand dollars. His deal with Alfa Romeo earned him somewhere in the friendly neighborhood of seventy-five hundred dollars a race, and he was paid when Alfa canceled out, even though he didn't have to drive.

So, from McLaren and Alfa, Revson probably earned $225,000 in 1973. In addition there was The Gnome of Cleveland, Bud Stanner, who was able to increase that by seventy-five thousand dollars from endorsements and merchandising income. Total: $300,000.

It did not make him the highest earner in Formula 1. But it made him the second- or third-highest. Jackie Stewart, Revson estimates, earned almost double that in the year he became world champion for the last time. Now that Stewart has retired, his income will still be at least equal to Revson's in 1973.

Not everyone in the Formula 1 circuit is a Revson or a Stewart. Howden Ganley, an ex-mechanic, drives for Frank Williams, an independent. He has a tough time making it.

Williams probably pays Ganley a small retainer, perhaps twenty-five thousand dollars. He may even pay Ganley about 40 per cent of the appearance money, out of which Ganley has to pay his own expenses. Ganley almost never wins any prize money.

Mike Hailwood, a former world's motorcycle champion, was with Surtees in 1973, and he was not being overpaid either. From the Surtees sponsor, Brooke Bond Oxo, Hailwood might have gotten as much as a twenty-five thousand dollar retainer. Surtees probably paid him another twenty-five thousand dollars. But that was about it, since Hailwood was not a participant in the appearance-money payments, as Ganley might have been, and he didn't win much via the purses.

In addition to his racing income, Revson had his partnership with Peyton Cramer. Since Revson was away from the dealerships, he was not paid a full-time salary. But he did participate in profits, and he was paid something in salary as well.

But even his racing income put him among the highest-paid athletes in the world. Arnold Palmer, the golfer, is also handled by Mark McCormack, and Revson guesses that he is at the top of the money pyramid. Revson estimates Palmer's income to be almost $2 million a year. Jack Nicklaus also makes more than Stewart. But that's about where it ends. Then come the racers.†

Revson, therefore, realized very well what Teddy was say-

† But they're pretty closely pushed by the basketball players, who, as a group, have the highest salaries of any players of team sports. The National Basketball Association *average* is over ninety thousand dollars, and some of the players get $250,000 or more. But their endorsement income, for some reason, is small—particularly if they're black. As a matter of interest, the next-highest-paid athletes are hockey players, only about two thousand dollars behind the basketball people. Then it drops way down. At the bottom of the list, oddly, are the players in the National Football League. L.M.

ing to him after the British Grand Prix. He understood what was at stake in terms of income. He understood, too, what was at stake in terms of his pleasure in his job, in his associates, and in his life.

The grand prix drivers are an elite. They are certainly the very best drivers in the world; even the bad ones are superb. They do not accept newcomers kindly. A driver just moving into their ranks works hard to be accepted and sometimes never is. They are well dressed, their wives and girlfriends are birds of the finest feather. In Europe, where they are all known wherever they go, their celebrity quotient is the equivalent of a top-flight television star's here.

In this extraordinary, proud, distinguished group, Revson is not only accepted, he is accepted as one of the best of the best. The institutions of the grand prix drivers, such as the GPDA, tend to perpetuate his high standing; the opinions and the regard in outer circles of the group, among the journalists, the camp followers, and the hangers-on, reinforce his ranking as well.

It is a tight, carefully ordered world, in which driving protocol is paramount and even social order is inflexible. There is not great interchange among grand prix drivers. In the first place, racing is an individual sport. It is also a dangerous one. Jackie Stewart knows best how painful it can be to have close friends among his fellow drivers. Until the gregarious and charming François Cevert became his Tyrrell teammate, Stewart had sworn never again to make a friend of another driver after his intimate Jochen Rindt was killed in the same year that saw the death of two other friends, Piers Courage and Mike Spence. Stewart relented to become both friend and teacher to Cevert. At Watkins Glen, in the final race of 1973, Cevert, too, was killed. A week later, Stewart announced his retirement from racing.

This sense of the relative order of things, this understanding of *position*, is made very clear when a Peter Revson describes what goes on in a Grand Prix Drivers' Association meeting. It becomes even clearer when he talks about some of the grand prix circus' supporting cast.

In one GPDA meeting, there arose the matter of Jody Scheckter's driving habits. Scheckter was in his first year in grand prix in 1973, and he was not on the circuit full time. There was great concern about his vigor. He blew an engine after doing well in South Africa. In France he had what Revson described as a "coming together" with Emerson Fittipaldi. Evidently, Fittipaldi was outraged by Scheckter's driving style. Jody, says Revson, is a hard guy to get around. In Revson's words, he doesn't know when it's correct to yield. He isn't aware that allowing himself to be passed is not "weak or feminine or cowardly." Then came Scheckter's accident at Silverstone, and then another at Canada, involving Cevert.

At Watkins Glen, the next grand prix, the GPDA had a meeting in which they discussed disciplining Scheckter, who was present. It was a bitter affair but Scheckter behaved in a "manly" fashion. At its end, Cevert and Scheckter shook hands. The next morning, Scheckter was the first man to arrive at the scene of Cevert's accident. He stopped his car, jumped out, and ran to try to help. What he saw was total disaster, a horror scene. Scheckter, the man who thought it was weak and feminine to allow himself to be passed, turned away and wept.

If the grand prix drivers are not close socially, they are inextricably tied spiritually.

Revson speaks often of the frequent display of "sportsmanlike behavior." He talks about a "universal code."

When he talks of his fellow drivers he makes clear that they are a pretty diversified group. Racing drivers, he says, are very independent types, they're not conformists. They differ physically. As an example, Revson says that if all the drivers in grands prix were standing around an airport, none of the other passengers could tell what they had in common. "We would look like eighteen different types."

He mentions the drivers with star quality: Jackie Stewart and Graham Hill. About Hill, who is the oldest and one of the best-known drivers, he says his presence creates a nice effect. He is very self-possessed, nicely dressed, very British. But, according to Revson, he can be a little overbearing too.

What is so impressive about all these observations is Revson's constant use of the word "we." Among American race drivers there is much of the same diversity as is found among the foreign drivers, but there is no sense of belonging, no "we."

It is popular to be cynical in bar conversations at the races in this country, whether you are a race driver, a journalist, or a team mechanic. Your willingness to be critical is somehow a measure of your independence, and your independence is the significant measure of your worth. Above all things, it is the driver or the mechanic who will tell his owner to get stuffed who is the most admired by his peers. All this is probably not very different from the behavior of other quasi-artistic, independent people: An extremely good screen writer or a very skilled NBA forward probably tends to use his insolence threshold as an index of his worth too.

So, much the same thing goes on among the grand prix teams as happens in Hollywood, in Milwaukee, or at Indianapolis (although not, oddly, in U.S. racing). But still, there is something about the bond of excellence, the worth of having arrived at the top, that holds them back from provoking the ultimate rupture. A grand prix driver rarely turns his back and walks away from his job. Hence the "we," the sense of belonging, the importance of the group.

This sense of belonging even affects the camp followers. The groupies at Indianapolis are recognizable right down to their '50s hairstyles and their wedgies. At American road racing tracks, they're infinitely more subtle in their appearance, but they have a kind of sameness and a kind of hardness.

For a long while, Judy Kondratieff was a prototypical American racing groupie. She began racing in small West Coast club events after her brother discovered road racing in the early '60s. She dragged her husband along. Wherever there was a race, there was also Judy Kondratieff. She was welcomed because she was a remarkably good-looking redhead. She had also decided she would be one of the boys, so she was game for anything. She had two young children, but nobody ever saw them.

Then, one day, she announced her divorce. Her husband disappeared and she entered the racing scene full time. She had a ride with the all-girl MacMillan Ring Free team at an international twelve-hour endurance race in Florida. She began to go everywhere in the United States and even, occasionally, to Europe.

No one remarked, soon after, when she said she would go to England for a few months to stay with her new friend Patty McLaren. Traveling in the same circles as Bruce's widow seemed to change Judy Kondratieff markedly. Instead of changing partners as though she were at a square dance, Judy was seen more and more often with one man, Howden Ganley.

These days, Revson, who never really knew her during her American racing days, says of Judy, "She is not a camp follower. She follows along because she is with Howden, but Judy is a very nice girl. Remember, it's tough to follow grand prix racing. It's tough and it's expensive. It's not like going from state to state. You go from country to country.

"That makes Judy a fairly worldly girl. She is definitely not the same as the girls who hang on the fences. Judy, remember, was a driver. She very much wanted to race. But now she's given it up; she's become more feminine. She used to be tough. Very hard. Not any more."

Judy Kondratieff, Revson seems to be saying, is one of us.

He also seems to be saying that, as a woman, she has a special, not-quite-so-good-as-us status. Despite his perceptiveness about people, despite his understanding of women, Revson is as much a chauvinist as the rest of the racing community. It is white chauvinist and male chauvinist. No one in racing has any interest in changing these aspects of it at all.‡

Perhaps a part of the group feeling among grand prix drivers is due to their traveling as much as to their feeling of being an elite. After all, the drivers pop in and out of strange countries with Kissinger-like regularity. No more than their crews, are the drivers likely to understand the language. Soon the

‡ It's only recently, for example, that women have been allowed in the pits at American oval-track races. The reason for keeping them out, the organizers say, is that they don't want women to have to hear the bad language of the garages. As for blacks, the only driver of any reputation at all is Wendell Scott, a southern NASCAR driver.   L.M.

hotels and pensions that are bearable near a given track are identified and become passwords that distinguish drivers and teams from ordinary tourists.

But the traveling is also a pure adventure to them all. There are Swedes and Frenchmen among the drivers, and drivers from New Zealand, Brazil, Argentina, Britain, and the United States—almost everywhere. Still, the circuit travels through so many countries that someone will always be seeing something for the first time.

That makes for a sense of belonging, too, the same kind of bond that exists between a cruise ship's passengers at the end of a cruise. Of course, these people have shared not only the voyage, but the status of an on-stage traveling troupe wherever they've gone.

And each weekend of racing, they've been brought closer in their sharing of the dangers of the sport too. When one of them is injured, they all feel the pain. When one of them is killed, some of the life goes out of all of them.

The wandering grand prix circus shares the joys of Monte Carlo and the miseries of Holland. They eat well together; all too frequently, they sleep uncomfortably together too.

Graham Hill can mention Kyalami to Jackie Stewart, and the two will know instantly the sharp pleasures and the bitter disappointments they both experienced in South Africa throughout their careers. They, and all the rest of the grand prix drivers, can do the same with Austria and Brazil, Mexico and Canada.

There is a story attributed to A. J. Foyt about his travels in the United States. The story is about his answer to a breathless question about the marvelous opportunities to experience the diversities of this country. The way it's told, Foyt's answer disabused the lady once and for all about the glamour of traveling to races: "You go to the same fuckin' airport and rent the same fuckin' rental car. You go to the same fuckin' track and when you're there you see the same fuckin' people. That's the way it is all year long."

The grand prix people would understand, but they wouldn't agree.

PART FIVE

Revson · Five

I was no longer a part of the family. It had been a long relationship and a good one. But I asked for my release and I got it.

I've been trying to see it Teddy's way. I see myself as a businessman engaged in a good business. Teddy says he thinks of himself in the same way, so that's the level on which I'm trying to understand.

But it's tough to swallow that, as of July 28, I became a lame duck at McLaren. It's hard. I've managed to tolerate the arguments, the friction, and the family quarreling. Until now I've felt a part of the team. We've all been working for the same things. But then, suddenly, I was excluded. It's hard to work toward the team's goals, because I've been told I'm not part of the family any more.

As difficult as it was in Europe, it became even tougher when the European part of the season ended and we came back to North America, because, somehow, I was in a part of the world I understood and among people I've known for a long time. The contrast between the security that gave me and the insecurity of my status with the team made things difficult.

It was particularly hard at Ontario for the California 500. Tyler didn't know I'd been released, so he couldn't understand my anger and resentment. I also confess that I was distracted, because Bud Stanner and I were negotiating with Ferrari, Eagle, and Shadow. There was even a moment when Graham Hill was talking to me about joining him with his sponsor, Embassy Cigarettes, to drive a new Lola Formula 1 car.

We started practice casually at Ontario. Tyler's schedule called for practice between 11 A.M. and 4 P.M., which were the hours during which the race itself would be run. The schedule also allowed the mechanics to have some free time. But Tyler also had managed to create a very deliberate atmosphere. We didn't waste any motion. I was living in my apartment at Redondo Beach, about one hour's drive from the track.

I arrived late on Tuesday, Wednesday, and Thursday before qualifying, and Teddy was exasperated. Tyler convinced him the schedule would work, so I think Teddy got used to the idea. We were doing well until Friday, when it seemed the track changed. The track started out being quite green—not too much rubber on it. As practice progressed, we got more and more rubber, so by Friday it changed the handling characteristics of the car substantially, perhaps drastically. We had to make some changes. Teddy went off to play golf in the afternoon, so Tyler and I made them without Teddy's help, as usual.

We decided to put a heavier right front spring on the car rather than mess around with wings and roll bars. That turned the trick, because Saturday morning, before qualifying, I ran 195+ without even touching the boost. Then we cranked in some boost and I did one lap at 199.4.

Friday night, I'd picked number two qualifying slot, behind Mario Andretti. I was a little concerned about going out behind Mario, because Monday, during early-morning practice, he'd had an oil leak. Since, I'd been assured his problem had been solved.

Having drawn number two, I got out before the wind came up and before the sun came out too brightly. I turned just on a 200-mph average. As the day wore on, that looked better and better. Then Bobby Unser went out on his second unsuccessful qualifying try and I had the pole. Very satisfying. It also meant I didn't have to run a qualifying race. That made it even better.

At dinner on Friday night, I talked over my situation with Larry Truesdale of Goodyear. I told Larry that with Teddy offering me Formula 5000 and USAC racing all but telling me I was off the Formula 1 team, he was trying to have his cake and eat it too. He would have Emerson and the Texaco/Marlboro sponsorship, which he desperately needed, and he would also have me in the United States, where I would be helpful to him with his search for sponsors here. Truesdale was sympathetic to my position. On the other hand, he is a man who understands all aspects of racing. He emphasized my value to the Goodyear USAC program.

But his conclusion was that I should do what I think is right. It was a difficult position for everyone involved. It was difficult for Teddy because he had no one lined up as a sponsor in the United States, so he couldn't make me any kind of offer at all. That meant I'd have to make my own decision about Ferrari, Shadow, and Eagle, because if I waited too long, Teddy would have me by the short hairs and I wouldn't have any choice but to drive for him—probably at much less money than I think I'm worth.

I went back to Redondo Beach after qualifying, and I got an interesting telephone call. It was from Boyd Jefferies, who was our only individual sponsor on Team McLaren. Boyd is a real sportsman and a very good friend of mine.

Boyd got into racing in 1969 with Marshall Robbins. I came along and drove the car and met Boyd at the same time. In 1970 I drove for Carl Haas, and he sponsored that effort too. Then, while I went with McLaren in 1971 and won the CanAm, he stayed with Haas, but the following year he came to McLaren with the idea of eventually buying part of the team.

Now, after two years of sponsorship of Team McLaren, he was calling about whether to consummate a deal to buy a good part of the operation. Considering my position, I appreciated the irony. I told him the team was well set up, that Teddy had managed to surround himself with key people, particularly Gordon Coppuck, the designer, whom I considered very good. I mentioned that Tyler Alexander was as good a practical engineer as there was in racing. I said that Gary Knudsen and Roger Bailey, of the engine shop, made it a really superior operation. But I also told him that I thought Teddy's ego demanded that he supply ideas and exert his influence on every area of the operation, whereas his forte was organization and administration and that's what he should stick to. That was a small problem, though, I told Boyd.

Boyd asked me my position, so I told him. Who would be driving Formula 1? he asked. My answer was Denny and Emerson Fittipaldi. I also assumed Jody Scheckter could be there if he was not too demanding in the way of money. Boyd asked me who I might be driving for next year, and I told him about my various negotiations. But I also said my preference continued to be Team McLaren, because I thought they would have the best car and the best engine in 1974.

Boyd concluded by saying that he and I were good friends, so he would stay out of my situation. He told me he appreciated my evaluation of the team. As it turned out, he decided against investing with Teddy.

Ontario carburetion tests were Thursday. I went out with a new engine and in no more than four or five laps scuffed a piston. It made for a mad scramble to get the qualifying engine back in so we could get another twenty-five minutes of running before the track closed. The engine we put back in probably only had sixty or seventy miles on it. I was told that if it was a good engine, it would live for at least one thousand miles—that if an engine is going to break, it'll break within the first one hundred miles.

On Friday I was invited to go out to Marina del Rey and try Roger Penske's new ocean racing boat. It was going to be the basis for a column I had started to do in *American Boating*. When I got there, Roger was in the engine compartment himself and there were obviously problems getting the boat started. It was a fuel-supply difficulty, and eventually I had to leave. But, until I did, I formed a part of Roger's audience, watching him tinker with his boat—which was not very exciting. I did think, though, that it was a beautiful boat. It was a 40-foot Cigarette, painted in the same colors as his race cars, blue and yellow. His crew told me it was an 80-mph boat out in the ocean and it was supposed to have an edge in the race that Roger was running on Saturday. Ever since he'd arrived, all he'd been able to talk about was his boat. Roger was probably as racy at Marina del Rey as he's ever been in sports cars.

Ontario ended in misfortune. After forty-three laps, the first nineteen in the lead, the engine gave up. It seemed like another dropped valve and it was only going to get worse, so we stopped the car before it blew up. That marked the fifth time in my most recent six races that I failed to finish because of engine failure. It was particularly unfortunate since it was probably Huey Absolom's last race as superchief. All in all, it was a sad day. John was running well until he hit some oil. He spun and got into the wall. John was not hurt, but the car was beyond repair.

Teddy is really unpredictable. I won the British Grand Prix and Teddy fired me. At Ontario I failed to finish and I wasn't out of the car ten minutes when he told me he wanted to make me an offer. I told him what I wanted and he said, fine, let me think it over. Then he complimented me on my driving during the previous two months. Since I was curious, I asked him what he would pay me to do the Formula 5000 alone, and he said thirty thousand dollars. I told him I'd already been offered seventy-five thousand dollars for the series and he just shook his head, not believing that anyone would pay a seventy-five thousand dollar retainer for that series only.

I suspected that Teddy was being conservative at the thirty thousand dollar figure because, although he was 95 per cent sure, he did not absolutely have his sponsors lined up. I had a word with Dan Gurney of Eagle, to whom I'd spoken earlier about a full program, including Formulas 1 and 5000. He continued to say he'd like to include me in his plans if he managed to put something together. But he didn't have his program underwritten yet either. Like Teddy, he was not in a position to make a firm offer.

Teddy and I talked that night about the team. He said he had a three-year contract with Jody, so I asked him what would happen if Jody made unreasonable demands. Teddy answered that he was free to do that, but if he did, he wouldn't be driving at all. He, Teddy, had the contract, and if he and Jody couldn't come to terms, that meant Jody would not be driving for anybody in any kind of car for the year that the contract had yet to run. I asked him with some surprise if he was really prepared to enforce that. He said he was and I believed him.

We talked quite openly about my offers. Teddy was very analytical about Ferrari and Shadow, in a disparaging kind of way. He kept pressing me to accept his offer to drive in the United States.

A week later, we continued the discussion over dinner in Milan, where we had flown for the Italian Grand Prix. Teddy told me Denny had sorted my car out in tests at Silverstone. That galled me. He was talking about the car I ran in Austria. I wasn't angry at the implication that I couldn't straighten it out myself, but I was very annoyed that Teddy was giving another example of his stubbornness. He had point-blank refused to acknowledge that there was anything wrong with it in Austria—or before. Now that Denny had tested in it, it was "straightened out." How could it be straightened out if there was nothing wrong with it in the first place? As we were walking up the hill from the restaurant, he said to me that I would have to learn how to use a clutch. At times, I thought, clenching my teeth, it gets so frustrating, I could just haul off and slug the little guy. But that's the way he is and that's the way he'll always be. I thought to myself after that dinner: Boy, I really have to consider getting away.

I was quickest in practice on Friday, second-quickest to Ronnie Peterson on Saturday.

Bad start again in the Italian Grand Prix. I concluded that caution is my problem with starts. I decided I was disgusted with myself and with lame excuses. The problem was that I had gotten so used to rolling starts that the standing-start system, with its violent demands on the car, seemed too abusive.

I decided after Italy that I'd stop worrying about the car—more wheelspin and more desire.

After having practically to stop behind Denny because he had spun right in front of me at the chicane at Monza, I finished twenty-five seconds behind the leaders at the end. My brakes started to fade. We were trying a new brake pad, and the puck material was a good bit harder. Toward the end, they started to glaze. I finished third, just ahead of Jackie Stewart, who was catching me at a great rate.

The Italian crowd is the most raucous and bullying crowd in the world. When they get near enough for an autograph, they push and shove. I needed a police escort from the impound area, because the crowd will just tear any driver apart. It was nice, it was flattering; but they're just too rough.

Denny had a bad weekend, and Denny is never very outgoing or agreeable, so far as the crowds are concerned anyway. He gets particularly annoyed in Italy. The crowds there really got his anger up. He pushed and shoved right back. In Italy he continually pushed people off as if he wanted to fight them. After the race, he was sitting by the truck and talking about Italy, and he said the best thing about the country was the border.

From Italy I went to London (just in time for a four-hour sauna and massage), then on to Toronto. At the airport in Toronto, I was met by the P.R. people for Labatt's, the sponsor of the Canadian Grand Prix. They immediately whisked me off to Montreal, where we met with press and broadcasters, stayed overnight, and then went back to Toronto to meet with more press. One thing they did that I thought considerate was to anchor me in a suite at the Sheraton Hotel and bring the people in. In the morning, we had newspapermen and then the TV group. Then came the radio people, and so it went through the day. Labatt's had chartered a Queenair twin-engined Beech for a whistle-stop promotion tour starting that evening. We went to Syracuse, Rochester, Buffalo, Cleveland, and Detroit.

In New York, after the tour, it was on to Mark McCormack's Manhattan office with George Lysle and then an Aurora Toy

Company father-and-son dinner. The next day, there was a lunch at Le Chanteclair, the racing hangout in New York, with René Dreyfus and his brother Maurice, who own it. I met there also with the Rolex people, for whom I had done a print ad. While in New York, I also did a couple of commercials for Aurora, and then George and I went to Lime Rock, Connecticut, to fulfill a commitment to race in a GT event in a Porsche Carrera.

The organizer was the International Motor Sports Association, the newest sanctioning body in the country. They specialize in what the British call saloon and GT racing. I must say their organization is somewhat loose. The Lime Rock race was particularly bad. I'd never seen such rank driving in all my life. It seemed to me if the organization was going to grow, it would have to be stricter with the cars and with the driving. Some of the people out there couldn't have managed to drive any worse if they had been paid to be rolling menaces.

The car I was assigned was not very good either. It was a '73 Carrera, but not nearly of the measure of the Carreras being raced by Michael Keyser and Peter Gregg, who were 1-2 in the IMSA standings. Obviously, with the very slack rules in IMSA, you were able to run anything that looked close to what it should have. Gregg's and Keyser's cars were probably a couple of hundred pounds lighter than the one I had, and they handled better.

Gregg's car had 14-inch rims at the back, mine had 11s. But I was happy to have the experience of running the car, because it was the same model as I would have to drive in the International Race of Champions, which was coming up.

I had very severe brake problems in qualifying and ended up fourth on the grid. But I still had to start thirty-third, thanks to the car owner's finish in a qualifying event. By the finish, I was up to sixth, which was no great accomplishment. Later on, I was able to take it philosophically, but right after the race, I was sore. I should have expected something of the sort— a one-shot deal with no knowledge of the background of the car and having to take someone's word for its worth. I certainly earned my three thousand dollars appearance money.

George and I had dinner at Sam Posey's house with Sam and his mother, Mrs. Moore. Peter Gregg showed up, and it seemed to me it was almost as though someone had talked to him about his attitude and his increasing notoriety as a result of it.

Peter has a rather egotistical personality. That night, though, it seemed as if he was taking pains to be a good guy and listen as well as speak. He is witty and he added to the amusement of the evening. Of course, Sam was his normal effervescent self and full of conversation. I'd always found Sam very amusing. Gregg was not at all overbearing. It was as though someone had slipped him some pills.

On the way home, George and I were talking about Sam's many talents. He is a fine artist; he planned to be the architect on the house his family was going to build on Maui, and the furniture he'd designed was impressive. If I had Sam's talent, I told George, that's what I'd be pursuing instead of motor racing. But Sam really enjoys racing, George pointed out, and he was right. I have always enjoyed music, and I said to George that if I were as talented a musician as Sam is an artist that's what I'd probably be doing. Well, he answered, why don't you do it now? I said that after fourteen years of racing I had too many motors ringing in my ears.

Spent a couple of days in Minneapolis for Goodyear at a tire dealers' convention in a Holiday Inn. Holiday Inn is a good name, but the quality varies drastically. The one in Minneapolis was terrible. Too bad the parent company can't exercise more control. Then I went to Cleveland to meet with Bud Stanner over upcoming contracts.

There were telephone talks with Ferrari and telexes as well. It didn't look as though we were going to be able to come to terms. In the meanwhile, I was talking to Shadow too. Then Larry Truesdale called saying he had a big meeting with Gurney coming up and he'd like to include me. Things were coming to a head.

The next day, we concluded a deal with Ferrari. The only thing we awaited was the arrival of the contract. A telex arrived requesting me to come to Italy to meet directly with Mr. Ferrari as per custom. He is a man of tradition.

I agreed to go over to Maranello and go through the formality of signing the contract. The specifics called for a $100,000 retainer for Formula 1, but there was an exclusion clause involving every other kind of racing but what Ferrari would offer. Still, it seemed like a good deal.

One thing that was very important was to keep the deal an absolute secret until after the United States Grand Prix. We felt that if Teddy became aware of it, his reaction might affect my chances of winning in Canada and the United States. My car might get only cursory preparation.

The terms and the agreement were verbal and I was leery, as I've always been, about things not committed to paper. I was reminded of a deal Bud and I made with Teddy at Riverside at the end of 1972. The deal was to go through 1974. We shook hands on a two-year deal with a minimum 10 per cent escalation for the '74 season. When it came to be signed, Teddy had second thoughts. I was surprised there had been a misunderstanding. In the first place, I hadn't wanted to make a two-year deal but it seemed to be a good idea. I figured then it would relieve me of having to go out the following year and renegotiate. But when the misunderstanding occurred, there wasn't much I could do. Now I don't believe anything unless it's in writing and signed.

Before we agreed with Ferrari, I had accepted an offer to go see John Logan, the president of Universal Oil Products, the sponsor for Shadow. He wanted to talk to me about how to improve the team. I told him I was only a driver and even if I were the finest driver who ever lived, there was only so much a driver was going to be able to do. But I was happy with the opportunity to meet him.

Now I had to cancel the appointment to see Mr. Logan. It seemed a 90 per cent certainty that I wouldn't be signing with Shadow no matter what happened.

I didn't feel disposed to tell UOP I was definitely not going to sign with them. In a way, I was sorry I couldn't. Don Nichols had done a great job with Shadow. He made it clear that 1974 would be a year of much change and substantial improvement. Any team that had the determination Shadow seemed to have was sure to get better.

The next morning, in Stanner's office, there sat the telexed contract, thirty-two minutes of it, from Ferrari. In New York, I again had lunch at Le Chanteclair with René Dreyfus. I told him I might be leaving Team McLaren. René, who is as knowledgeable about racing as any man alive, asked me for whom, Lotus? I said I didn't think I'd ever go to Lotus, so he said who else, Ferrari? I said perhaps, and he just looked at me smiling and said, just make sure they pay you. There was a time when people would drive for Ferrari for nothing, they were doing so well. These days, any good driver anywhere won't drive unless he's well paid.

Eppie Wietzes is a great pace-car driver. Thanks to Eppie, I won the Canadian Grand Prix. When everything is pieced together, it will turn out that when the pace car was brought out it was put in front of the wrong car, and that determined the race. The pace car is supposed to go in front of the leader, but the leader was farther in back of the pack than indicated by the pace car. The fact that the pace car went in front of the wrong car meant that Emerson Fittipaldi never got to catch up to the back of the pack. That lost him too much time. So I won the race. As they say, take them any way you can get them.

We all started out on rain tires. When the rain stopped and Emerson came in to pit for drys and to hook up his roll bars, his pit stop was about sixty seconds longer than mine, which was only for a quick tire change. We had decided to sacrifice handling for time on the track and let the roll bars go. It turned out Emerson couldn't make up the difference he lost in the pits.

Jackie Oliver, in the Shadow, was third.

The weekend was very odd and very tense. There had been a lot of movement pending between teams, a lot of closed-door negotiations, and everyone was preoccupied.

Emerson had not told Lotus about joining McLaren. Teddy had not said anything to Jody about his plans. I'd been on the bubble, the odd pig in the litter, for so long, I was getting used to it, but it wasn't any more pleasant for all the others than it had been all those weeks for me.

John Logan came to Canada and I met him. He was impressive. He was a gentleman and I thought he must be a very good businessman to be in the position he was in. Ferrari had a bad weekend, with its single entry, driven by Arturo Merzario, encountering a lot of problems.

There was a great deal of intrigue and it was all coming to a head.

The day after Canada, the contract situation took a totally new turn. Teddy had put the Texaco/Marlboro package together on one team, but he had satisfied Yardley with the promise to run a *separate* team under its name. Teddy made me an offer to be on the one-car Yardley team. I would have a car and a backup to run as a separate entity. That looked like a perfect deal. So I concluded I'd hold off on closing anything else until the middle of the week, when Teddy would be able to confirm everything.

Bud Stanner was in Canada, and he said he'd never seen anything like it. Everyone was so preoccupied with the behind-the-scenes happenings that the race seemed almost secondary. Of course, the big question was Jackie. He hadn't even given a hint about whether he was going to retire. It seemed time for him to quit, having just won the world championship for the third time. But no one knew if he would.

Bud called me in New York to tell me he had sent off his revisions to my Ferrari contract and—at first—had received no answer. When the answer *did* come, it said the revisions were understood and that I should come over and something could be worked out. That was neither an acceptance nor a rejection of our revisions. I was not disposed to go over to Italy until the matter was settled. It seemed to me the problem was probably with Mr. Ferrari. He was a bit old-fashioned, which went back to the old days when Ferrari was supreme and could get away with one-sided contracts. Not any more.

The same day, I got The Buffalo's telegram, which said that no matter what happened at Watkins Glen, since I'd won the British and the Canadian GPs I was champion of the

English-speaking world. That was heartening, and it was something I hadn't figured out for myself—perhaps I wasn't so imaginative as I thought I was.

I had another long talk with Dan Gurney. He told me there was no way he could be prepared to do a full Formula 1 season in 1974. He said he intended to take the basic chassis of his new car, develop it as a Formula 5000 car through the 1974 season, and when it became competitive, try to turn it into a Formula 1 car for 1975. That's what Lola did and it made sense to me. He talked to me about driving the car in Formula 5000 and I said I'd be interested so long as it didn't conflict with Formula 1. We left it on that basis, both of us being aware that getting a sponsor was crucial both to his plans and to mine.

By midweek, people were still in confusion about the Canadian Grand Prix, so I tried to reconstruct it in my mind. The confusion at the outcome (they waited an hour and a half to announce the results) was due to two things, I concluded. First, a grand prix is a 200-mile race and there are rarely pit stops. But since it rained and then dried up, everyone had to stop to change tires. The second reason was that, for the first time ever, there was a pace car in the grand prix racing, as a new safety measure. So we had these two factors, which shuffled the field quite a bit. Most of the teams weren't used to keeping track of a lot of stops and lost track on their lap charts. But the officials did not. There were three official lap charts and they all showed me the winner.

I started on rain tires, so when it began to dry I could not have stayed out without really instantaneous, critical wear. The wet tire is far less durable on a dry track than a dry. It's a super-soft compound with only half the rubber. It's grooved more or less like a passenger-car tire, and it wears rubber off at a great rate on a dry track.

When it began to dry up, our crew was really the key. With their Indianapolis experience, they made the right decision, pitting me as soon as possible and getting me back out on the race track. More than anything else (more, even, than the pace car mixup) that won the race for me. The quick stop meant that we didn't connect the roll bars when it got dry, and since we didn't correct the very steep wing angle either, I was very slow on the straightaway. The car was also just careering all over the road and bouncing off the bottom of the suspension. It wouldn't point too well and the front end was a little bit nose high and light in the turns. But I could still drive the car, and I drove it as hard as I could.

The end of the week after the Canadian GP was hectic. I was literally standing by ready to go either to Italy or Chicago to sign with either Ferrari or Shadow. In the meanwhile, I was *also* waiting to have the McLaren-Yardley deal confirmed. Finally, I ruled the Ferrari contract out on the basis of its exclusivity clause. I would have had to make up for the reduction in income it imposed somehow, but I didn't see how. The original deal was $100,000 for Formula 1 only. But that meant no other racing for any other team. The $100,000 would have been almost enough, if Ferrari had been willing to add for prototype racing with their sports car. But they came back and said it would *include* driving the sports car. All of a sudden the deal started to look less attractive. All of a sudden I was not going to be paid very well. If Ferrari had upped the ante to $150,000, it would have made sense. But in this business, exclusivity is pretty sticky. I sent Ferrari a specific telex and again they wouldn't answer. So I postponed my trip to Italy indefinitely.

When I finally heard that Teddy would be able to complete his negotiations favorably, I called Don Nichols at Shadow and told him I'd be staying with Team McLaren. I said I didn't know exactly what the format of the team would be for 1974, but that I'd hear at Watkins Glen. He said he was sorry and if by any chance we had problems signing a contract, by all means to get in touch with him again. He told me the offer would remain open, which was very flattering.

I didn't think that would happen. Teddy and I had been together for more than three years and we understood each other.

When I got back to California for a few days, the first hint that I was wrong appeared. Ed Stallanwerk, the advertising manager of Gulf U.S., said Gulf might be interested in doing something with me in their advertising. Of course I talked to Teddy. He admitted that even though Texaco was not part of the Yardley-McLaren Team, he had agreed that Yardley-McLaren would not advertise another fuel—even though the team did not intend to use Texaco. Teddy boxed me in without my knowing it.

The preoccupation of everyone at Canada with the future continued at Watkins Glen.

Our thoughts were soon taken up with something sadder and more immediate, when François Cevert had his fatal accident.

François was coming up the hill over the bridge. It is probably the most dangerous place in racing. You come up the hill blind, and you are just about flat out, using the whole road and drifting to right. Just as you exit the turn, you come up on top of a bridge with nowhere to go on either side.

From the skid marks, it looked as though François might have slid a little bit too far, tried to correct, and hit the upper railing of the Armco barrier. When the car hit the barrier it apparently sprung the bolts of the barrier, which were loose fifty feet before and after the impact mark. The result is that Armco didn't do what it was intended to do, which was to contain the car. The barrier collapsed. Evidently, the car disintegrated and rolled over on its cockpit, killing François.

For that afternoon's practice session, everyone just went through the motions.

The next morning, race morning, the Tyrrell team withdrew from the race as a tribute to François, so we started without Stewart and Amon. My chance to win faded right on the starting line. I couldn't disengage my clutch again, just as in Austria. That made the second time this had happened in four races. But this time, instead of holding the car on the brake, I just stuck it in neutral and threw my arm in the air, waiting for everyone to go by. Then I jammed it into gear, but of course my clutch wasn't working cleanly for the rest of the race.

After my car cooled down in the garage, the mechanics

shook their heads and told me everything was working perfectly. I had no explanation for it, although the situation was very real. Maybe when the fluid got hot the lines expanded and there was a bit of a leak. I just don't know.

When you realize you've lost the race before you even start, a lot of adrenalin and enthusiasm drains out of your system. It becomes harder to concentrate and harder to bear down.

As the race wore on I got back into the swing of things, but it was too late. I ended fifth, behind my teammate, Denny Hulme. It was an unsatisfactory end to an unsatisfactory weekend.

What with the death of François, my own disappointing performance, and the pressure over the contract negotiations, which approached their climax outside the Kendall Service Center, it was one of the most difficult weekends of my life.

To go back: Teddy had told me in Canada not to do anything, he was negotiating with Yardley. Then he called that week from Europe to say he would be able to give me a contract to drive Formula 1 for McLaren in the Yardley-sponsored car. What this meant was that Yardley had allowed Teddy to accept another sponsor. That must have represented considerable compromise on their part. Yardley had at least an option (which even Teddy admitted) to continue with McLaren. They might have been difficult and insisted on their rights. But they graciously accepted Teddy's proposal to split Team McLaren in two: one branch with two Marlboro/Texaco cars and one with the Yardley car.

Yardley could have made life very hard for Teddy. Their lawyers were advising them that they had not just an option but an exclusive right to sponsor McLaren for the remaining year (1974) of a three-year contract. But they were more concerned with harmony with Teddy and acquiesced in his proposal of a divided entry. Teddy evidently claimed hardship, which, comparing his revenue to the income to Lotus and Tyrrell, was understandable.

Given Yardley's racing budget, the company simply could not match the large sponsorship figures Marlboro and Texaco were offering. Yardley's only stipulation in allowing Teddy to run two teams was that they get parity across the board: in the cars, maintenance, and management. Dennis Matthews, the managing director of Yardley, wrote that to Teddy in August; Teddy replied there would be no problem.

Now it gets a little complicated. When Teddy got the new sponsorships, he didn't actually sign with Texaco and Marlboro. As I understood it, McLaren signed a contract with Emerson Fittipaldi. In turn, Emerson had contracts with Texaco and Marlboro. The key to the whole thing was that in *Emerson's* contracts there seemed to be certain stipulations and conditions to which Teddy agreed. What those conditions amounted to was that Yardley would *not* get the same treatment as Texaco and Marlboro were getting.

But I didn't know that at Watkins Glen, and neither, evidently, did Yardley. Teddy asked that Yardley show good faith in his ability to run three cars without asking specific questions about team management. But Yardley began asking for guarantees that Teddy couldn't provide. Teddy then suggested that the Yardley car might even have to be disassociated from Team McLaren.

All of this did not boil over until the Thursday after the race. During the weekend, I had signed a McLaren contract for 1974 on the basis of my belief that the Yardley contract was firm. Teddy told me that the only thing that was holding him up from closing the deal with Yardley was my assurance to Dennis Matthews that I would be co-operative with promotions and publicity.

I was a little puzzled by that, since it seemed to me my record with Yardley was more than ample proof of my willingness to be co-operative. But I said I would be glad to provide those reassurances. So we had a meeting in a camper at the race track.

Teddy was there with Phil Kerr, Bruce McLaren's friend and also a director of McLaren. With Dennis Matthews was Martin Cartwright, the racing publicist for Yardley. Dennis was happy to know that I'd signed the McLaren contract and it was pretty obvious that he wanted me as the driver for the Yardley car.

It seemed clear we were all there to witness my assurance to Yardley of my co-operation—the only detail left before the whole package could be put together on the spot.

That was when Dennis Matthews surprised me. He said he was glad to have my assurances, but that was not the only problem. Evidently Teddy hadn't given Yardley any guarantees at all. Teddy had refused to name a team manager, saying that the Yardley contract only specified that the running of the team be left to his discretion.

It all made for a very bitter weekend. Matters were left unresolved pending a meeting in the New York McCormack offices scheduled for the following Thursday. In the interim I got one of the least pleasant letters I have ever received. It was from Teddy. In it, he accused me of about everything in the book.

Here are some of my sins of omission and commission, according to Teddy: I had made an agreement on the Yardley program, then changed my mind and asked for more money, which jeopardized the sponsorship. I was demanding a say (on Yardley's behalf admittedly) in the running of the team. I had accused Teddy of lying. I put the blame on the team when I made mistakes on the track. I was very bothersome in my constant requests for expense money. Besides all that, I didn't know how to operate a clutch pedal.

Given all that, according to Teddy, I had singlehandedly driven Yardley away from his door. And so, if Yardley *did* come back with their purse open (a highly unlikely happening, Teddy made clear), I would be held responsible if they were unhappy. And if they did become unhappy, I would be replaced.

Teddy's letter didn't say, but it certainly seemed to imply, that I could make Yardley unhappy (and therefore I would be replaced) if I did such awful things as be late for practice, ask for expense money, or lie to him.

Teddy also seemed to be saying that I would be making Yardley unhappy if I continued to ask for some control by them of their own racing team.

It was not a letter particularly calculated to reassure me—or Yardley for that matter—that Teddy was prepared to treat the Yardley entry on the same basis as his two-car Texaco/Marlboro team.

Teddy obviously sincerely believed what he was writing me. But his thinking that I corrupted his deal because I stood behind Yardley and wanted to be protected with them by guarantees seemed to me a distortion.

We had been able to solve a lot of the problems we had encountered over the past year. Some of the personal differences had been more difficult to resolve. After all, we had achieved a great familiarity, having known each other for many years. Theretofore we had always been able to bury the hatchet when it came to personal quarrels, and get the job done. Lately, though, it seemed to me Teddy had been under great stress from trying to juggle two sponsors and make them both happy.

Nonetheless, I bitterly resented being dragged in and accused of acting with questionable motives. That letter made me think I shouldn't drive for Teddy after all. Teddy once said to me that this was a tough business. Unless you're winning a lot (and it looked as though with Yardley's car we wouldn't be in a position to) life was unpleasant, Teddy had said.

I read the letter several times and figured it would be best for the team and best for me if we parted company.

On that note we met in New York.

We gathered in the offices of Motor Marketing: Teddy, Tyler, and Bill Smith for McLaren; Dennis Matthews; Stanner, and I. Dennis spent the first hour or so trying to resolve some of the questions in his mind about the conditions under which he could sponsor a car.

When Teddy was unable to satisfy his demands, it became very clear that the deal had blown up. I concede I did not have an open mind going into the meeting. I wanted out of the contract, out from under Teddy Mayer's management.

I listened for a while, then interrupted to bring up the specifics of the letter. At that moment, Tyler made a really heroic attempt to reconcile the differences between Teddy and me. Even Teddy got caught up in it. Teddy paid me more compliments in half an hour in that meeting than he had paid me in the three and a half years I had been driving for him. It was gratifying, but it was also too late.

Tyler said he hated to see the team lose me. I answered I hated to go. It had been a long relationship and, on balance, a very good one. I found myself getting far more emotional than I expected, but I asked for my release and got it.

The next day, I was at Laguna Seca, in Monterey, California, to meet Don Nichols of Shadow, whom I had called later in the afternoon of the meeting day. I had won the next-to-the-last CanAm for McLaren at Laguna in 1971, the year I won the championship with them. McLaren had dominated the CanAm with its orange cars for so long, it came as a shock to me to be at a CanAm and not see a single team car representing them. Roger Penske's Porsches had pushed them completely out of the series.

Bud Stanner told me after I left that Tyler had asked if I would consider signing to drive with his end of the McLaren operation—the 500-mile races in the United States. But it was too late for that as well. I had already signed with Roger Penske to drive for him at Indianapolis in 1974.

At Laguna, too, I signed with Shadow for Formula 1.

Mandel · Five

One of these days the racing people are going to drive out a race track access road to the main highway to find nothing but wisps of smoke, some blackened fields, and a twisted tree.

It was not that the extraordinary social cacophony of the United States Grand Prix at Watkins Glen had failed to penetrate the consciousness of Peter Revson. But when you're driving in your twenty-fifth grand prix, having seen God knows how many before, when a friend is killed and when your future is being decided in the rental cars parked along the garages, you manage to somehow miss the color, the sights, and the sounds.

Sid Collins, The Voice Of The Five Hundred, is not exactly right. Indianapolis has a serious rival as the greatest spectacle in racing. It depends on your tastes, your income, your education, and—quite literally—how deep you want to sink. But a college kid, a time-and-motion-study man, a zodiac acid pusher, or any suburban dweller anywhere would probably think the United States Grand Prix had a great deal more to offer than the Indianapolis 500.

You don't live much better on the rolling infield of the Glen than you do in the quagmire at the Speedway, but it's a European-style adventure, which means that every one of those 125,000 people at the Glen is spending some part of the weekend reassuring his neighbors that they are all having *fun*.

Most particularly, the people in The Bog are having fun. The Glen management created The Bog inadvertently: By building a new access road on the pit straight side of the track, they managed to gouge out a hollow. There followed a general submergence of the terrain around it, and the result was a large and permanent mud-sink.

The locals are very proud of The Bog. They look forward to Sunday not because it's race day, but because on Sunday they can finally add up the score of destruction the Bog People have wrought.

On Sunday morning, before the sun comes up, the aging sheriff's deputies who man the long garage called the Kendall Service Center rub the night's grime out of their eyes and await the first visitor to tell him what they've done in The Bog this year. The flags above the pit grandstand are barely waving; it will probably be a calm day. The paddock is quiet, peaceful, and filled with twenty-thousand dollar campers with their nubby polyester drapes closed. Only the occasional headlight swings through the morning darkness; in the concession stands, the attendants are halfheartedly scraping off last night's grease from the stoves. Soon, as the campers from the tents and the motor homes begin arriving, they will start preparing the faintly greenish omelet they advertise as scrambled eggs.

Inside the service center a man of perhaps seventy, his gray uniform sadly rumpled but his badge still bright, talks about last night in The Bog. He speaks of it with awe. To him, it is obviously western New York's Grand Canyon.

There are three or four hundred people who rush to get places in The Bog the Wednesday before the race. They fight each other to get in. They submerge themselves in the slime, are covered with mud the whole weekend long. They get stoned on drugs and drunk on wine. They sleep in the slime and make love in it. The drugs and the wine make them more and more twisted. By Friday morning they are throwing mud at each other, tearing hoods off their own cars, and shooting rockets at the faces that pop up on The Bog's other side, protecting themselves with shields made from the hoods of the cars. The next step is to use cherry bombs as mortars to lob over the shields. The bombs explode on the people they hit.

Anyone who gets close to The Bog is fair game. Mostly, though, the Bog People hope that cars will drive innocently along the road. When they do, the Bog People rise from the mud and capture them. And then they burn the cars. In 1973 the Bog People burned twelve cars over the grand prix weekend—an all-time record. The sheriff's deputies, who will not go within one hundred yards of The Bog under any circumstances, were very proud.

There were also a record number of Bog People taken to the track hospital. As the weekend wears on, the accumulation of shattered bottles in the mud gets larger; great, jagged edges begin to stick up from the mud like shark fins. By Saturday, when the Bog Denizens are totally twisted, they begin to stage competitive swims across The Bog, climbing up the other side with their bodies torn and bleeding from the glass. They don't seem to notice.

One Watkins Glen deputy has a theory about the Bog People. He thinks they are representative suburbanites. He thinks the demographics (he actually used the word) of The Bog are exactly the same as those of White Plains or Burlingame. They take to The Bog, he says, because it's the most outrageous thing they can do. No insurance salesman or ad man could afford to be a visible political activist, say. Instead, says the deputy, such people sink into the mud and chant, "The Bog wants the Porsche, The Bog wants the Impala, The Bog wants the Toyota" along with the other crazies from the split-level colonials. Then, anonymously and covered in slime, they rise out of the muck to burn all three.

The Bog People are caked in mud. Almost everyone else wears the standard university uniform: work shirts and jeans. There are a lot of body shirts and tank tops, some bare feet but mainly sandals. Watkins Glen is a place to go camping, and you do not wear ermine in a shelter half. All the way up the hill from the Finger Lakes town, there are signs advertising firewood. The tents begin the moment you enter track grounds. Most of the campers are there for three days. Perhaps they have come for the race, perhaps not. As you drive into the paddock, almost two miles from the track entrance, more people are playing volleyball than leaning on the fences. The Frisbee is at least as popular a device as the race car at Watkins Glen, if the number of its devotees is any measure. The cars pulled up alongside the tents don't give much of a clue about the fanaticism of their owners. There are a lot of vans and many dirt bikes. The place is clotted with motor homes. If there seem to be two representative cars, they are the Datsun 240Z and the Camaro. There are some Porsches and a sprinkling of Ferraris. But where are the Alfa Veloces? the Citroën SM's? the restored HRG's?

If the deputy is right about his demographics, the parents are in The Bog and their children are swarming around the rolling countryside of the race course.

But there is a sprinkling of the ultrafashionable Juan-les-Pins people too. Mainly, they stay up near the pits and around the Paddock Club. It is dusty and hilly around the course. They wear jeans too, but theirs have been bought used, look like velveteen, and are sprinkled with sequins. The men have on rough Harris tweed hacking coats or blazers and flannels. On their feet they wear scotch-grain lotus veldschoens. They don't arrive before noon, and they leave at three whether the race is over or not.

Not so much to the pure racing people as to the ad men and the P.R. types, is it vital to be at Watkins Glen for the Grand Prix. *Car and Driver* magazine used to take a whole house for the week to entertain clients. Because in the East road racing has now become a tradition—Cameron Argetsinger started the Glen in 1948—it is traditional for elegant people to go to the Grand Prix in a way that is true of no other race in the country.

The Glen even smells different from any other race in the United States. There is the sharp autumn tang of New York State, made up partly of the smoke of ten thousand campfires. Instead of the eye-watering fumes of the alcohol fuel at

Indianapolis, you inhale castor oil from some spectator and veteran cars, a bittersweet evocation of childhood for the middle-aged. The outdoor privies are no more benign than at Indianapolis, but you are expected to be polite and not notice them. So you are careful to walk to windward. Instead of fried-chicken remains, the Glen offers the astringent smell of apples freshly bitten into.

The sounds are different too. Pete Lyons, the American reporter who follows the grands prix, once wrote about race car sounds in a way no one has ever written about a road-racing car before. No one will ever do better. "You [sneak] through [the trees] up to the guardrail. Not *right* up to it because of fear, but nearly. If you're lucky, there will be a pause in the 180mph traffic, and you'll hear [a car] coming.

"It starts far down through the forest, just a thin shapeless noise, a shrill cry broken by a million tree trunks into 'white noise' like the sound of falling water. Very rapidly it swells in volume . . . until the noise rises to become the only noise in the world. A sudden thrill of panic seizes your heart . . . it's like the last instant standing under the glide path as a 747 comes down on you, and it's too late to run away.

"By now through the rushing noise you can distinguish the central shriek of the engine, eight or twelve tiny pistons straining at top speed and angry they can't go faster. . . ."

"For just an instant you glimpse the car, a flash like sunshine on a bullet. . . . The noise, beamed straight back at you now by two long exhaust pipes, is pure and clean but astonishingly lower in pitch. It fades away rapidly, but you can still hear it for a long, long time."

Martin Revson, dressed in a gray tweed jacket and gray worsted trousers, arrived from New York City on Sunday morning in a rented helicopter with his wife, Eleanor, and their two children.

The elder Revsons go racing in style, although they are not always aware of what has been accomplished backstage so that life can be civilized for them at the track. Martin Revson flew from New York to the Glen in a helicopter. As we've seen, his brother Charles chartered a jet to go to Indianapolis, where he was met by Danny Folsom's man Jim, the chicken deliverer. Of course, Charles was no more aware of Jim's real job than he was of the fact that the limousine that picked him up belonged to the classiest funeral parlor in town.

Martin deposited his family with George Lysle and swam upstream through the swirling crowds around the service center to look for Peter. He was upset when he couldn't find him, but he was considerably less upset than his sole surviving son had been all weekend.

Peter had arrived at the Glen Motor Lodge with Marji Wallace on Thursday. Peter was in from Redondo Beach, Marji had come from nearby Binghamton, where she had just won Miss U.S.A. on her way toward the Miss World title. Although Peter had been under pressure all season long, the squeeze had really begun in Canada.

Revson and Bud Stanner had the first of their meetings with Teddy on Friday night at Watkins Glen.

It is crisp in October in the Finger Lakes region of New York. There is no other part of the country so splendid in the fall. The old, glacially worn hills roll softly beneath the greens and yellows and reds of the foliage. Most of the roads remain ancient two-laners, and they break startlingly around a wooden corner above Lake Cayuga or Lake Seneca again and again as they weave through the region. The countryside is quiet and content. The people who live there do not lead dramatic lives. Their pace is slow, their worries and their pleasures are on a human scale, and their placid faces show it.

On Saturday it was cold and it threatened to rain. The crews arrived late, perhaps 8 A.M., at the service center, where their cars had been unloaded into the sharply defined stalls along both sides. Running through the center of the building is the aisle where spectators who pay one dollar each can walk. Only a few campers wandered there on Saturday morning, up early after a fairly peaceful night. Sheriff's deputies at either end were drowsy, having sat guard all night. The ticket sellers were rolled up asleep alongside their tables in pink and blue blankets.

Along the outside of the service center, at its back, was a

row of pastel-colored rental cars: Furys and Satellites, Galaxies and Lagunas. Most of them were filthy and many had Ontario plates, having been picked up at the Toronto airport before the Canadian Grand Prix by the teams to keep for the North American swing.

Teddy was sitting in his blue Fury outside the McLaren stalls. Ken Tyrrell's car was alongside his, and on the other side, with a gap left open for the race cars to get out, was the car Colin Chapman was using.

There is a deceptive laziness to the atmosphere of a grand prix practice/qualifying session. Unlike the system used in many American races, where the cars go out one at a time to turn official qualifying laps, the grand prix cars are all out together. They are timed on every lap. The teams are very professional and seem relaxed. Someone goes out to the wall occasionally to signal his driver with a chalk board. Every once in a while a car comes in and the driver has a conference with his crew chief. The morning unwinds slowly and gently, despite its punctuation by the bark of race-car exhausts.

Late Saturday morning at Watkins Glen there was a sudden stillness. A race track is not meant to be quiet on a busy weekend. When it is, the quiet suddenly translates into a terrible chill. It means everyone on the track has stopped, and cars at work stop for only one reason. The crews seem to coalesce around the team manager, everyone turns up his collar and seeks the warmth of other humans. They stand there in the pits, in clumps, waiting to hear.

Jackie Stewart's car, the dark-blue Elf Team Tyrrell, was one of the first in. The whole crew, along with members of other crews, closed in on the car. Jackie's wife, Helen, offered her hand to him as he stepped out. He pushed her aside, pushed away the crowd in front of him, and walked to the pit counter. "Where's Helen?" he asked as though at that moment he was only just returning to consciousness. Helen took his hand and led him around to the back of the pit. Although it is said that their relationship is perfunctory, now, he clearly looked to her for help. She responded with cool, calm strength. Somebody gave Stewart a sedative.

Revson was one of the last to come in. Immediately, Teddy asked him what had happened and there was a brief conference after he pulled off his helmet with the lollipop shapes on it. Then he walked slowly to the pit counter where a terrified Marji Wallace was sitting. "Cevert" he said. "It's a bad one. It really is a bad one."

George Lysle was standing behind them. "We've got a serious thing here," he said. And Bud Stanner, next to him, added, "The public relations on this looks very bad."

Revson said he wanted to walk down to the Paddock Club. There was a one-man show of motor-racing paintings there he wanted to see. He seemed unaware or unconcerned that he would have to walk a half mile or more through the crowds and that when he got there, he would be facing a window that looked out upon the spot where Cevert had died.

Revson and Marji Wallace had barely begun their long walk when a man in a green Chevelle stopped and offered them a lift. It was David Phipps, an enormously tall English racing writer. Phipps had been reporting grand prix racing for many years. He had often been at races where drivers had been killed. Very matter-of-factly he asked if Revson knew how Cevert's crash had happened; very matter-of-factly, Revson said he did not. Phipps stopped at the entrance to the Paddock Club, reached back, and opened the rear door from the inside. It was a more than perfunctory gesture which communicated a solicitude Phipps could not manage to convey in any other way. Revson's thanks were warm, but when he stepped out of the car, he was faced by the sight of a large, dirty man carrying a beer can and wearing a sweat shirt that read KEEP ON BALLING.

"Nice," said Revson and walked into the Paddock Club to look at the paintings of race cars.

Revson paused during lunch to wonder about Cevert's crash. He speculated about its cause; he talked about Cevert's considerable ability as a driver, wondering about the possibility of human error. He spoke almost as though Cevert had been a man he'd never known. He didn't mention Cevert's death again.

Marji Wallace seemed stunned. Perhaps not so much by the fact of death as by the attitudes of those around her. She was bewildered by the calmness of the grand prix people, their refusal to display grief. It seemed grim and callous to her. Not even Revson, who had shown himself capable of tenderness and understanding, was willing to offer solace.

When Revson went off to practice again, and to have his conference in Bill Smith's camper, she walked to the yellow Satellite he had rented, sat in the driver's seat, and stared numbly through the windshield. They had had breakfast with François, she said. Everyone knew about his charm and his vitality; why were they all acting this way? She watched Jody Scheckter emerge from the McLaren stalls and walk to a car nearby. She turned her head as he opened its door and she saw Scheckter's fiancée inside, weeping. She remained still for a moment longer, and then began to cry quietly.

Meanwhile, although the practice was going on, the doors of the pastel rental cars, parked nose in to the service center, were opening and closing regularly as first one driver then the next slipped into the front seat to talk to Teddy, to Ken Tyrrell, or to Colin Chapman.

In the field between the top of the pit straight and the service center stood one of the car owners from the Formula 5000 series. He was wearing a red knit shirt and dove-gray checkered trousers. His arms crossed in front of him, he stood peering through enormously thick glasses at the activity by the garages.

"Fittipaldi has signed with Tyrrell," he announced, turning his head and nodding yes, as though to reassure himself that he was right. Five minutes later, a smaller, rounder man with long hair, a mustache, and a notebook ran up breathlessly to tell him that the man who used to own Jochen Rindt's car had just arrived from England and was walking up and down the pits with Dan Gurney.

"It's very clear," intoned the man in the glasses, "that Peter Revson has just signed with Gurney to run the Eagle."

At that moment a mechanic drove Ronnie Peterson's black

Lotus at a breath-taking speed along the road by the side of the service center.

"Were you aware that Peterson will be with McLaren next year?" asked the man in the glasses.

The smaller man disagreed. Gurney, he said, would be coming out of retirement. His cars were to be sponsored by Universal Oil Products. The Shadows would be driven by Brian Redman and Jackie Oliver. Jody Scheckter, of course, was going to Brabham.

It was not surprising that even the racing establishment's own people didn't know what was going on. After all, inside the camper, parked within view of the man in the checkered gray trousers and his friends, Revson, Teddy, and Dennis Matthews didn't know either. All they knew was that something had gone awfully wrong. Revson accused Teddy of lying when Dennis Matthews said no guarantees had been forthcoming to Yardley. "You've lied, Teddy, you've lied," he said, reminding Teddy of his assurance the night before that the Yardley deal was done.

The door of the camper banged open and Teddy exploded outward, walking in his curious, high-buttocked way to the garages. When Revson came out he looked terribly tired and terribly angry. "There are times I feel like punching the little white-haired guy right in the mouth," he said bitterly, walking by. Two or three steps farther on, he stopped and turned around. "I'm sure he feels the same about me."

The sun had come out earlier. Marji Wallace had taken control of herself. Her questions still remained, but it was clear there would be no solutions this day. Practice was over, and inside the garage, the McLaren crew were eating a combination lunch and tea.

After practice or after a race at a road course, there descends a warmth and a friendliness offered at no other time. It does not last long, and as the darkness comes, people leave the circles of drivers and crews reluctantly, knowing such moments are rare.

At Watkins Glen on Saturday afternoon, the concern with racing chit-chat was puzzling. I had driven out of the track early in the morning to buy some sandwich meat for the McLaren crew. On my way back, I turned on the radio and heard the first sketchy reports of the Yom Kippur War.

Now, as I stood with a beer in my hand watching the joking and laughing in the pits, I wondered about the racers and their world. It seemed to me they were so out of touch with everything that did not concern racing that they were taking a terrible chance. One of these days, I thought, these people are going to drive down a race track access road that leads to the main highway, and when they get there, they are going to find the highway is gone. There will be nothing but wisps of smoke, some blackened fields, and a twisted tree. While World War III had started and ended, these people will have been playing their reckless game, unaware they are the last humans left alive. Only the racers, their crews, and their hangers-on would be left to wind out their lives gossiping about automobiles and racing, never realizing that the world had ended. It would probably serve them right to have to spend the rest of their lives in each other's company, I thought. Since I had discovered a war had started that morning, only because I had driven into town on a racer's mission, I suddenly realized I would no more be aware the world had ended than anyone else. Well, I thought, at least I would have survived.

The same day the Yom Kippur War started in the Middle East, the Mets were playing Cincinnati and the Orioles were at Oakland. "How's the war going?" I asked Revson.

"The war. Oh, the war!" He looked at the Rolex he'd gotten as payment for appearing in a Rolex ad in *Sports Illustrated*. "You're right. The ball game's on."

"No, no," I said, "I mean the war. The goddamn war, Peter, the war between the Jews and the Arabs."

"Oh, *that* war," he answered. "The Jews will win the war," he said positively and put his head to the side almost as though he were denying what he had just said. "The Jews always win when they play at home, don't they?" he asked.

On Sunday, Peter and Teddy Mayer were not speaking away from the racing pits. Revson's whole life had come into focus over the weekend, and the picture was not pleasant. There were uncharacteristic cracks in the smooth Revson façade as the day wore on, and then his father, whose helicopter had deposited him on the grass outside the track, found him and rushed up to take his arm.

Martin Revson's questions were persistent and came tumbling insistently from his lips. All the while, he held his son by the arm, so even if he had wanted to, he could not have gotten away. Peter was very patient with his father, his voice was quiet, and he answered slowly and fully about the weekend negotiations. After ten minutes or so, he told his father he had to go to his car now, he'd be back after the race. Watching him walk away, Martin Revson spoke Teddy Mayer's name and something else: "Street fighter," he said over and over again.

Revson kept his word to his father after the race. Taking only time to accept the cup awarded for the best combined finishes in the Canadian and U.S. GP's, he spent half an hour in close conversation with Martin Revson just outside the garage. After thirty minutes or so, he looked up to see they were tightly ringed by spectators, most of them with pens and scraps of paper. "You're too famous, dad," he said to his father and led him into the garage.

In the stall next to the McLarens was a medium-sized wooden crate, perhaps five by three by three feet, its sides covered only by some rough cross members with an address in England scrawled on them. Inside the crate were the remains of Cevert's Tyrrell.

The last grand prix of an unsettling year had ended. During the year, some people had died, some people had won. Some people had entered the grand prix ranks, some people had retired from them.

Jackie Stewart retired. Jody Scheckter signed with Ken Tyrrell, who also brought Patrick Depaillier up from Formula 2. Emerson Fittipaldi and Denny Hulme joined to form the new McLaren team. Teddy worked out his problems with Yardley and entered a third car for Mike Hailwood. Jacky Ickx went to Lotus, replacing Fittipaldi. Revson, of course, signed with

Shadow, where his new teammate was another Formula 2 star, Jean Pierre Jarier.

The season was over for Revson, although he would compete at Riverside in the International Race of Champions against drivers from all sectors of the sport. In February, in the finals at Daytona, he would finish second to Mark Donohue and ahead of A. J. Foyt, George Follmer, Bobby Unser, and David Pearson. Emerson Fittipaldi and Denny Hulme did not make it as far as Daytona. They were eliminated in the semifinals.

While Revson and his father talked at the back of the garages, out by the fence near the spectator aisle the McLaren mechanics were auctioning off Team McLaren stickers to the crowd for the year-end crew pool. When they ran out of stickers, they sold a spare windshield from Revson's car. Seeing the price it brought, Revson reached into his helmet bag and gave them a visor and a pair of gloves to sell too.

Footnote

In 1967 Revson went to San Jose State College to take a battery of tests being given to a group of about four hundred drivers by Dr. Keith Johnsgard of the Department of Psychology.

A colleague of Johnsgard's had been working with the San Francisco Giants and the San Francisco 49ers, achieving remarkable results. He had been able to predict which rookies would make good in the professional ranks. He had also indicated solutions to some of the problems the coaching staffs were facing.

Johnsgard was a motor-racing fan as well as a psychologist. He had been involved in some of the work with the Giants and the 49ers, and he began to wonder if the same techniques could not be applied to racing drivers.

His objective was to arrive at a point where he could make some judgments about the potential of any driver: his potential for self-destruction as well as for success.

In general, Johnsgard's tests told him that top-level racing drivers were the *least* self-destructive people he had ever measured. As compared to his control group (graduate students at San Jose State), they were considerably more independent and self-assertive. They measured as high in intelligence.

Revson's profile was extraordinary. He scored highest in self-sufficiency, intelligence, stability, assertiveness, willingness to experiment, and self-control. He was scored as very tough-minded. The tests showed he had great poise. He was not, according to the tests, emotional, forthright, or casual.

Johnsgard's work has been significant. The drivers tested have proved his testing techniques sound. One of the statistical samples he found encouraging was Revson's. Johnsgard's tests indicated, during the time that Revson was still much in the background, that he had world-championship potential.